PROFESSIONAL WRESTLING
COLLECTIBLES

Kristian Pope & Ray Whebbe Jr.

Published by

krause publications

700 East State Street, Iola, WI 54990-0001
Telephone (715) 445-2214
www.krause.com

Please call or write for our free catalog of publications. Our toll-free number to place an order or obtain a free catalog is (800) 258-0929 or please use our regular business telephone (715) 445-2214 for editorial comment and further information.

Library of Congress Catalog Card Number: 99-68109
ISBN: 0-87341-878-6
Printed in the United States of America

Acknowledgments

When I started watching wrestling in the early 1980s, little did I know I would one day be writing a book about it. But here it is, and what a blast it has been. There are so many people I wish to thank for making this project possible. The most important thanks and love goes out to my family. To mom and dad, your loving, continued support was so encouraging through the years and you never minded that your son watched wrestling. Thanks for all the trips to the matches as a kid. I know you hated it, but were willing to sit through it for me. Thanks to my brothers Jeff and Darrell for all the times they, too, took their younger brother to the wrestling matches. Those times that we shared together will forever be great memories for me. Thanks to Krause Publications, Paul Kennedy and Kris Manty for having confidence and patience in us two amateurs. To the special friends for the ages: Mike Saindon, Joe Christensen, Paul McEnroe and family, Jeff Sherry, Ben Wilinski, Mick Karch, Todd Zolecki, Chris Ison, George Dohrmann, Peter Barzilai, John Bisognano, Dan Reines, Geoff Ooley, Tod Leonard, Tony Friedman and family, Emilio Garcia Ruiz, Steve Scott, Ray Whebbe and his generous and loving family, Eddie Sharkey, Steve Anderson, the Berend family, Julie and Ellen, Nick and Natalie, the Dinan family, the Baker family and Aunt Pat. You all have special meaning for me. Thank you to everyone who helped along the way in making this dream come true.

—Kris Pope

To thank or not to thank, that is the question. First thanks to Paul Kennedy at Krause Publications. Without them, I wouldn't be a published author. A special thanks goes out to those who have helped us by giving their valuable time and information. I owe them big time. I'd be a bad son if I didn't dedicate this book to my mother, Ida. She did more for me than I would ever dream of. Without her guidance, I wouldn't be here. Thank you to the people who have helped give us valuable information: Mike Chapman, Pat Hollis, Mick Karch, Marvin Joel, Don Laible, Tom Burke, Mike Rogers and Royal Duncan. A special thank you goes out to my mentors, the late Chuck Van Avery and Jim O'Connell, Al McFarlane, Pat Reusse, Dr. Greg Olson, Don Del Fiaco, Doug Grow, Ed Sharkey, General Adnan, Don Riley, Bill Corrigan, The Pope and his family, my Uncle Les and my pop. Others who have stood by me through thick and thin: Richie and family, S.P.C.W., Steve Anderson, Ricky "the Prophet" Rice, Derrick Dukes, Fancy Ray McCloney, Bill Borea, Viva and Jerry, Rob Russen, Terry Katzman, Johnny Love, Dorean Porter, Roger Keller, David Boyd, General Chang, Jon Harberts, Bruce Hart, Jim Cornette, Steve Beverly, Paul E., Jeff Mullin, Pulse, Bob Clossen, Dave Meltzer and the rest of the posse. Printed wrestling history is sparse. If in some small way we can do this as well as those trailblazers have, we probably did a decent job. Read on!

—Ray Whebbe Jr.

Special thanks to these special people who sacrificed time and money to help contribute to this endeavor. Without your graciousness, our work would not have been possible: "Killer" Ken Raftery, "Dueling" David Olson, "The Stomper" Sheldon Goldberg, "Terrific" Tom Burke, Dr. of Style Bob Bryla, "Ripper" Rob Feinstein, Terry "DJ" Katzman, John "The King" Pantozzi, Sheik Ed Farhat, Figures Inc., "Stormin'" Norman Kietzer, "Fabulous" Phyllis Gould, ToyBiz, Jakks Pacific, Chaos Comics, "Queen" Francisca Pulido, "Crabby" Steve Carroll, ECW, The Nashville Network, "Fast" Tom Chipetta, "The Genius" Dave Meltzer, The Wrestling Observer, "Stone Cold" Steve Anderson, WOW Magazine, "Dapper" Donny Laible, "Dangerous" Dave Scherer, "The Golden Greek" Georgann Makropolous, 1Wrestling.com, The International Wrestling Institute and Museum, "Shooter" Mike Chapman, "Puffin'" Pat Hollis, Tony "Don't Call Me Lance Russell" Friedman, "Slick" Mick Karch, the World Wrestling Federation, World Championship Wrestling, "Booker" Paul Heyman, Highspots, "Dandy" Chris Perry, Jay "Da Best" DeChellis, "Jumpin'" Joel Held, "Dangerous" D.E. Mueller, "Pounding" Pedro Martinez, P.M. Video and the millions (and millions!) of fans who added their support.

Contents

Introduction, 6

Chapter 1

The Kings of Wrestling Collecting, 8

Chapter 2

Some Superstars Worth Collecting, 18

Chapter 3

The Video Market, 34

Chapter 4

Valley of the Dolls, 44

Chapter 5

Card Collecting and Knickknacks, 72

Chapter 6

The Wrestling Museum, 90

Chapter 7

Books, Magazines and Programs, 96

Chapter 8

Wrestling and the Silver Screen, 124

Chapter 9

The Rock & Wrestling Connection, 132

Chapter 10

Autographs, 136

Chapter 11

The Internet, 150

Chapter 12

To Know Your Role,
You Must Know Your Past, 158

Introduction

Collecting memorabilia means many different things to many different people. Some folks collect for the sheer joy of maintaining a collection of specialized items. Some folks collect with the hope that the item will increase in value. And others collect because of their strong connection to a specific genre of pop culture, be it television shows like the "A-Team" and "Charlie's Angels" or old B-grade Godzilla flicks.

In the last 20 years, the sports-memorabilia market has seen both exceptional and lean years for investing. The volume of merchandise with which fans have access to is rather astounding. Upon any visit to sports-memorabilia stores, one can find a myriad of different items from all different sports. Cards, figurines, one-of-a-kinds, autographs and more are all for the taking for any virtual category of discriminating tastes.

However, one market that has not been tapped into is that of professional-wrestling collectibles. Wrestling is purely unique in that it has the enviable position of combining the best of the so-called "traditional sports" market, as well as the television-collectibles market phenomenon. Wrestling shows have been part of a recent boom in popularity that is without rival and has seriously competed for the dollars of fans from traditional sports areas. The television shows like the ones staged by the World Wrestling Federation and World Championship Wrestling rank as the top-rated cable programs and nowadays it is truly difficult to keep up with the never-ending line of new merchandise that is generated. Increasingly, collectibles shops around the country have added pro-wrestling memorabilia out of fear for losing out on this pop-culture craze.

True wrestling fans know, however, that the sport has seen more than 50 years of great popularity. The fact that wrestling is getting mainstream media attention is new, but wrestling has always been a popular spectator sport. Wrestling memorabilia has been bought, sold and talked about in underground circles for years. Wrestlers have appeared in advertising, movies, have figures made of them, and have been cover stories in thousands of magazines around the globe. That, truly, just scratches the surface of the appeal wrestling has to millions of fans. Even today, with the wrestling-collectibles market at record levels of popularity, the sport has not been officially recognized as a viable part of the memorabilia marketplace.

That's why we are thrilled to be the first authors to take it upon ourselves to write one book, as comprehensive as possible, to chronicle the pro-wrestling collectibles market. We are pleased you decided to buy our book, check it out, and be one of the many who will be part of a first-of-its-kind manual of wrestling collectibles for both wrestling and non-wrestling fans alike. When Krause Publications approached us in 1999 about doing this project, little did we know what a chore (but fun) putting together a book like this would become. With very little sourcing and established pricing available, the work put into this book cannot be described. However, we hope you'll see the love and passion that went into making this book possible. What we hoped to provide for fans was an introduction into the wrestling-collectibles market that would suit both old-time enthusiasts and newcomers to this great "Sport of Kings."

We clearly felt a price guide alone would not do the marketplace justice. That's why, on our pages, you will see many tidbits of information on different stars of the past and present, and why they are important for collectors. From pioneers like George Hackenschmidt and Frank Gotch to classics like Lou Thesz and Bruno Sammartino to modern-day heroes like Hulk Hogan and Steve Austin, we tried diligently to incorporate a mix of new and old.

One thing to keep in mind about the wrestling market: there were thousands of individual items that could be considered for inclusion in this book; but sadly, we could not fit everything. From old photos to programs from different territories to posters to one-of-a-kind items to today's mass-marketed items and video collecting, the number of items available within wrestling is quite staggering. So what we do, however, is give readers an idea of the different categories within wrestling collecting and what fans may find in that area. So, if you rummage through your attic some Saturday afternoon and find a gem of a collectible, hopefully, through this book, you may have a better idea of its worth and significance to other collectors.

But that's not all we hoped to accomplish. We thought, and our publisher agreed, this book should take both the new and trident wrestling fans on a walking history of pro wrestling. Without question, the history of the sport is vast and entertaining. While doing our research, we stumbled on some fantastic photographs that are fit for a wrestling Smithsonian. Through these pages, you the fan can go on a brief (but thorough as possible) walking history of pro wrestling. A lot can be learned about where wrestling is today by looking at our past. Obviously, there just aren't enough pages to cover every important name. And every fan has reason to believe their favorite is a legend. But we tried to give credit to the great stars who helped induct fans into the wild world of pro wrestling through their athleticism, humor and outrageousness. Hopefully, you will find your favorite star somewhere on these wonderful pages.

If you have an item in your basement that is not in here, don't be surprised. That's the great thing about collectibles: There are literally hundreds of undiscovered treasures out there just waiting for a new home on a bookshelf or office desk. Our one ultimate goal was to create a book that fans will read, enjoy, learn a thing or two, and have a few laughs during a walk down memory lane. We hope you like this book enough to give it a special place in your personal library. If you have any questions or comments about the book, please send e-mail to: kristianpope@earthlink.net.

So let the opening bell ring loud and clear. And thanks for being a part of history.

Kristian Pope and Ray Whebbe Jr.

chapter 1

The Kings of Collecting

There are basically three kinds of pro-wrestling fans: Those who watch it on occasion, but can take it or leave it; the casual fan who may enjoy a pay event or live show from time to time; and those who are truly addicted, those who are bitten by the bug. You may find them surfing the Internet for all the latest gossip. They drive for hours to take part in an independent card. They sometimes become involved in the sport in one way or another (Paul E. Dangerously was once a ringside photographer!) or they become collectors.

Most collectors begin gathering things at a leisurely pace and soon entire rooms of houses become shrines to the sport. Take John Pantozzi. He never dreamed he would become one of the sport's most noted collectors. But he has. Pantozzi's two sons share an interest in professional wrestling, but it's doubtful they will ever be bitten by the bug like their father. "My kids like wrestling, but thank God they didn't go crazy like I did," Pantozzi said, in a somewhat sighed relief. "My wife has been very good about it, but it has taken on a life of its own."

Pantozzi says his Fabulous Moolah and Buddy Rogers ring jackets are two of his most treasured items. Both items have serious historical value. Why? Because for years, the state of New York had a law against women wrestling before live crowds. But Moolah fought the law and eventually became the first woman ever to wrestle at the Mecca of wrestling, Madison Square Garden. The "Nature Boy" Buddy Rogers' (a legendary NWA champ) jacket carries historic value. The "Nature Boy" was one of the first to wear a sequined jacket. Many wrestlers had flashy robes during the '50s and '60s, but none wore them with more class than Rogers. His jacket had a

Tommy Rich's autographed boots that he wore when he won the NWA World Title bout against Harley Race in 1981, $250. Photo courtesy of Chris Perry.

waistline cut with a zipper. By today's standards, it would be considered quite tame. But the flamboyant Rogers wore it well.

This jacket also comes with quite a story. Rogers, though he played the role of a strong heel, made sure, in no uncertain terms, that he would never lay down. Yet, in his match in 1963 at MSG against Bruno Sammartino, he might have done just that. Sammartino won the match in mere seconds and still boasts that he simply out-muscled Rogers. But truth be known, it was a miracle Rogers could even walk to the ring, much less fight before 18,000 screaming fans. Historians claim the Nature Boy had a mild heart attack prior to the match and was under strict doctors orders to quit the sport. Many believe Rogers agreed to the creative finish, which, as history shows, helped sew the beginnings of Sammartino's legacy. With the added mystique that surrounded the match, Rogers' trademark jacket has skyrocketed in value.

Dr. Bob Bryla of Utica, New York, was introduced to wrestling at age seven. His father, at the time, was the ringside physician for the New York State Athletic Commission and always had a front-row seat to the local matches. "I had a lump in my throat," recalls the younger Bryla. "I

"Dr. Wrestling" (Dr. Bob Bryla) holds Jackie Fargo's trunks, tights and belt the wrestler used to wear, $300. Photo courtesy of Dr. Bob Bryla.

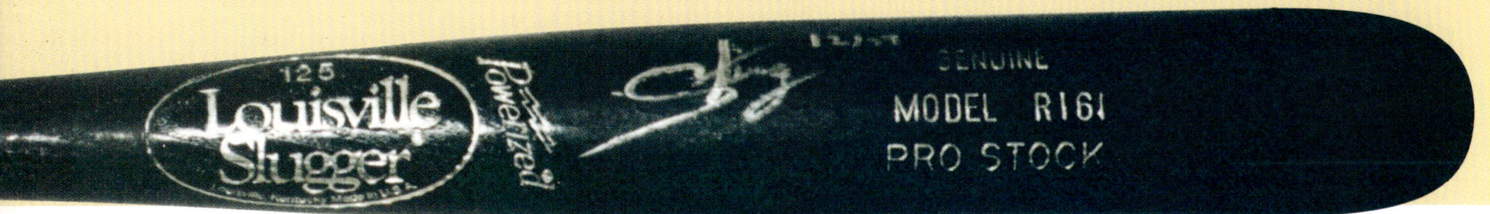

An autographed Sting bat, $100.
Photo courtesy of Chris Perry.

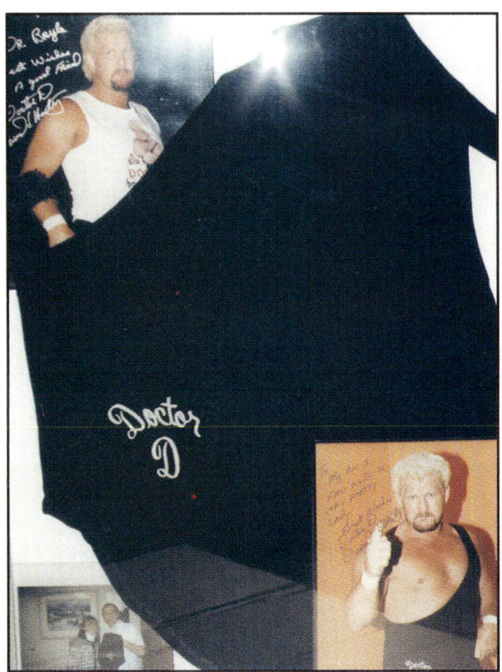

"Dr. D." David Schultz ring attire, photograph and autograph, $275.
Photo courtesy of Dr. Bob Bryla.

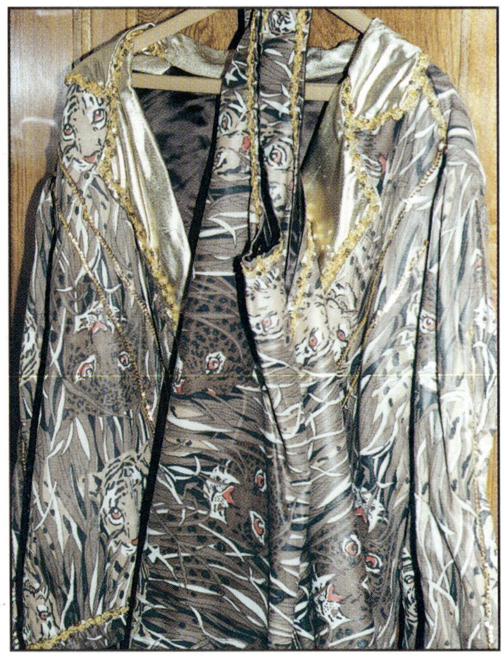

Superfly Jimmy Snuka's ring attire, $150.
Photo courtesy of Dr. Bob Bryla.

thought the wrestlers were killing each other." One night, Bryla asked his father to escort him to the bathroom. Instead of using the arena's facilities, Pop took his son to the back, where all the wrestlers prepared for their matches. "They were all sitting around, talking with one another and being normal. I knew right there that it was all entertainment."

And he was hooked ever since. Bryla began collecting the programs his dad would bring home for him. Now, his collection, which boasts some of the most unique and one-of-a-kind items there are, consists of several thousand items. His most prized possession is an old advertisement for "Gotch Socks," a product placard that the legendary Frank Gotch pitched in the 1920s. It is the only one that exists. "I knew an antique seller from Iowa and I bought what I thought was a picture of Gotch. When I went to put it in a new frame, I realized it was an ad for these socks. I didn't even know that I bought it." One couldn't put a value on an item like that, but it shows the power of collecting. Bryla continues to amass items today, but prefers the older stuff, like from when he was a kid. His outfit worn by Jackie Fargo (given to him from Fargo through his sister, who was Fargo's veterinarian) is another one-of-a-kinder and treasured item. Bryla is now a chiropractor and physical therapist in Utica, and remains an avid fan. But it all started from collecting.

Tom Burke has done a little bit of everything in pro wrestling. He has operated fan clubs, dabbled a bit on the business end of the sport, published a fine newsletter that networked a group of fanat-

Terry Funk's cattle prod, $150.
Photo courtesy of Chris Perry.

ical fans (of which many became wrestlers), is active in the Cauliflower Alley Club and last, but not least, is an avid collector. Burke owns a library full of magazines from the '20s to present day, a wrestling business-card collection, and has hundreds of postcards and posters. It's a living, breathing collection that grows daily. Among some of Burke's most cherished treasures are two world title belts (the WWWF's and Grand Prix's), masks worn by Killer Kowalski when he was a member of the championship team the Executioners, and a classic fez worn by the always wacky, Grand Wizard.

Mick Karch has been following wrestling since he was in diapers. "I learned how to read by figuring out the words of wrestling programs," said the 40-year-old lifelong Minnesotan. Karch's addiction has taken him into locker rooms and arenas as a photographer, journalist, and collector. Later on, as his interest in the sport increased, Karch became an award-winning television talk-show host, ring announcer, play by play commentator, and interviewer. He is without a doubt the finest announcer the independent scene has. He has also worked for Verne Gagne's AWA, Windy City Wrestling and Rob Russen's IWA. Karch, who was the founding president of Nick Bockwinkel's fan club called the "Bockwinkel Brigade," has an entire room dedicated to pro wrestling.

"The collection tells my entire life story," he said. "It has truly been my passion and I am thankful to have become a small part of the business. Unfortunately, when you're doing some interior decorating, most wives would prefer to

Chastity's ECW dress, $300.
Photo courtesy of Chris Perry.

Balls Mahoney chair from November to Remember PPV, 1997, $150. Photo courtesy of Chris Perry.

have armoires or a crystal collection rather than a bleeding fork used by Abdullah the Butcher."

Karch has many programs from the Minneapolis-St. Paul area, where he grew up. Karch remembers waiting to get into old television tapings at a local hotel in the '60s. That passion he had for wrestling way back when is still evident in Karch, as the sport reaches a new era. "I love the Golden Days," Karch said, "but I love what the current promotions are doing now. Needless to say, I will always collect."

Chris Perry of Virginia is quite a unique character. His area of interest is in collecting one-of-a-kind and rare items. Some of his best items are an autographed pair of boots used by Tommy Rich when he won the NWA World title from Harley Race as a teenager, a metal folding chair painted and signed by ECW's Balls Mahoney, and a Calgary Hitmen (the team that Bret Hart was part-owner of) hockey sweater autographed by all the Hart brothers, including the late Owen Hart. "These are all special things and I treasure them dearly," Perry said. "Some of these things I bought at auctions and I got to meet the wrestler who the item belonged to." Perry also has a real outfit worn by "Goldust" Dustin Runnels that is worth around

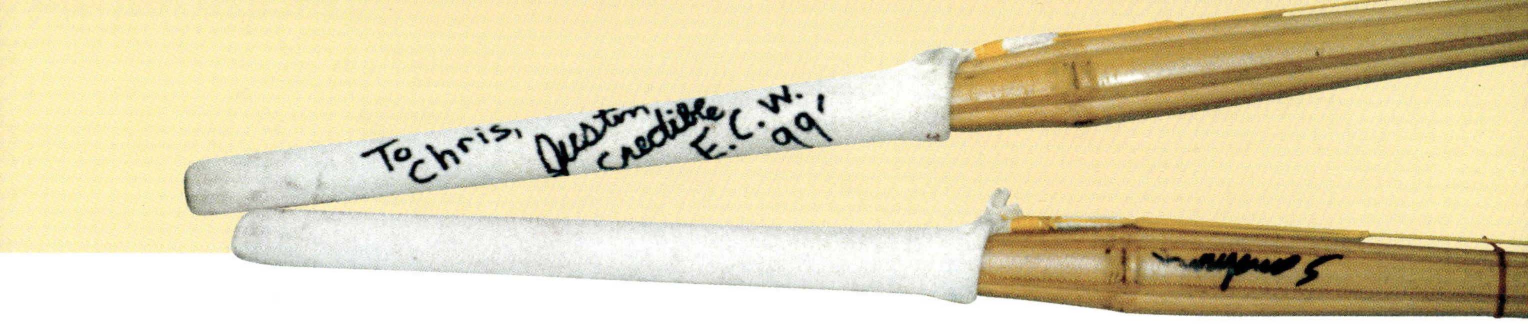

(Above) Singapore canes autographed by Sandman/Justin Credible, $150 each. Photo courtesy of Chris Perry.

$300 and two Singapore canes used by Sandman and Justin Credible.

Dennis Corraluzzo is another lifelong fan who made the big leap from fandom to working in the wrestling business. He has been instrumental in promoting independent cards on the East Coast and has cemented his name in history by beating his own drum. He has promoted pivotal matches involving X Pac, Sabu and Jerry Lynn and at one time he worked with Eastern Championship Wrestling (which later, Paul Dangerously formed into Extreme Championship Wrestling). Coraluzzo is a solid family man and owns an insurance business, but it's wrestling that gets his blood going.

"I've had a lot of fun promoting and always enjoy meeting the guys," he said. "If I retired from promoting tomorrow, I would still be happy with my family and business. You've got to be able to draw the line between the two. But no matter what, I'll never give up my poster collection." Corraluzzo has one of the largest collections of wrestling posters found anywhere. "The posters are an invaluable piece of history and tell a story like nothing else can. Reading a poster allows the mind to be creative, visualize what could have happened on that particular evening and to me that's better that any written report or video tape. The

Sheik Adnan Al Kassie's tank, worn during his famous bouts in Iraq, $150.

Another ring shirt worn by WWF's General Adnan, $125.

Sheik Adnan Al Kassie's ring robe, $75.

WWF's General Adnan's ring shirt, $125.

poster puts us into a frozen time warp. For those minutes we're reading that poster, all other thoughts cease."

No doubt, it was the art of the poster which sold the show. A well-done poster could make the card seem larger than life. Some promoters enjoy the multi-color posters that have roots traced to the '20s. Others enjoy using action-photo posters, while some use basic ring shots. For years, Calgary's Stampede Wrestling had a basic poster with the Hart family on it and simply left space to write in the date and site. Mexican posters are often quite ragged, but always show a facial shot of a masked Luchadore. Japanese posters are truly works of art.

Rob Martinez inherited the wrestling bug from his father, Pedro, who wrestled, refereed and promoted in the '60s. Papa Martinez not only broke racial barriers, but through his grit and fortitude, became a promoter in a field that at the time was limited to a select few. Today, the younger Martinez oversees P.M. Video, which has been successful in marketing the "Golden Age" and "Wrestling Gold" video series. He also has countless hours of great matches including Eddie Einhorn's ultra-rare 1975 IWA group. P.M. Video also sells custom-made tapes and offers only the highest quality of videos for sale.

Martinez was once a ring announcer, referee, and promoter for his father's group, which was based in Buffalo. He says his fix comes from being able to share these classics matches with other fans. P.M. has several collectible matches that include the likes of the Original Sheik, Dick the Bruiser, Bobo Brazil, and Pat O'Connor. His most cherished video is a first-generation copy of the 32-minute Chicago Comiskey Park battle between O'Connor and "Nature Boy" Rogers. In the last few years, Martinez has had his collection seen on MSNBC, A&E and now has a contract with ESPN's Classic Sports Network.

Like Martinez, for David Krause, the passion for wrestling comes from video tapes. Krause's collection has become known as "the beast that ate Ohio." "I can't count how many tapes I have," he said. "I started in the '80s. I wanted to see the

Americans work in Japan, a Madison Square Garden show or two, and get a look at the independents. As I started trading tapes of young stars like Sean Waltman and Jerry Lynn, I started getting tapes from all over the world. I am not even actively trading now and I still get boxes and boxes every week. People think I'm some kind of tape guru or something. I'm not. I'm just a fan with more tapes than I know what to do with."

There are countless numbers of fans, who began their interest in wrestling, who have similar stories as the gentlemen mentioned. Marvin Joel began his involvement as a fan some 30 years ago. He, too, developed into a promoter, booking agent and tape collector. He was the one who believed in X-Pac and gave him a shot in Minnesota. He also played an instrumental part in getting Erin O'Grady a place in the WWF as Crash Holly. Among Joel's prized possessions are tapes of a 12-year-old X-Pac cutting Randy Savage's grass and an O'Grady early career promo tape.

Jim Cornette and Paul E. Dangerously began their illustrious careers in wrestling as photojournalists and many of their photos were seen in Norman Kietzer's "Wrestling News." Mike Rogers

Sheik Kassie's boots, $100.

Autographed Calgary Hitmen hockey jersey, $350. Photo courtesy of Chris Perry.

Goldust's WWF ring costume, worth around $300. Photo courtesy of Chris Perry.

of Oregon is a school teacher and family man. Wrestling fans throughout the world know him for his wide array of photos and his great newsletter "Ring Around the Northwest." Rogers enjoys the piece of history that photos tell. He offers photos of Northwest mainstays like Billy Jack Haynes, Diamond Tim Flowers, Bret Sawyer, and the Barr family. He also has classic shots of Bruiser Brody, Ricky Vaughn (who later became Lance Von Erich), Pedro Morales, Hulk Hogan and countless others.

"Photos tell another part of the wrestling story," Rogers said. "It's especially fun to collect photos of wrestlers at different parts of their careers. Especially interesting are pictures of wrestlers who are just beginning to find their niche, or in gimmicks that just didn't work."

Don Laible is another fan and collector. He has written hundreds of published articles about wrestlers and has even become a book author. For Donny, it's been fun. But like all other collectors, he often wonders where it began—and how it will end. "I've been fortunate enough to personally meet many of the wrestlers and establish some good friendships within the business," Laible said. "But as far as collecting, I don't even know what I have. There are boxes here, and boxes there. Just tons of stuff. It just keeps growing." He also has more than 300 Japanese wrestling magazines in mint condition that go back to 1968. The quality of these magazines is impeccable. In the Orient, wrestlers are treated as icons

Billy Whitewolf's ring headdress, $175.

and the pictures in the national weekly magazines are of the caliber found in National Geographic. Laible also has more than 3,000 American wrestling magazines and 1970s' programs from Sam Muchnick's storied St. Louis promotion.

Many collectors, like those mentioned, began corresponding with other fans in the '60s. It was an era where promoters only released information they saw fit. Many fans were led to believe the world champion seen on their local television show was the true champion. Information was hard to get. What resulted was a network of pen pals who traded everything from photos to video tapes. Newsletters, and now the Internet, have followed in that tradition and have made a huge impact on the sport.

In the 1960s, corresponding was essential for those who had a thirst for more wrestling information. Burke's newsletter and Kietzer's publications were must-reads for those seeking gossip from the major companies like the NWA, AWA and World Wide Wrestling Federation (now the WWF). Many collectors and pen pals were only closet wrestling fans. Most had real jobs as nurses, doctors, social workers and laborers. But when it came to wrestling, all seemed to have one common bond—an unbridled passion for the sport of professional wrestling.

Billy Whitewolf's ring attire, $125.

2 chapter Some Superstars worth Collecting

Most collectors—new and old—always ask themselves one question when collecting wrestling memorabilia: which wrestler should I collect? That, my friends, is not always an easy answer. Some would argue the older fellows, while some would say the money is with the new generation.

Convincing arguments can be made either way. The "most popular" wrestler is not always the one who will get you the best return in later years (if that's why you collect). Generally, a fail-safe method is to choose from all over. The legends, the hall of famers, the young hot shots—they're all worthy investments. It should be noted, however, that most items of current superstars are only worth their market value.

To make it easier, we have comprised a list of our most favorite personalities from wrestling and why they are important to collecting. We are positive you will disagree with this list. It's not intended to be the end-all list, merely a sampling of some names that you may want to be on the look out for. As you'll see, this list is made up of everybody—from pioneers like Lou Thesz and George Hackenschmidt, to the wild personalities like Andre the Giant and Abdullah the Butcher. Sure, we are biased and these are our favorites. But in the case of these gentlemen (and one woman), you can't go wrong. So without further adieu...

Steve Austin in his days with WCW, when he was known as "Stunning" Steve Austin. Note the long blonde hair.

Steve Austin

Casual fans and diehards can't agree on much, but they do when it comes to Steve Austin: this guy has incredible talent. A mix of Terry Funk and Roddy Piper, Austin deserves the top spot he has—so it's not surprising to find many items out there for Stone Cold. Fans won't find any pre-WWF figures, but his WCW cards are available. His early days in World Class Championship Wrestling in Dallas supply fans with posters and programs. But don't expect to find anything spectacular. The real supply comes from recent years. Go to any store and Austin paraphernalia can be found. He has everything from dolls, to candy to posters to specialized toys. The Jakks Austin dolls are particular favorites among collectors. Like Hulk Hogan's merchandise from the early 1980s, there is a glut of Austin stuff, from shot glasses to doormats. But he is the biggest star ever seen and count on some items getting a nice price down the line.

The Rock battles Jerry Lawler.

The Rock

This third-generation grappler has overnight become one of the greatest attractions the sport has ever seen. The Rock calls himself the most electrifying man in sports entertainment, but he's not the most marketed—not yet anyway. Fans will be hard pressed to find any pre-WWF items; but if you look hard, you may find a gem. His days in Memphis are not forgotten by fans. His videos and programs are readily available from collectors. Some fans are now beginning to take notice of the Miami Hurricanes football media guide where he played in his college days. Like every WWF wrestler, fans can find many items for him now, from T-shirts to his trademark sunglasses.

Hulk Hogan

Probably the most mass-marketed wrestler in the history of the sport, the Hulkster's likeness has graced everything from candy to bath soap to video games. Most Hogan-related merchandise has a collector's value, so fans are encouraged to snap up what they can because it will probably increase in price. Hogan was a key man in bringing wrestling to the mainstream. Fans can find movies with Hogan, cartoons with Hogan, lunch boxes with Hogan. You get the message. His cover article in a 1984 Sports Illustrated is coveted.

Hulk Hogan is the most mass-marketed face in wrestling history.

Abdullah the Butcher in action.

Abdullah the Butcher

Where is he? What is he thinking? Who will be his next folly? Only Abdullah the Butcher knows for sure. One thing we do know is this ever-lasting cult favorite is the living legend of hardcore wrestling. Abdullah made his mark while wrestling in Japan since the mid-1970s. Over there, he is a major star. Fans can find hundreds of items from Japan, such as magazines. His travels in the U.S., most specifically through the Detroit area in the '70s, are perhaps the most sought-after items his fans look for today. If it's a doll you are looking for, you're in luck. Abby has two: a Remco doll from 1984 which is very rare, and a recently issued doll through Figures Inc. Promoters loved the Butcher because his look was great. There are hundreds of photos out there which give proof to his legendary appearance, which made him one of the most-feared wrestlers ever.

Jerry Lawler

He likes to call himself the King. For collectors, he's known as the Joker. There are lots of fun items out there of Jerry Lawler from his early days all the way to present. Fans can find videos, dolls and much more. The best items, if you can ever find one, is some original artwork by Lawler himself. His cartoons are very well done and there's no question Lawler is an accomplished artist (two examples of his artwork are in Chapter 5). However, most, if not all, of his work is unavailable to the general public. If you are lucky to come into contact with one, expect to pay a few hundred dollars for it. New items of Lawler have sprouted up as a result of his 1999 bid to become mayor of his hometown, Memphis, Tennessee.

Jerry "The King" Lawler.
Jim Cornette photo.

Kerry Von Erich.

Kerry Von Erich

The Texas Tornado was the icon of the fabled Von Erich family of Dallas, Texas-based World Class wrestling, and items from their wrestling heyday are readily available still. The Parade of Champions spectacular, when Kerry won the NWA World title in 1984, stands as the man's defining moment in the sport. Programs from the event are must-have's to be sure.

Paul Heyman

Paul E., as everyone knows him, has a foundation in wrestling rooted in fandom. Now co-owner and matchmaker for Extreme Championship Wrestling out of Philadelphia, Heyman got his start as a ringside photographer. As a teen-ager, Heyman was a resourceful young journalist, snapping photos for some of the top wrestling magazines the world over. He also penned many articles for those magazines in the early 1980s. His accomplishments on the printed page make him a big part of the collectibles market today. Often, those classic pictures in old Pro Wrestling Illustrated magazines were taken by Paul E. But it wasn't until the mid-to-late '80s, that Paul E. would begin what has turned into an illustrious career on the TV screen. He started managing wrestlers, instead of writing about them, and created the ever-lasting gimmick Paul E. Dangerously. Through the years, he managed such greats as the Original Midnight Express, Austin Idol, Tommy Rich, and a young Mark Callous (The Undertaker). He entertained audiences in the AWA, Mid-South region, NWA and, of course, the East Coast. Now, a behind-the-scenes maven of the sport, Paul E's great works continue. It's hard to think the brash, outspoken manager was once a quiet fan just like many of us fans today.

Paul E. Dangerously.

As people on the street stop to look, 6-foot 10-inch Japanese wrestler Shohei Baba gives Michelle Amour, hostess at the Golden Violin Restaurant, a bird's-eye view of Sunset Strip.

Shohei "Giant" Baba

Seen here outside Hollywood's Golden Violin Restaurant circa 1963 while on a promotional tour in the states, Baba was, and remains in his own wake, an endearing pro-wrestling legend. In Japan, and even to many U.S. fans, Baba is synonymous with the sport. At nearly 7-feet tall, Baba was truly a giant in the Land of the Rising Sun—not only for his wrestling stature, but for his humanitarian efforts as well. Baba's funeral in 1998 left his entire nation in mourning and was carried live on national TV. Obviously, fans can easily find many items on Baba, including literally thousands of magazine and program covers. In his later years, Baba's likeness was even made into a doll. His battles with such U.S. greats as Bruiser Brody, Abdullah the Butch and Andre the Giant are timeless classics and fitting for a place on any collector's shelf.

A Verne Gagne magazine ad, $5. Photo courtesy of Mick Karch.

Verne Gagne

One of the real stars of the sport, Gagne was a hero to many. An NCAA heavyweight champion, his wrestling skills were hard to match. He became AWA world champion and was followed by son Greg into the ring. Gagne is the subject of many items. A board game was made in his honor in the 1960s and he was the pitch-man for a diet product called Geraspeed. Magazine ads with Gagne are a favorite among some fans. Gagne also trained many stars including Ric Flair and the late Chris Taylor. His AWA territory brought to prominence such stars as the Road Warriors and Hulk Hogan. Verne's group was the first to mass-market a line of wrestling dolls in the mid 1980s. The dolls may not have looked good compared to today's standards, but they are revered by doll collector's.

Mankind and "Socko" put a finishing move on an opponent.

Mick Foley

Mick Foley has taken wrestling to heights and places no other wrestler has been before—namely, his book, Blood and Sweatsocks, was the first-ever wrestling book to reach No. 1 on the national best-seller lists. But that is because the path to stardom for Foley (a.k.a. Mankind, Cactus Jack, Dude Love) has been so fascinating. He began in the '80s under the tutelage of Dominic DeNucci. He traveled all the small circuits and then WCW before getting a big break in the WWF as Mankind. His tours took him to Japan, where he became 'King of the Death" matches. Videos of Foley are very hot, namely his fire matches with Terry Funk. Expect to pay close to $45 for these. Posters from his ECW days can get around $20 and footage from his teen-age "backyard wrestling" days would command several hundred dollars if they could ever be found. Autograph seekers love this guy because with his three names, the challenge to get them all is high. But whichever name he chooses, Mick Foley will always be a fan favorite.

Bobby "The Brain" Heenan.

Bobby Heenan

The greatest manager ever to grace the sport, Heenan stands as a legend. He got his start in the sport by cutting Dick the Bruiser's lawn in Indianapolis. His talents on the mike and in the ring were unparalleled. The cerebral and quick-witted Heenan is the reason why many of us watched wrestling. Even in his later days in the WWF, Heenan was still at the top of his game. Collector's are constantly on the lookout for interviews of his because they are truly classic. In this day when the manager has seen a diminishing role, Heenan's efforts stand as a testament to how important the manager can be in wrestling. One of Heenan's most prized recruits was the eloquent and sharp-tongued Nick Bockwinkel. Through most of the '80s, Bockwinkel and Heenan were inseparable in the AWA, where Bock was world champ and tag-team champ. Together, they made the sport's best speaking tandem for the better part of 10 years.

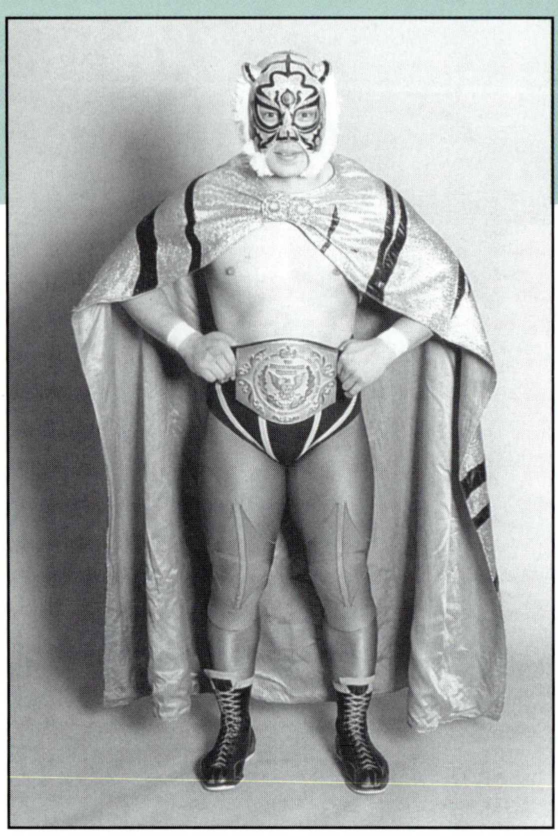

Tiger Mask.

Tiger Mask

One of the first real superstars of the modern era in Japan, Tiger Mask's bouts are widely regarded as some of the greatest of all time. As a junior heavyweight, Tiger Mask pioneered the diving moves of today's high flyers and paved the way for the smaller wrestlers to become legitimate stars in the land of big men. Perhaps his most sought-after videos are against Dynamite Kid, one-half of the British Bulldogs. Tiger Mask was also a superhero character in Japan and as a result, is seen on countless mass-marketed items. The Kid-Tiger Mask videos from 1981-83 are must-see matches for any fan. Collectors have built entire collections by trading these matches for others on their want list.

Freddie Blassie

Newer fans may only remember Blassie has an older manager from the WWF, but he stands as a true novelty in the land of wanna-be novelties. Blassie's record deals from the 1980s are priceless to real collectors, although they can really be had for $50. Who wouldn't have a place for "Pencil Neck Geek" and other classics. Blassie has a doll made in his likeness, too.

Freddie Blassie.

Bruno Sammartino.

Bruno Sammartino

No one questions the importance Bruno Sammartino had on pro wrestling in the United States. He was a multiple-time WWF championship holder and put a stranglehold on New Yorkers for the better part of a decade. His main events at Madison Square Garden are fondly remembered by collectors. His bout with Larry Zbyszko at Shea Stadium in 1979 drew what was then a record crowd. Fans can find the program from that classic match for a pretty reasonable price. In this photo, he is in all his glory with a pre-disco-era "mod" haircut.

Stu Hart gets ready to take on Chi-Chi.

Stu Hart

One of the toughest men of any era and father of wrestling's first family, Hart is a patriarch in the world of wrestling. Here he is battling Chi-Chi, a 500-pound Bengal tiger. But Hart is more widely known for training his famous sons, Bret, Bruce, Keith and the late Owen Hart. Each one of his sons wrestled and each daughter married a pro wrestler, including Davey Boy Smith and Jim Neidhart. The famous Hart family dungeon, which was actually the basement of his Calgary mansion, was the training ground for the sport's most elite and accomplished stars. The creaky dungeon was featured in a 1997 WWF match between Owen and Ken Shamrock.

Bruiser Brody

Frank "Bruiser Brody" Goodish, one of the sport's brawling icons and truly independent men, was respected worldwide for doing things his way in and out of the ring. He made phenomenally large purses in Japan and Puerto Rico and helped independent promoters fight the Turner and McMahon-led corporate takeovers by refusing to join either the WWF or WCW. Tragically, in 1988, Brody was slain while in Puerto Rico, but his legacy still stands as tall as the man lived his life. Tapes of his matches are among the most traded and sought after, in particular the All-Japan tag-team tournaments from the early '80s. Brody also went under the name, "King Kong Brody." Posters and programs from his Japan days are coveted by collectors, as is the memorial issue of Gong Magazine that paid tribute to this warrior after his death. Known as a brutal opponent, he was the gentlest of men in real life. His battles against Antonio Inoki and Abdullah the Butcher are classics.

A classic pose from the late Bruiser Brody.

The Fabulous Freebirds in their "war paint." Paul Heyman photo.

The Fabulous Freebirds

The Freebirds were arguably the greatest tag team of all time. They were the first to utilize "rock and wrestling" to their benefit. Comprised of Michael Hayes, Terry Gordy and Buddy Roberts, the 'Birds visited virtually every territory and were always part of the big-time feuds during the '80s. Videos of the boys from the early '80s on WTBS are in high demand. Many present-day wrestlers still visit those tapes to see how important the "interview" can be. Hayes turned interviews in works of art. Hayes and Co. recorded a record in the mid-'80s called "Bad Street." Those are rare, but can be found for around $35. Old pictures of the trio are great additions to any collection. The Freebirds had legendary meetings in Dallas against the Von Erich family. Novelties from those days are in high demand and any of the beautiful robes which Hayes wore to the ring during his career are worth hundreds of dollars.

Mil Mascaras

A worldwide star during the 1970s, Mascaras began as a bodybuilder who later was hired to fill the "Mil" part in the movies which also encompassed pro wrestling. He was one of the first high-fliers. Mil was part of the fascinating culture of the masked men in Mexico. Replicas of his masks have been sold all over the world, and he rarely, if ever, wore the same costume twice. Original versions of his mask are priceless. Mil was in numerous movies in Mexico and, although his better days are behind him, he is still considered a legend south of the border. Anything with the likeness of Mascaras is worth keeping.

The masked Mil Mascaras.

Hart (bottom row, center), with his First Family.

Jimmy Hart

This was one of Hart's first wrestling dynasties called the First Family. Hart, a manager from the Memphis area, started after fellow wrestler Jerry Lawler asked his friend, lead singer of the rock band the Gentry's, to do some managing. In the 1980s, Hart was the game's top manager and he is still a presence behind-the-scenes in WCW.

Terry Funk with his AWA belt.

Terry Funk

Here, Funk is seen with a belt worth more money on an Internet auction now than it was when it was used. Today, Funk is the one wrestler who connects many new fans with the "old" days. Terry is a world-renowned superstar and near-legend in Japan. Through 30-plus years of action, Funk just recently became known for his hardcore style. His matches with Cactus Jack and Atsushi Onita, among others, sell for around $30. Once you see one of his fire bouts, or barbed-wire wars, you will be hooked on Funk for life. His Japanese match against the Sheik and Sabu is a must-see, as the ring they were in caught fire and quickly went out of control. Funk suffered severe burns, but it had no effect in slowing down the veteran. Old posters during Funk's days in Amarillo, Texas, are very rare.

Jesse "The Body" Ventura strikes a pose in his earlier wrestling days.

Jesse "the Body" Ventura

A shameless self-promoter, Ventura has become a legend in his own time. As a wrestler, he shocked and stirred thousands of people during the '80s. Now that he is an aspiring president of our country, all of Jesse's merchandise has been increasing in value of late. His early WWF dolls are popular, as are his early collector cards. New Ventura action figures are being marketed and he has a full line of merchandise in an attempt to capitalize on his new-found career. Ventura wouldn't have it any other way. Because of his enormous off-screen success as Minnesota's governor, everything with Ventura has been seen with an inflated value. If he really does run for president, the sky is the limit (wouldn't that make a great wrestling angle!).

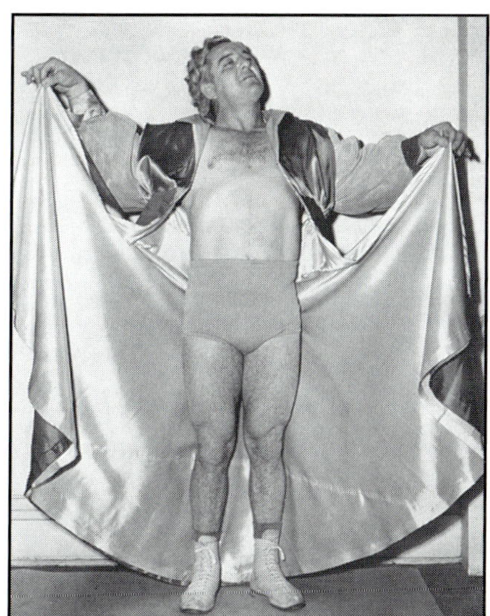
The theatrical Gorgeous George.

Gorgeous George

George was perhaps the original showman in a field that didn't quite know what to do with "showmen." He was the first TV star and was part of wrestling's first boom due to the advent of television. His old gowns and personal effects are kept alive and well through Slammer's Wrestling Gym in Los Angeles. In a testament to his legacy, George was past his prime physically when he attained his biggest successes. The fact that fans were still willing to buy tickets to see this man stands as the proof to his meaning in wrestling. Everything with his face on it is rare and highly valuable.

Bill Goldberg.

Goldberg

There is very little history when one speaks of Bill Goldberg. But that is not to say there is no future. Goldberg, a former professional football player with the Atlanta Falcons, burst onto the pro wrestling scene in 1996 and, along with Steve Austin, brought the sport back to No. 1. When Goldberg is interviewed about his shocking success, he says he never dreamed he would be making millions of dollars by parading around in his underwear. Truly, this phenom is as taken by his popularity as are the fans. There is no denying his talent. He is huge, has mega-charisma, and has already been the world champion. That's why he is extremely popular among collectors. His trading cards, autographs and dolls are hot. But because he has not been around long, true collectors must get creative when adding to their Goldberg collection. Here's an idea: an Atlanta Falcons media guide from his playing days is sure to fetch close to $50 on the open market.

Andre the Giant

Andre was an anomaly in pro wrestling. For the better part of his career, the happy Frenchman was used sparingly by regional promoters who wanted to draw a sell-out crowd for an important event. Andre usually wrestled in Battle Royals and six-man tag-team matches. He wrestled in virtually every part of the country at one point or another and was an international star. Posters advertising the Giant are popular for collectors because the man was not only a giant, but a very special individual. His autograph is highly sought after and is getting anywhere from $110 to $150.

Andre and the ladies.

An original photo of George Hackenschmidt, $35. Photo courtesy of Mike Chapman.

George Hackenschmidt

In the early 1900s, in an era gone by, just two names were the ones to know in wrestling: Frank Gotch and the "Russian Lion" George Hackenschmidt. Hackenschmidt was the European champion, having won every major tournament there. Gotch was widely considered the "world" champion. Naturally, these two men would have to meet in the ring. Three years in the making, the first Gotch-Hackenschmidt bout was scheduled for a capacity crowd at Chicago's Comiskey Park in 1908. In a war-like three-hour match, Gotch prevailed. But Hackenschmidt's memory lives on. Items from the historic match-up, such as promotional fliers, can get up to $100 from serious collectors. His autograph is worth close to $100, since it is such a hard find. Footage of the legendary match-up is very rare, but if one searches hard enough, who knows?

World heavyweight champion Lou Thesz wearing the NWA title belt he won from Buddy Rogers in a 1963 match.

Lou Thesz

Few can argue that Thesz was not the greatest professional wrestler of all-time. The six-time world champion won his titles in an era where championship belts were not traded just on Monday nights. He was a protégé of former champ Strangler Lewis. His first title was won in 1937 and even seven decades later, he still stepped between the ropes. Before men like Harley Race and Ric Flair, Thesz was the icon of the National Wrestling Alliance, which was the most prestigious sanctioning body of the day. Because of his relevance to the sport, Thesz is a popular name in collecting. His book, Hooker, is a detailed account of his career. Many photos and programs can be found with Thesz and most are inexpensive. Expect to pay in the $15-$20 range for programs. His autograph is fetching $50 on the open market. His best years came between the 1940s and '60s. Because of that, not many Thesz items are available, but of the ones that are, they are truly wrestling treasures, for Thesz was the jewel of the ring.

D-Generation X: Chyna, Triple H and Shawn Michaels.

Chyna and Hunter Hearst Helmsley

Joannie Lauer always considered herself to be athletic. At 6-1 and 190 pounds, she possessed the strength and size to star in a gladiator film. Instead, she was bitten by the wrestling bug. As Chyna, Lauer has become the prototypical WWF athlete for the new millennium: bold, powerful and in your face. Trained by Killer Kowalski, she learned the ropes alongside future boyfriend Triple H. Shortly after, she caught the eye of Vince McMahon and she became the bodyguard for Degeneration X. In 1999, she stood tall on her own, becoming the first woman to win the Intercontinental title. Lately, Chyna has become a cross-over star and a subject for collectors. She has graced the cover of TV Guide and Newsweek and can be seen on different network TV specials. Her dolls and merchandise is widely available and an autobiography should be out by the time this book is published.

Best known as Triple H, Paul Leveque epitomizes the WWF "attitude." He's brash and cocky on screen, but in real life is a level-headed 30-year-old who is on top of his game and loving every minute of it. After toiling in WCW, he ventured to the WWF in 1994-95, where he learned how to be "Triple H." After forming DX, his career skyrocketed. Now, he calls himself "The Game" and he is arguably WWF's top bad guy. Not many mass-produced Triple H items are available before his WWF days. His autograph is worth about $35 and his action figures are extremely popular. But fans enjoy this entertainer and those values are sure to increase, given time.

Diamond Dallas Page

He's known as DDP in wrestling circles and at one time was considered the people's wrestler. Page started as a manager in Florida and the AWA. But he always wanted to be in the ring, rather than outside. In the WCW and at age 35, Page did the unthinkable and trained to be a wrestler. He studied tapes religiously, trained hard and yearned to prove his critics wrong. By the mid-'90s, Page's work had paid off. Since then, he has established himself as one of the few stars of WCW. No one can dispute his success. He teamed with Jay Leno against Hulk Hogan and Dennis Rodman and appeared in the cable movie "First Daughter." Collectors can find many of the typical items like programs, photos and videos. Most are in the $20-$30 range. His book, Positively Page, sells for about $25.

Diamond Dallas Page and his "little buddy," a 10-inch sculpture in his likeness created by Creative License. The cold-cast porcelain figure, limited to 5,000, sells for $95.

Roddy Piper

If there is any wrestler who has ever "been there, done that," it's Roddy Piper. He helped catapult the WWF into the mainstream in the early '80s and his effect is still being felt. As the story goes, Piper started as a Golden Gloves boxer when he was 14 and eventually turned to wrestling professionally at age 15. By the late '70s, Piper had developed his ring persona of the loud mouth in a Scottish kilt. He earned a reputation for doing whatever it took to sell the show to the TV viewers. Tape traders relish his interview from that era when he broke a beer bottle over his head. He moved on to the NWA and Mid-Atlantic areas and in 1984 he moved to the big-time, the WWF. Fans can find hundreds of hours of great Piper moments on video. He has also been a major cross-over star, having starred in more than 20 feature films like "Hell Comes to Frogtown" and "They Live." Wrestlemania I programs, when he fought Mr. T and Hulk Hogan, sell for about $50. There are lots of fun Piper items available.

Roddy Piper, as action figure.

The colorful Randy Savage wearing his title belt.

Randy Savage

Randy "Macho Man" Savage has lived a life many only dream of having. He has been the main event on pay-per-view, played baseball professionally, had a few acting jobs and became one of the bigger-than-life stars created by the WWF in the mid-'80s. His aggressive attacks on Hulk Hogan, wildly colorful outfits, trademarked "Ohhhhhh yeeeeeah" interviews and sheer talent made him a household name. Savage was born into a wrestling family. His father, Angelo Poffo, is a legendary figure who held the record for most consecutive push ups and wrestled worldwide in the '60s and '70s. His brother, Lanny Poffo, also enjoyed a long ring career. Collectors are always looking for Savage baseball cards (he was signed to the Cincinnati Reds) which will fetch close to $100. Savage also has been the pitch-man for Slim Jims, so any advertising with his likeness can be sold for $20-$30.

Road Warriors

Animal and Hawk, better known as The Road Warriors.

In 1981, Joe Laurinidas and Mike Hegstrand graduated from Ed Sharkey's Minneapolis wrestling camp. It wasn't long before Georgia Championship Wrestling matchmaker Ole Anderson saw Mel Gibson's hit movie "Road Warrior" and slapped Laurinidas and Hegstrand with the name and the rest was history for these two men. Together, as the Road Warriors, they became the hottest tag team in wrestling history and changed the face of wrestling as fans knew it. These two spawned many offshoots around the country, but none were as successful as Hawk and Animal. Later, known as the Legion of Doom, the team won numerous world titles in the NWA, WCW and WWF. Their dolls from 1984, made by Remco, are true collector's items and get anywhere from $20-$75 today. Magazines like Pro Wrestling Illustrated with the "Roadies" are in high demand, as are snapshots of these painted warriors of the ring.

Undertaker

Mark Calloway set out to become a professional wrestler and after being scoffed at by critics, he found his niche in the WWF as the Undertaker. The first publicity photos of 'Taker showed a 6-8, 220-pound skinny kid. Bruce Hart of Stampede promotions put the photo in the "never will be a star" file and has regretted it ever since. The rejection obviously motivated Calloway, who worked small territories for years perfecting his craft before 1990, when he was given the creative Undertaker gimmick. Lots of Undertaker novelties are available, from key chains to shirts to mugs. The Undertaker comic book is a hit at conventions and gets close to $20 already. Programs from the USWA and WCW when Calloway wrestled under different names are very rare. Nowadays, Undertaker dolls are very hot and worth the small investment. If you're looking for a "Mark Calloway" autograph now, forget it. The Undertaker claims that person no longer exists.

The Undertaker strikes a menacing pose.

Antonino Rocca

Many consider Rocca the first wrestler turned marketer. In the Northeast area, Rocca was synonymous with local advertising. Rocca even recorded his own album. But his true fame happened in the ring, where he became a huge star of the '60s. He enticed fans with his acrobatic style and his drop kicks were second to none. He fought all the greatest names of his time and then some. Old posters and advertisements with his likeness are hard to come by for fans outside the Northeast.

Antonino Rocca unleashes a high-flyin' kick to Verne Gagne during a bout in 1953.

Sting in his earlier wrestling days.

Sting

Another of the new-era mass-marketed stars, Sting was WCW's first legitimate mega-star. Fans are hard-pressed not to find Sting's collectibles. Fans can also find some out-of the-ordinary things. He was discovered originally has a member of a weight-lifting squad called the American Warriors in the early 1980s. From these salad days, the Stinger is in several photos with his partner at the time, the Ultimate Warrior. Warrior would later team with Sting as the Blade Runners for Bill Watts' UWF. Now, Sting's line of merchandise is as easy to find as a trip to your local super store.

chapter 3 The Video Tape Market

For the most part, since the Great Depression, mainstream media has treated pro wrestling quite unfairly. Most television news and sports programs overlook the "Sport of Kings." Once in a great while, TV stations would carry a clip or two from a sold-out wrestling card. To be sure, the anchors would present the news with their tongues firmly planted in their cheeks. Some newspapers would even go so far as to promote an upcoming event in a simple, three-paragraph story. Not exactly Super Bowl coverage here, folks.

The immense history of wrestling has been covered and documented with equal ineptitude. To be certain, wrestling magazines have been better sellers on the newsstand than half of the general topic publications, but prior to the 1960s, there were few wrestling magazines published for the fans.

With the birth of the video era in the 1980s, the history of the sport found its chance to be preserved for generations to come. The 1970s, '80s and '90s created an astounding video boom for wrestling fans and collectors. Thousands of pay-per-view and specialty-made videos have been released by Coliseum Video (Titan Sports/WWF), Turner Home Video (NWA, WCW), USWA (Memphis), ECW and numerous independents. Many are available at local video stores. There are probably close to 5,000 matches from the 1950s' Golden Age converted from black-and-white film to video. Unfortunately, very few matches held prior to that time are available on video. If they exist, film of the Gotch, Hackenschmidt, Londos and Lewis bouts would be quite costly and run between $100-$200.

The video market is vital to any collector, and to some extent, even the casual fans. The greatest feuds, biggest blood baths, origins of superstars, best interviews, top matches, and virtually every aspect of professional wrestling are all well documented on video tapes.

Most commercially released video tapes that feature wrestling sell in the $20 to $30 range. Almost every pay-per-view spectacular ever held in the United States is available either via the Internet or through your hometown video store. The sales of wrestling videos have surpassed most critics' expectations. In Variety Magazine's weekly listings of the top-selling videos, wrestling ruled the roost and had as many as the top 16 of 20 selling videos on the chart throughout the entire year of 1999.

The most popular, and important, craze throughout the world for wrestling fans is that of tape collecting. Tapes of various territories, best-of compilations, local wrestling programs and cable access-oriented videos are swapped and sold in virtually every state and country in the world. This has allowed the wrestling underground to see any wrestler in any match from anywhere in the world. The average fan-based tapes sell for about $20; however, very rare and mint-condition videos can sell for as much as $100. This is certainly considered a very good price, especially if you keep in mind that many new-release movies can sell for as high as $79.95, give or take a few dollars.

Some collectors want every match or every weekly series from a specific region. Others prefer best-of compilations. The matches that are highest in demand are brawls, classics and also great interviews. It's extremely difficult to say exactly what the best videos are because it all depends on an individual's taste. However, the most meaningful to collectors are their favorite matches and wrestlers that drew them into the sport as a child or teen-ager.

Therefore, it is extremely difficult, almost impossible, to put values on tapes. To someone

Tapes of Bobo Brazil and the Sheik, shown here in a wrestling match, can fetch up to $50.

who grew up in the Detroit area, tapes of Bobo Brazil and the Sheik may be worth $50. To a child of the 1980s, Hulk Hogan's tremendous feuds with Paul Orndorff, Randy Savage or Roddy Piper may be their cup of tea. A fan from the 1990s may go gaga over a Stone Cold, Rock or Undertaker video.

But, as our experience notes, videos of several vintage wrestlers of the 1980s have been traded more than any wrestlers alive. Names like Dynamite Kid, Davey Boy Smith, Tiger Mask, the Freebirds, the Funks, Ric Flair, Harley Race, Bruiser Brody, Abdullah the Butcher, Giant Baba, Akira Maeda and Antonio Inoki are just a smattering of the all-time favorites. Tapes of Bruno Sammartino are in high demand but are also very rare.

Rob Feinstein's RF Video and Pedro Martinez' P.M. Video are two of the most successful businesses which sell wrestling collections, interviews, entire cards and television programs. Feinstein also sells a "shoot" interview series, where superstars such as Abdullah the Butcher, Sid Vicious and Terry Funk are interviewed out of character. The wrestlers are asked questions in a straight, no-holds-barred fashion that brings fans into the minds and hearts of these amazing stars.

Feinstein has virtually every inch of film shot by Extreme Championship Wrestling. For those new to ECW, the promotion is seen on the Nashville Network. RF Video also features many Japanese matches, entire cards and compilations. RF has preserved the history of the 1990s well, but it also has tapes from the 1950s through '80s in its catalog. It also recently acquired the rights to the Florida territory from the 1980s, where future stars Rick Rude, Lex Luger, and the Nasty Boys battled against, and alongside, greats like Blackjack Mulligan, Dusty Rhodes, and Kevin Sullivan.

On the other hand, PM Video features mostly '60s and '70s stars. Among the stars it features are Ernie Ladd, the Sheik and Bobo Brazil. Tapes of Lou Thesz, Gorgeous George, a young Verne Gagne, Gene Kiniski, Whipper Watson, Rikidozan, Buddy Rogers, and other late, or retired greats, are very rare. Nick Bockwinkel recently acquired the collection of late Houston promoter Paul Boesch. Hopefully, tapes of world-class superstars like Thesz will be found there someday.

What follows below are some various categories that we believe are some of the most popular videos available via the current marketplace:

Roots of Wrestling

"Stone Cold" Steve Austin is a true phenomenon. His 1998 income has been estimated to be in the $8 to $10 million range. He has become a counter-culture cult hero to the masses and he has name recognition parallel to the biggest names in sports and entertainment.

What videos offer is the chance to see how a wrestler grew into the character he is today.

In Austin's case, his lineage goes back to the late 1980s in Dallas, Texas, when he wrestled for the USWA. His long hair and colorful trunks were a far cry from the bald,

Stone Sold Steve Austin vs. Savio Vega in WrestleMania XII in 1996.

The Rock and Jerry Lawler in a match.

Brett Hart in his Calgary days. Hart and his family are very popular with collectors.

black-trunked and bold personality that he exudes now. He then went to WCW and teamed with Brian Pillman as the great tag team the Hollywood Blondes. He even went to ECW for a short time, where, many say, "Stone Cold" was born. But that's the great thing about videos. Most fans enjoy keeping on record the past of their favorites and tape traders are more than willing to accommodate other fans in making their collections complete.

The Rock

Rocky Maivia certainly has the lineage to be a wrestling superstar. His father is Rocky Johnson and his uncle was Chief Peter Maivia. He is a former collegiate football player and has the body to back up his talk. However, when most saw his 1996 USWA performances as Flex Cavana, they could not foresee how big a star he would become. Therefore, his career as Flex is much sought after by collectors.

Owen Hart & Brian Pillman

As in any other collectible genre, footage of those who have died in their prime are some of the most popular to obtain. Guitar god Jimi Hendrix made only four albums while he was alive, but since he died, more than 40 albums have been issued. His licensed merchandise sells more today than ever. That's why tapes of Owen Hart and Brian Pillman are worth more today than ever before. Fortunately, both of these great stars, who both began their careers in the Calgary Stampede promotion, have had dozens of great matches that are available on video. Owen was well schooled in every aspect of the sport. He wrestled as an amateur in college. Bret Hart is certainly the most successful of the Harts; however, Owen's late '80s and early '90s matches are the family's best. In those years, he was considered to be the best overall wrestler by numerous collectors and writers. Owen won major championships in England, Mexico, Europe, Japan and Canada to prove he was far from the "baby" of this great wrestling family. In 1999, Owen was killed when a cable, that was dropping him down into the ring before a match, broke and sent him plummeting to his death. Collectors have always kept Owen's tapes close to their hearts.

Like Owen, Pillman, a former Cincinnati Bengal, was trained by Bruce Hart. In the mid to late '80s, Pillman and Bruce Hart were inseparable. They ran the Stampede training camp together by day and battled a wide array of villains as Bad Company in the evening. Even today, many say Bad Company was Calgary's most beloved tag team. Flyin' Brian left the Calgary area to chase bigger dreams in WCW. There, he had many memorable matches with partners Tom Zenk and Steve Austin. Sadly, in 1998, his heart gave out, while he was a contract wrestler with the WWF. Owen Hart and Brian Pillman may be gone, but through video tapes, collectors will never forget them.

Bruiser Brody

Prior to his death in 1988 in Puerto Rico, collectors believed Brody was the greatest brawler of all time. Before it became in vogue to battle outside the ring into crowds, Brody was making it a habit. His interviews were believable, and at

King Kong Brody.

times, even scared local fans and interviewers. Brody was a star in every region he performed. When crowds were down, local promoters utilized this 6-foot-6 madman to bring them back. He was also the '80s' top free agent. In real life, Frank Goodish was a loving father and devoted family man. In the ring, he knew no boundaries. Tape collectors go crazy over Brody's battles in St. Louis with Ric Flair, in Japan with the Funks, and in Puerto Rico with his pal Abdullah. The legend is honored yearly when the Wrestling Observer Newsletter's fans vote for the Best Brawler of the Year and honor them with an award named on behalf of Brody.

Ric Flair

Very few wrestlers of the past three decades had as many great matches and interviews as the "Nature Boy" himself. As a regional NWA star, he packed them in and made promoter Jim Crockett millions. His matches often went 20 to 30 minutes and he also had many time-limit draws. The 14-time world champion also fared well in Japan. He drew 44,000 fans to Texas Stadium to fight Kerry Von Erich in 1984. He has had great feuds with the likes of Curt Hennig, Ricky Steamboat, Dusty Rhodes, Bret Hart, Harley Race, Barry Windham, Sting and Wahoo McDaniel.

Ric Flair before a match in St. Paul, Minn.

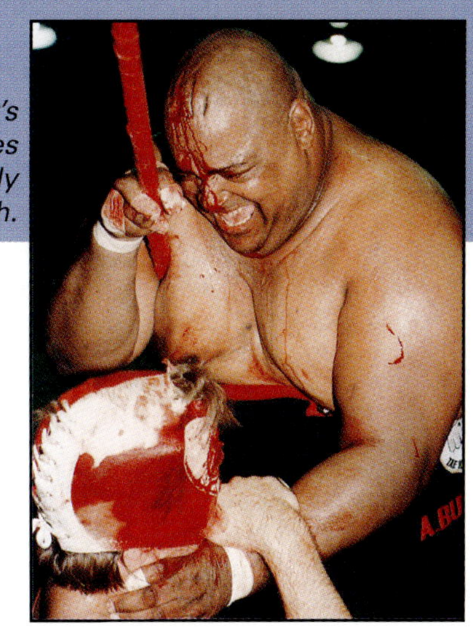

Abdullah the Butcher's bloody battles are spectacles to behold, but not necessarily for the squeamish.

Antonio Inoki

Although he didn't capture stardom in the States like he did in his homeland, no one can deny the international star, Inoki. He was Rikidozan's heir apparent, a role he ultimately shared with another Japanese legend, Giant Baba. Eventually, Inoki went his own way with New Japan and Baba went his own with All Japan. Inoki became a bigger headliner and even went on to become a politician. Tape collectors cherish his mixed matches, most notably the late '70s, and his 15-round draw with Muhammad Ali. One of the most interesting tapes in history is a match held in the '80s on an island, as Inoki faced the menacing Mr. Saito. The two warriors fought on the island for several hours. Special trainers and members of the media were the only people invited to witness this bizarre event. Onlookers arrived at the island on shrimp boats, planes and helicopters. Even though the buildup and commentary was done in Japanese, viewers of all languages could appreciate the unique drama demonstrated by this unusual war. The match began in daylight and ended in the dark. Edited tapes in the 120-minute range are the easiest to obtain. But raw footage of the entire three-hour match is also available through various collectors. This tape has been found for as high as $100.

Abdullah the Butcher

This madman is an icon in Japan and to many tape collectors in the U.S. He is easily the most identifiable wildman the ring has ever produced and he is still going strong in his fifth decade of wrestling. Abby's blood baths in Japan and Puerto Rico fill dozens of tapes. His U.S. battles

Jerry Lawler, leader of the Memphis mayhem.

"The General" Jerry Lawler, trading in his king crown for camo gear, complains about the "conspiracy" against his men.

are every bit as much fun. The 400-pound Sudanese warrior is a former karate instructor whose trademark is blood, blood, and more blood. He has also starred in at least two Japanese movies as a villain and is the topic of several commercially released videos (including "Halloween Havoc," where he was allegedly put into an electric chair).

Memphis Mayhem

The Memphis region has taken on many forms but has always provided countless hours of unmitigated fun. Jerry "The King" Lawler, and the recently retired Jerry Jarrett (father of Jeff), created most of the hijinx that mostly centered around Lawler. Many of the things we see on the tube today were first seen in Memphis and many superstars got their first break or developed their talents there. The Fabulous Ones and Kimala the Ugandan Giant had their careers take off in Memphis. Paul E. Dangerously, the Rock, Michael Hayes, King Kong Bundy, Jim Cornette, Honky Tonk Man, Jackie Fargo, Randy Savage, Bill Dundee, Austin Idol, Rick Rude, Tommy Rich, the Rock & Roll Express, The Road Warriors and countless others had career-defining positions and roles in this area. And who could ever forget the "Man on the Moon" himself, and Andy Kaufman, and his battle with the King? The first broken table ever recorded happened in a Memphis arena, when Savage piledrove Robert Gibson onto a nearby table in the early 1980s. That one move was a major event in the '80s. Nowadays, it seems no table is safe near a wrestling match. Hair versus hair bouts, cage matches and loser-leaves-town matches were regular fare in Memphis' heyday. The history of Memphis wrestling is rich, wild and often comical. Thankfully, much of it is available through tape trading.

Jackie Fargo was also part of the Memphis mayhem.

All Japan

Some of America's top stars—Brody, Stan Hansen, Steve Williams, the Destroyer, Bruno Sammartino and the Funks—all had great matches for the mighty Japanese All Japan promotion led by Giant Baba. Most of their tag team matches, like the annual tag-team tournaments tapes show, included good, stiff wrestling that all collectors and tape viewers would find to be interesting, worthy and believable.

New Japan

Antonio Inoki has been one of the most progressive promoters and wrestlers of all time. Inoki had mixed matches against boxers Leon Spinks and Muhammad Ali, he battled martial artists and promoted young bucks like the Great Muto. For the curious newcomers, start with a "Best of Inoki" collection of matches. Riki Choshu and Akira Maeda's shoot matches are also high on collectors' must-have lists.

Giant Baba holds the trophy he wins after defeating Jack Brisco for the NWA world title in 1974.

Barbed Wire, Broken Glass and Blood

There have been dozens (and dozens!) of Japanese off-shoot promotions over the past few years. Some groups preach honest, technical mat wrestling. But others hold dear the philosophy that more gore makes for more viewers. Groups like the IWA, FMW, Big Japan and several others offer bizarre-o garbage matches which are very violent. The uncrowned king of violence is Frontier Martial Arts' Atsushi Onita. He's gone as far as being attacked in a hospital, has had bombs blow up around his face, has set himself on fire, has stepped on landmines, has been wrapped with miles of barbed wire and has been known to bleed from time to time. Matsunaga is another hardcore legend (sorry Mick Foley). He calls himself "Danger Man" and has done all that Onita has done and then some. These are the promotions in which Cactus Jack displayed his fighting ways and became a hardcore freak. Because they are so popular, tapes are very easy to find. But be warned: They are not for the squeamish.

Territories

Any regional promotion, be it Verne Gagne's AWA, Bill Watts' Mid-South, Eddie Graham's Florida, Stu Hart's Stampede, Vince McMahon Sr.'s WWWF, Montreal's mixed bunch, Sam Muchnick's St. Louis "Wrestling at the Chase" or Don Owens' Portland group, holds its place in history. Older tapes will show wrestlers having less to work with, but getting powerful ratings. Tapes of these bouts are hard to find in good quality, but they are true testaments to the history of the sport.

Death-defying leaps

Certainly, our favorite high-risk leap of all-time was Jimmy "Superfly" Snuka's leap off the top of a 12-foot cage against Bob Backlund in the early 1980s in Madison Square Garden. Nowadays, it seems tame, but thanks to the slow, methodical and deliberate buildup to the leap, as Snuka climbed up the cage inch by inch, it was one of the most dramatic moments in wrestling history. Mick Foley topped the feat in the 1998 Hell in a Cell match, falling from the top of the cage through a ringside table, literally risking life and limb to please onlookers. He did something that evening that no other athlete (or lunatic) should ever attempt to top. Thank goodness, all can see these amazing stunts forever on video.

Freebird Fantasia

In this classic Georgia wrestling interview, Michael Hayes goes into a 10-minute speech that's part Southern Baptist, part Disney and all wrestling. He talks about how he is not backing down from the threats of former partner and life-long pal, Terry "Bam Bam" Gordy. Hayes tugs at our hearts as he talks about their family lives, his younger brother who needs a role model and

Harry Thornton interviews Freebirds Michael Hayes and Terry Gordy.

how "Freebird Fantasia" lives on, all while Lynard Skynard's anthem "Freebird" is playing in the background. Whether you say hallelujah, cry or cheer, this interview is bound to move those who still have a pulse.

The Shoot

The brawl between karate kick-fighting champion Don "Nakoya" Neilson of Canada and Japanese star Akira Maeda, who has been known to "shoot" from time to time, was intense and brutal. Was it a "shoot?" You decide. But be certain that this bout, in many ways, opened the floodgates to the Ultimate Fighting Championships and mixed martial arts matches becoming so in vogue.

Japanese Light Heavyweight Battles from Early 1980s

Great names like Davey Boy Smith, Dynamite Kid, The Cobra, Rollerball Rocco and Tiger Mask were staples of these all-out wars. No matter who wrestled who, these were amazing performances. The drama was high and the action was non-stop. Calgary trainer Bruce Hart influenced Kid and Smith to utilize high-flying moves in ways fans had yet to be exposed to. They also blended in American build-ups, English grappling, and the Japanese style. When one of them, especially Tiger Mask, leapt over the top rope onto a foe with reckless abandon, collectors called them must-see suicidal performances. Today, nearly every wrestler has emulated their pioneering moves.

Nick Bockwinkel and Bobby Heenan.

Dusty Rhodes was part of a classic "turn" with Ric Flair.

Interviews

Be it Bobby Heenan, Don Muraco, Roddy Piper, Bruiser Brody, Nick Bockwinkel, Jesse Ventura or any other of the sport's great talkers, interviews were often the most entertaining, if not the most believable, aspects of pro wrestling. Things were slow for awhile in the early 1990s until Cactus Jack and Terry Funk were let loose in ECW, which helped make the WWF's now-bold, brash style the success that it is. The new great interview men are led by throwback loner Steve Austin, the hilarious, but powerful, Rock and the off-kilter Mankind-Dude Love-Cactus Jack persona of Mick Foley.

The Turn

Prior to the '90s, anytime a "babyface" turned on his fans or a "heel" saved the "babyface," box office ticket sales soared. Today, wrestlers change their ways more often than they change their gym shorts. Nearly every major turn in modern history has been seen or documented through video. Whether it's Zbyszko turning on Sammartino, Diesel on Shawn Michaels, or Ric Flair on Dusty Rhodes, they are all available.

Managers

These gentleman, to put it nicely, have always had a major part in selling the live shows. Their role was much more important to a promoter before pay-per-view became the big money machine but even today, their ability to sell a feud can bring people to the arena like nothing

Jesse Ventura vs. Mad Dog.

else. Bobby Heenan and Sheik Adnan Al Kassey held court in the AWA, Classy Freddie Blassie, Lou Albano and the Wizard dominated the WWWF, Wild Red Berry appeared throughout the United States, Jimmy Hart was the "Mouth of the South" in Memphis and the No. 1 heel manager of the '80s was probably that lovable loudmouth himself, Jim Cornette. All of these men had a flair for the dramatic and could make a soggy diaper seem vicious.

Announcers

We all have those we have hated, loved, loved to hate and hated to love. Ed Whalen drove the promoters and wrestlers nuts with his power trips in Calgary, Marty O'Neil taught the world how to be subtle and Ken Resnick and Gene Okerlund mastered "over the top" in the AWA, Lance Russell was a master and maestro in Memphis, Boyd Pierce and Jim Ross brought dignity to the Mid-South and nobody knew how to sell the show better than the WWF's Vince McMahon. Whichever TV wrestling program we watched as kids, the announcers became a part of our lives. For most tape collectors, just hearing those voices can bring back memories of Saturday afternoons watching wrestling.

Houston promoter Paul Boesch arm wrestles Superstar Billy Graham.

With literally thousands of hours of wrestling action preserved through video, we have compiled a short (as short as possible) list of our favorite moments that have a small, but important, place on our video bookshelves:

Our Favorites

Tommy Rich winning the NWA title at age 18...anything Terry Funk has ever said or done...ECW and FMW's hardcore influence that changed wrestling forever...Ken Patera's feats of strength and turning his back on the U.S. to become a Sheik...Kimala the Ugandan Giant patting his bulbous belly...the rise and fall of the Von Erich and Gagne families...Mad Dog Vachone building a casket for Jerry Blackwell...Road Warrior Animal powerslamming Terry Gordy not once, but twice...Hulk Hogan's ear to the fans...Roddy Piper announcing his tearful retirement at age 30...any Piper's Pit...Paul Orndorf , and later, Ernest Miller's exercise classes...Ted DiBiase feuding with Hacksaw Duggan in tuxedo and coal miner's glove matches in Mid-South...the sound of glass breaking and the Titan Tron's depiction of Steve Austin as he enters the arena...the Rock's eyebrow and interviews...Ric Flair earning the moniker "the 60 minute man" in hundreds of televised Hall of Fame matches...Flair being hauled off into a mental ward...Gorgeous George (Wagner's) golden locks and hair pins...great submission moves like Rick Martel's "Boston Crab," Nick Bockwinkel's "Piledriver," Baron Von Raschke's "Claw," Stan Stasiak's "Heart Punch," or Bobo Brazil's "Cocobutt"...the blood baths of Fred Blassie, The Sheik, Cactus Jack, Abdullah the Butcher, Terry Funk, Sandman, Dusty Rhodes and the FMW crew...great tag-team matches and title champs...

Ox Baker vs. The Crusher.

Randy "Macho Man" Savage, as the ICW world heavyweight champion.

Andre the Giant winning a Battle Royal...early Clash of Champions shows...the WWF's bizarre talk program called TNT...Sgt. Slaughter's turn on the fans (in favor of Iraq with General Adnan) and his never-to-be-forgotten "Boot Camp" match against Pat Patterson...Puerto Rico blood baths featuring its favorite son, Carlos Colon...the Four Horsemen...the late Freddie Miller's signature line, "Be there!"...Joe Pedicino and Bonnie Blackstone...cable-access wrestling from the banal to the bizarre...primetime wrestling on NBC, UPN, USA, TNT, and TBS...the aura of the Wild Samoans...the wrestling "Mummy" in Memphis...Andy Kaufman and Jerry Lawler on David Letterman...Lou Albano in Cyndi Lauper's music video, "Girls Just Want to have Fun"...the dropkick of either Ricky Rice or Jim Brunzell...Bruno Sammartino slamming the 600-pound Haystacks Calhoun...Shane McMahon's flying and his dad's crazy falls...Austin kidnapping Vince and using his fake 3:16 gun..."Big Juice" and "Beetlejuice"...Hulk Hogan cartoons...Paul Dangerously's cell phone...Missy Hyatt...Bobby Heenan wearing a weasel suit...the Randy Savage-Ricky Steamboat series..."Da Crusher's" cigars.

"Freebird creme" and the Junkyard Dog going blind..."Hello Ladies"..."Do You Smell What the Rock is Cookin'?"..."Cause Stone Cold Said So"...the unbelievably powerful matches of All Japan and New Japan...Abdullah the Butcher being placed in an electric chair...a younger Diamond Dallas Page doing the ring announcing at a George Foreman fight...the classy, but over-used, Michael Buffer's "Let's get Ready to Rumble"...Billy White Wolf, Jay Strongbow, Charlie Norris, Billy Red Cloud, and Wahoo McDaniel's chops...Mando, Chavo and Hector Guererro...Bruno breaking his neck...Marty O'Neil's signature line, "Run, don't walk, to get your tickets"...Fred Blassie's jackets, the Wizard's sunglasses, and Lou Albano's rubber bands...the Gagne "Sleeper" hold...wrestlers coming out of the audience...midget performers...wrestling bears...the hope (that our man can win) and the hype (of a loser leaves town)...the feuds and their finishes...the Strong Machines...Eddie Gilbert being interviewed from a hospital bed...Don Owens trying to be dramatic...the gruff-sounding Gordon Solie describing what a particular move is doing to a specific body part...WWF's satire of the aging Hulkster and Macho Man..."The Fink"...The Rock and Mankind's battle during half-time of the Super Bowl...Roddy Piper breaking a bottle over his head...Killer Khan and Terry Gordy's gore-fest in World Class...heroes and friends...tipsy announcers...JYD chomping at the bit.

Jerry Lawler and Terry Funk beating the hell out of each other in their famous "empty arena" match...Sabu's scarred body...Elizabeth's fearful gasps...the Boiler Room matches...Hardcore Holly "picking on" larger men...the Crusher and the Bruiser smacking each other to get warmed up for a match...the Slammy's...Larry "the Axe" Hennig, a lifetime Verne Gagne hater, saving Greg Gagne and saying, "What if that was my kid"...Ali vs. Kenny Jay, Ali vs. Antonio Inoki, and Ali vs. Gorilla Monsoon...Bruiser Brody with a garbage pail in hand and a map of his head declaring he was going to clean up the NWA...the

Road Dogg vs. Double J.

Clowns, Doink and Dink...the Gobbledygooker and the Red Rooster...D-Lo Brown shaking his head like a cartoon character...Jerry Lawler's one-liners on commentary...the beatings taken by Rodney and Pete Gas...Jeff Jarrett and Honky Tonk Man's guitars...Butterbean nearly beheading Bart Gunn in a boxing match...the "Is it real or is it Memorex" award-winning "Wrestling With Shadows" flick...the WWF's very vulnerable Spanish announcer table.

Jesse Ventura's interviews and commentary where he truly honed his skills to become a politician...Jim Ross blending the grace of the 1950s with the madness of the new millennium...The Crush Gals, Dump Matsumoto and the unbelievably talented Japanese women wrestlers of the late 1980s and early 1990s...AWA's Superclash brawl from old Comisky Park... Brody destroying rows of seats in Japanese arenas and watching him swing his chain at the fans...Bobby Heenan breaking Buck Zumhoff's boom box...a suplex from Taz...Brother Love...Lenny and Lodi...the eyes of Viscera, any Sheik, the Rock, Mad Dog Vachone and the Undertaker...casket matches...Mick Karch's Saturday Night at Ringside TV show...any Wrestlemania. And that's just to name a "few."

Commercial Videos

"Best of Wrestling Gold," Volumes 1-4, 1992
"Bloody Side of Blood Wars," 1992
"Bloopers, Bleeps and Bodyslams," 1988
"Danger Zone/NWA Wrestling," 1997
"Diesel: Big Daddy Cool," 1995
"GLOW Gorgeous Ladies of Wrestling," 1990
"GLOW" Volumes 1-3, 1997
"Golden Age of Wrestling," Volume 2, 1986
"Masters of Mayhem," 1991
"NWA Bash Wargames," 1988
"NWA Price of Freedom," 1988
"NWA Ringmasters: Great American Bas," 1996
"NWA Starrcade 1986," 1987
"NWA Starrcade 1989," 1990
"NWA Terror Rules the Ring," 1990
"Pro Wrestling Hall of Fame," Volumes 1-3, 1998
"Rock & Roll Wrestling: Women vs. Aztec," 1990
"The Wrestling Match," 1983
"Trashy Ladies of Wrestling," 1987
"UWF Beach Brawl," 1993
"UWF Best of Paul Orndorf," 1992
"UWF Combo Pack 1," 1994
"UWF Combo Pack 2," 1994
"UWF Lumberjack Matches," 1997
"UWF Steel Cage Matches," 1994
"UWF Tag Team Tandems," 1994
"Women's 3-D Wrestling," 1993
"Women's Championship Wrestling," 1994
"World Class Wrestling," Volume 1
"World Class Wrestling," Volume 2
"World Class Wrestling," Volume 3
"World Class Wrestling," Volume 4
"World Class Wrestling," Volume 5
"World Class Wrestling," Volume 6
"Wrestling Bloopers," 1997
"Wrestling Classics: 6 Man Tag Team," 1994
"Wrestling Classics: Buddy Rogers," 1994
"Wrestling Classics: The Kangaroos," 1994
"Wrestling Classics: Haystacks Calhoun," 1994
"Wrestling Classics: Strangest Matches," 1994
"Wrestling Classics: The Sheik," 1994
"Wrestling Funnies," 1994
"Wrestling's Greatest Blood Baths," 1993

chapter 4

Valley of the Dolls

One of the more popular items in wrestling collecting is, without question, the doll and action-figure market. The first question fans ask is, Are they dolls or action figures? The macho thing to call them would be action figures. But some of the earlier versions of this collectible are clearly dolls. So we'll leave that distinction up to the fans.

For our purposes (and we want to feel macho), we'll call them action figures. One thing is for certain though—the action-figure market is seeing great success, as the market has exploded in popularity. Jakks Pacific, makers of the WWF line of merchandise, recently bragged about reaching nearly $100 million in sales last year. And not too long ago, collectible-maker heavy-hitter Marvel Comics took over the rights to make the WCW line of toys. It used to be that the wrestling action-figure market was somewhat of a joke. Now, the companies are laughing all the way to the bank.

One intriguing aspect to the figure market is how much premium fans are currently placing on these figures. Even older dolls, which have discontinued production, are nabbing hundreds of dollars on the open market. While most fans have been introduced to the current realistic lines of WWF and WCW figures, the market actually began with a much more conservative American Wrestling Association line produced by that old toy company relic, Remco.

In its heyday, Remco produced many different lines of all types of figures, such as superheroes and TV stars. But in the early 1980s, in an attempt to save a struggling company, Remco approached Verne Gagne's AWA after seeing the immense popularity of TV wrestling. The AWA, while not the most widely seen product, was a solid choice with its catalog of major wrestling stars like the Road Warriors and Freebirds. So, in 1984, Remco released the first-ever mass-produced line of wrestling figures. In actuality, there were a few names, like Ric Flair, who were not AWA property but were major players in the wrestling industry nonetheless.

The first line produced such classics as Greg Gagne (the son of AWA owner Verne), Larry Zbyszko, Curt Hennig and the Fabulous Ones. Action figures were very different then, when compared to today's products. The detail of the figures left a little bit to be desired, and the AWA line was no exception. The running joke was that all the bodies were from the same mold and only the heads of the different figures were different from character to character. The Remco line was met with a lukewarm reception. But today, these dolls are very rare and are fetching high prices by sellers. While both the AWA and Remco went out of business in later years, the wheels for future wrestling figures were set in motion.

The Remco line, little did we know, would be the trend-setter in an industry filled with products. Just a few years later, when the WWF was taking its show national and into the living rooms of millions of fans around the world, it summoned the company LJN to produce an exclusive line of WWF figures. Still, today, this line is widely considered the most popular line ever produced because these characters are the ones many fans grew up watching. All the WWF regulars, and not-so-regulars, were part of the production line. Standbys like Hulk Hogan, Andre the Giant and The Iron Sheik were produced alongside classics like Bruno Sammartino and Terry Funk. These figures are a sight to behold. They are made of all rubber and have no moving parts and the detail, while not a total disaster, is less than lifelike. But that is why they remain popular. Truly, the style that makes them a classic will probably never be seen again. The all-rubber, non-articulating bodies of the LJN line are classics. They are a style which we will probably never see again. Included in this line was the very first, and only, Jesse Ventura figure. Nowadays, the Minnesota governor is fetching almost $50 for a mint, in-package doll.

Steve Anderson, who writes a weekly wrestling collectibles column for Wrestleline (www.wrestline.com) called Toy Story, is a 20-year wrestling fan and has been collecting these figures since 1992. He is not unlike a lot of fans who are now purchasing these figures as a testament to their days as a youngster. "Being a fan of wrestling, obviously, these figures are fun to collect," he said. "Why did I start? A lot had to do with the LJN craze which I missed out on. Plus, my son likes the toys, too."

Anderson's interest in the figures leapt when he picked up an old Hasbro Dusty Rhodes doll in the bargain bin at a local discount store. When he took the doll home, he was shocked to find out that fans were getting close to $100 for the figure. In just a few years' time, that figure alone is worth $300. "That's what got me into the selling side," laughed the wrestling journalist.

Since the LJN line was released, the major wrestling companies have churned out a steady stream of wrestling figures. Several lines were produced in the 1990s to little fan fare. Different companies have taken over the publishing rights through the years, which have seen some stinker lines, as well as big-time money producers. A Hasbro line of WWF dolls, which closely resembled Weebells, showcased 100 different WWF characters. With no moving body parts and a very cartoonish look, most fans were turned off from the size of the doll. Most are about four and a half inches tall, although the color is superb. Galoob put out a WCW line of dolls that are also short, but rather realistic looking. Today, the Hasbro line is buffered by several heavy hitters on the market, topped by the Dusty Rhodes doll. Meanwhile, the WCW line fetches only a little more than the original asking price.

WCW, WWF and, of late, ECW, are producing lines of their current superstars. Without question, the king of all figures makers is Jakks Pacific. Since 1996, it has been making WWF figures exclusively and fans have flocked to the stores looking for their favorites. As we went to press, the volume of figures being produced by Jakks was a little overwhelming. The newer lines are more poseable and the latest lines are being packaged with lots of bonus toys like baseball bats (for whacking of course) dumpsters and toilet seats. For the sick fans of hardcore wrestling, that's cause enough to collect these dolls. But there certainly is a market, even for the newer dolls, that cannot be denied.

Now, wrestling figures are as popular as, if not more, than mainstream superheroes. Sales in 1998 were topped only by the Star Wars line. Our favorite, for detail alone, is the Jakks Maximum Sweat line.

"I see Jakks continuing their success because they have so many variations,"

Anderson said. "But as long as wrestling is strong, there will always be a need and desire for these figures."

Toy Biz/Marvel has closed the gap somewhat on Jakks with its recent lines of WCW figures. The detail has been improving greatly, but the different lines are hit and miss. Some, like the Ring Masters' line, are super. Others, like the Chris Benoit doll, could pass as a homemade doll. And no company can seem to perfect the likeness of Lex Lugar. Even still, fans are snapping them up at a record pace. Resale value has proved to be a worth-while investment.

Other figures that have value are ones that are specialty items. The Phoenix Toys' "Thunderlips" figure, based on the character that Hulk Hogan played in the movie "Rocky III," is getting about $40. And just last year, Jesse Ventura introduced his own line of action figures to capitalize on his new life as a politician. Jesse's dolls have been extremely hot. As of October 1999, Ventura had sold more than $800,000 worth in figures. About 10 percent of sales goes to charity. So far, there are three renditions of Jesse: the governor, football coach, and Navy SEAL. If you're looking for a new Ventura "wrestling" doll, don't hold your breath.

"It was under consideration, but then they decided to hold off because of the negative publicity," said Ventura's doll manufacturer, Steve Tierschel. In 2000, three new Ventura figures are set to hit the market, including a buckskin jacketed Jesse, Jesse in lighter-colored fatigues from his Navy days, and another look as governor. Other future plans include a Jesse in a compete SEAL outfit, with goggles, fins and all. Tierschel also is close to producing a Ventura family collection, complete with wife, kids, family dog and horse. Oh my God!

One thing to ask yourself when seeking out these figures is, how many were made? That fact can be a strong factor (as can appearance) in the eventual resale price. Anderson says seek out the figures that are produced in a "short pack," meaning, fewer numbers of that version were made. Most short packs, while not a guarantee of the resale value, increase in value. Take the Jakks Blue Blazer doll, for example. After Owen Hart (the wrestler who used that gimmick) died, the value of the doll increased. But adding to that was the fact Blue Blazer was part of a short pack.

The Remco and LJN lines were produced at a time when no one, not company nor wrestler, knew wrestling dolls would become such a hot-selling market. After the success of LJN, the WWF and WCW have nearly made it company policy to continue churning out new product every year. With new product being cranked out about every month, it's hard to keep up pace with it all. But, no doubt, that's what is driving the dollars up on a lot of these items and it doesn't appear the market will cool off any time soon.

Series 4

Ric Flair (Remco).

Buddy Roberts (Remco).

Remco, AWA All-Star Wrestling, 1985
2-Packs
Series 1

Fabulous Ones, Steve Keirn & Stan Lane $70.00

High Flyers, Greg Gagne & Jim Brunzell $70.00

Road Warriors, Hawk & Animal $50.00

Grudge Match, Ric Flair vs. Larry Zbyszko $50.00

Grudge Match, Rick Martel vs. Baron Von Raschke . . .$50.00

Series 2

Gagne's Raiders, Greg Gagne & Curt Henning $60.00

Long Riders, Bill & Scott Irwin $60.00

Managers

Michael Hayes, Terry Gordy, Buddy Roberts $80.00

Jimmy Garvin, Steve Regal, Precious $80.00

Road Warrior Hawk & Animal, Paul Ellering $70.00

Series 3

Abdullah the Butcher vs. Carlos Colon $90.00

Scott Hall vs. Jimmy Garvin $80.00

Nick Bockwinkel vs. Larry Zbyszko $80.00

Jerry Blackwell vs. Stan Hansen $90.00

Series 4

Boris Zuchov $130.00

Buddy Rose $100.00

Doug Somers $100.00

Nord the Barbarian . .$120.00

Referee $100.00

Sheik Adnan Al-Kaissey $130.00

Midnight Rocker Shawn Michaels $120.00

Midnight Rocker Marty Janetty $100.00

Remco AWA Thumb Wrestlers

Ric Flair vs. Larry Zbyszko $20.00

Greg Gagne vs. Hawk .$20.00

Rick Martel vs. Animal $20.00

Remco AWA Mini Mashers 8-Pack

Scott Hall, Curt Hennig, Boris Zukoff, Nord the Barbarian, Larry Zbyszko, Nick Bockwinkel, Ric Flair, Stan Hansen $30.00

12-Pack

Hawk, Animal, Larry Zbyszko, Nick Bockwinkel, Ric Flair, Stan Hansen, Boris Zukoff, John Nord, Shawn Michaels, Marty Janetty, Scott Hall, Curt Hennig $35.00

LJN, World Wrestling Federation, 1985-1987

Adrian Adonis $50.00

Andre the Giant
(long hair) $60.00
(short hair) $60.00
(strap) $200.00

Ax of Demolition $100.00

Bam Bam Bigelow . . .$100.00

Big Boss Man (night stick) $150.00

Big John Stud $30.00

Billy Jack Haynes $60.00

Bobby Heenan
(brown hair w/design on shoulders) $30.00
(blonde hair w/o design on shoulders) $30.00

Bob Orton Jr. 40.00

Bruno Sammartino . . .$50.00

Brutus Beefcake $50.00

Cpt. Lou Albano
(pic on shirt, has red vest and cumberbund) $35.00
(pic on shirt, has white vest/cumberbund) $35.00

Classy Freddy Blassie .$30.00

Cpl. Kirschner
(cleanly shaven) $20.00
(stubble) $20.00
(beard) $20.00

Elizabeth
(gold skirt) $75.00
(purple skirt) $75.00

George the Animal Steele
(clear chest hair) $30.00
(colored chest hair) . . .$30.00

Greg the Hammer Valentine
(light blonde hair) $40.00
(dark blonde hair) $40.00

Hacksaw Jim Duggan .$50.00

Haku $75.00

Hercules Hernandez . .$30.00

Hillbilly Jim $25.00

Honky Tonk Man $60.00

Hulk Hogan
(yellow trunks, light blonde hair) $50.00
(yellow trunks, dark blonde hair) $50.00
(white shirt) $250.00
(red shirt) $50.00

Iron Sheik
(orange design on tights) $30.00
(yellow design on tights) $30.00

Jake Roberts $75.00

Jesse Ventura
(blonde hair) $40.00
(brown hair, same color as mustache) . . . $40.00

Jimmy Hart
(Mega w/no hearts) . . . $30.00
(Red Mega w/pink hearts) $30.00

Jimmy Superfly Snuka $60.00

Johnny Valiant $40.00

Junkyard Dog
(w/silver chain) $40.00
(w/black chain) $40.00
(w/red chain) $40.00

Kamala $100.00

Ken Patera $50.00

King Harley Race $200.00

King Kong Bundy $50.00

Koko B. Ware $100.00

Magnificent Muraco . . $25.00

Gene Okerlund
(logo on mic) $30.00
(no logo on mic) $30.00

Mr. Fuji $30.00

Paul Orndorff $30.00

Nikolai Volkoff $25.00

One Man Gang $80.00

Outback Jack $40.00

Randy Savage $60.00

Referee
(blue shirt) $100.00
(white shirt) $100.00

Rick Rude $110

Rick Martel $125.00

Ricky The Dragon Steamboat $35.00

Rowdy Roddy Piper
(red boots) $35.00
(brown boots) $35.00

Slick $55.00

S.D. Jones
(red shirt) $30.00
(Hawaiian shirt) $30.00

Ted Arcidi $50.00

Ted DiBiase $50.00

Terry Funk $35.00

Tito Santana
(purple trunks) $50.00
(white trunks) $50.00

Ultimate Warrior $150.00

Vince McMahon $40.00

Warlord $100.00

Sgt. Slaughter (Made by Hasbro for LJN) $100.00

Tag Teams

British Bulldogs $200.00

Hart Foundation $600.00

Killer Bees $200.00

Strike Force $400.00

LJN, WWF 14 inch, 1985

Roddy Piper $50.00

Hulk Hogan $75.00

LJN, WWF Bendies, 1986

Cpt. Lou Albano $20.00

Hulk Hogan $20.00

Hillbilly Jim $20.00

Big John Stud $20.00

Randy Savage $20.00

Junkyard Dog $20.00

Paul Orndorf $20.00

Roddy Piper $20.00

Iron Sheik $20.00

Cpl Kirchner $20.00

Ricky Steamboat $20.00

Andre the Giant $20.00

George Steele $20.00

Bobby Heenan $30.00

Nikolai Volkoff $20.00

Brutus Beefcake $20.00

Jesse Ventura $20.00

King Kong Bundy $20.00

LJN, WWF Thumbwrestlers, 1985

Jake Roberts $15.00

Iron Sheik $15.00

Hulk Hogan $15.00

Ricky Steamboat $15.00

Nikolai Volkoff $15.00

Roddy Piper $15.00

Hillbilly Jim $15.00

Randy Savage $15.00

Big John Stud $15.00

Junkyard Dog $15.00

Paul Orndorf $15.00

King Kong Bundy $15.00

Hasbro, WWF 1990-1994 Series 1

Akeem $100.00

Andre The Giant $150.00

Ax $50.00

Big Boss Man $25.00

Brutus Beefcake $30.00

Hulk Hogan $25.00
Jake Roberts $25.00
Macho Man $30.00

Million Dollar Man $25.00
Rick Rude $50.00
Smash $30.00
Ultimate Warrior $30.00

Series 2

Dusty Rhodes $300.00

Hacksaw Duggan $20.00

Honky Tonk Man $30.00
Hulk Hogan $25.00

Macho King $20.00
Million Dollar Man $20.00
Rowdy Roddy Piper . . .$20.00

Superfly Jimmy Snuka $20.00
Ultimate Warrior $50.00

Series 3

Big Bossman $15.00
Brutus Beefcake $75.00

Earthquake $30.00
Greg Valentine $25.00
Hulk Hogan $20.00
Koko B. Ware $75.00
Macho Man $50.00
Mr. Perfect $50.00
Sgt. Slaughter $30.00
Texas Tornado $30.00

Typhoon $30.00
Ultimate Warrior $50.00

Series 4

Bret Hart $25.00
British Bulldog $30.00
Ricky Steamboat $20.00
Undertaker $25.00

Series 5

Hulk Hogan $20.00
I.R.S $20.00
Macho Man $30.00
Rick Martel $20.00
Skinner $20.00
Sid Justice $20.00
The Mountie $20.00
Virgil $20.00
Warlord $20.00

Series 6

Berzerker $20.00
El Matador $20.00
Jim Neidhart $20.00
Papa Shango $20.00
Repo Man $20.00
Ric Flair $20.00
Tatanka $20.00

Series 7

Crush $20.00
Kamala $20.00
Nailz $20.00
Owen Hart $20.00
Razor Ramon $20.00
Shawn Michaels $20.00

Series 8

Bam Bam Bigelow $15.00
Bret Hart $15.00
Lex Luger $20.00

Hasbro's Dusty Rhodes.

Mr. Perfect $15.00
Undertaker $20.00
Yokozuna $20.00

Series 9

Doink the Clown $12.00
Hacksaw Jim Duggan .$12.00
Million Dollar Man $15.00
Rick Steiner $12.00
Scott Steiner $12.00
Tatanka (re-release) . . .$10.00

Series 10

Butch #2 . . . .$10.00
Fatu $12.00
Giant Gonzalez $12.00
Marty Jannety $12.00
Luke $10.00
Razor Ramon
(re-release) $20.00
(purple) $20.00
Samu $12.00
Shawn Michaels
(black) $25.00
(re-release) $20.00

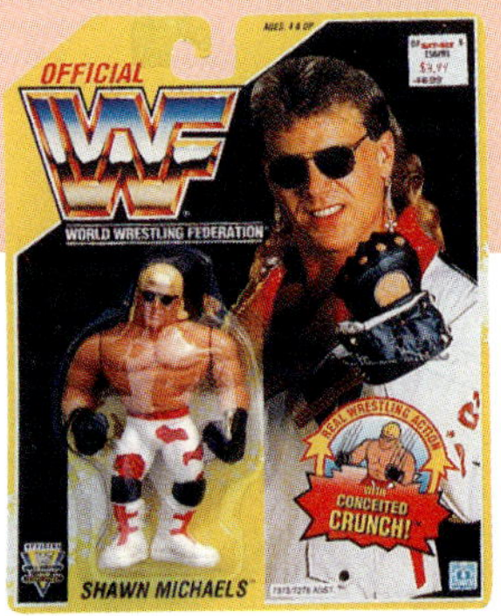
Hasbro's Shawn Michaels.

Series 11

1-2-3 Kid $45.00
Adam Bomb $30.00
Bart Gunn $20.00
Billy Gunn $25.00
Crush $30.00
Ludvig Borga $30.00
Yokozuna $20.00

Tag Teams

Bushwackers $20.00

Demolition $40.00
Legion of Doom $50.00
Nasty Boys $50.00
Rockers $20.00

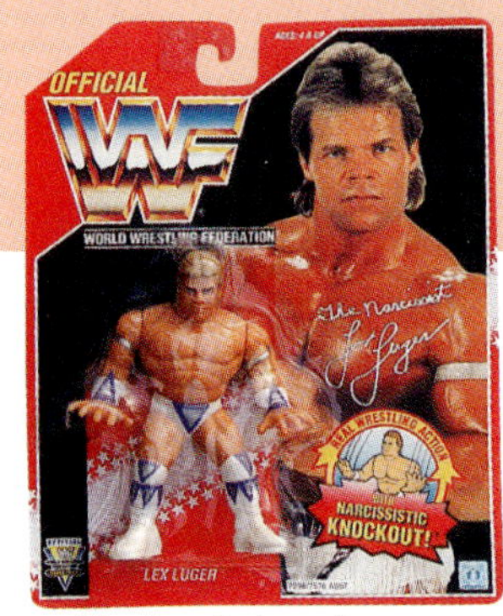
Hasbro's Lex Lugar.

Mail-Away

Bret Hart $75.00
Hulk Hogan $60.00
Undertaker $80.00

Hasbro, WWF 12-inch Talking Figures

Hulk Hogan $40.00
Ultimate Warrior $40.00

Hasbro, WWF Royal Rumble Mini Ring

Hulk Hogan, Big Bossman, Jake Roberts,
Sgt. Slaughter, Million Dollar Man $80.00

Hasbro, WWF Royal Rumble Mini 4-Pack

Roddy Piper, Texas Tornado, Mr. Perfect & Jim Duggan $20.00
LOD, Typhoon and Earthquake $20.00
Beefcake, Valentine, Bushwackers $20.00

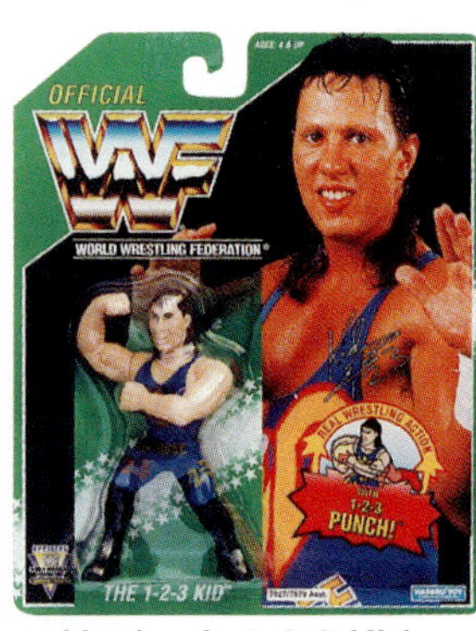
Hasbro's 1-2-3 Kid.

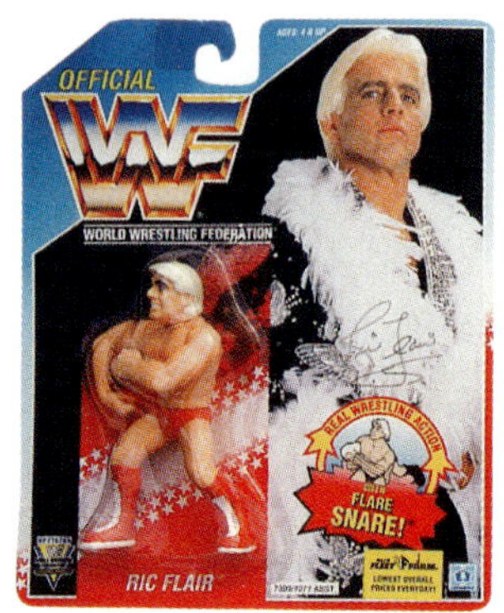
Hasbro's Ric Flair.

Hasbro's Razor Ramon.

JusToys WWF Bendables 1994-current
Series 1

Diesel $10.00
Doink $15.00
Razor Ramon $10.00
Bret Hart
(purple) $8.00
(pink) $20.00
Lex Lugar $15.00

Series 2

1-2-3 Kid $4.00
Mable $4.00
Undertaker $6.00
Bulldog $4.00

Series 3

Shawn Michaels $4.00
Yokozuna $4.00
Goldust $4.00
Amhed Johnson $4.00

Series 4

Sunny $4.00
Sid $4.00
Marc Mero $4.00
Vader $4.00

Series 5

Farooq $4.00
Rocky Maivia $6.00
Mankind $4.00
Steve Austin $4.00

Series 6

Hawk $4.00
Animal $4.00
Triple H $4.00
Undertaker $4.00

Series 7

Owen Hart $4.00
The Patriot $4.00
Crush $4.00
Ken Shamrock $4.00

Series 8

Chyna $4.00
Kane $4.00
Double J $4.00
Taka Michinoku $4.00

Series 9

Brian Christopher $4.00
X-Pac $4.00
Cactus Jack $4.00
Sable $4.00

Series 10

Billy Gunn $4.00
Road Dogg $4.00
Steve Blackman $4.00
Edge $4.00

Series 11

Vince McMahon $4.00
The Godfather $4.00
Val Venis $4.00
Al Snow $4.00

Star Toys (Spain), WWF 1990 12-inch w/hair

Ultimate Warrior $125
Hulk Hogan $125
Jake Roberts $125
Hacksaw $125
Big Bossman $125

JAKKS, WWF 1997-current Superstars Series
Series 1

Bret Hart $15.00
Diesel $45.00
Goldust $25.00
Razor Ramon $55.00
Shawn Michaels $20.00
Undertaker 20.00

Series 2

Bret Hart $8.00
Owen Hart $20.00
Shawn Michaels $8.00
Ultimate Warrior $30.00
Undertaker $8.00
Vader $8.00

Series 3

Ahmed Johnson $6.00
Bret Hart $6.00
British Bulldog $6.00
Diesel $50.00
Goldust $10.00
Mankind $6.00
Shawn Michaels $6.00
Sycho Sid $6.00

Series 4

Farooq $6.00
Triple H $6.00
Jerry Lawler $6.00
Justin Hawk Bradshaw .$6.00
Steve Austin $12.00
Vader $6.00

Series 5

Sycho Sid $6.00
Flash Funk $6.00
The Rock $6.00
Steve Austin $12.00
Savio Vega $6.00
Ken Shamrock $6.00

Series 6

Marc Mero $6.00
Steve Blackman $6.00

Mark Henry $6.00
Triple H $6.00
Jeff Jarrett $6.00

Series 7

Steve Austin $6.00
Steve Williams $6.00
Undertaker $6.00

Edge $6.00
X-Pac $12.00
Val Venis $6.00

Series 8

Kane $6.00

The Rock $6.00
Ken Shamrock $6.00

Shawn Michaels $6.00
Shane McMahon $6.00

Big Boss Man $6.00

Series 9

Gangrel $6.00
Christian $6.00

Big Show $6.00
Vince McMahon $6.00

Hardcore Holly $6.00
Undertaker $6.00

2-Tuff Series
Series 1

Triple H/Chyna $12.00

Truth Commission $12.00

Chainz/8-Ball $12.00

Marlena/Goldust $12.00

Series 2

New Age Outlaws $20.00

Kurrgan/Jackyl $12.00

Brian Christopher/
Jerry Lawler $12.00
Kama/D-Lo Brown $12.00

Series 3

Rock/Owen Hart $12.00
Austin/Undertaker $20.00
Legion of Doom 2000 .$12.00
Kane/Mankind $12.00

Series 4

Austin/Bossman $12.00
Kane/Undertaker $12.00
Rock/Mankind $12.00
Bad Ass/Val Venis $12.00

Series 5

Undertaker/Viscera . . . $12.00

Bad Ass/Road Dogg . . . $12.00

Austin/The Rock $12.00

Debra/Jeff Jarrett $12.00

STOMP Series
Series 1

Steve Austin $12.00

Crush $6.00

Ahmed Johnson $6.00

Brian Pillman $6.00

Undertaker $6.00

Ken Shamrock $6.00

Series 2

The Rock $6.00

Steve Austin $12.00

Chyna $6.00

Owen Hart $6.00

Mosh $6.00

Thrasher $6.00

Series 3

Sable $6.00

Kane $10.00

Undertaker $10.00

Hawk $6.00

Animal $6.00

Marc Mero $6.00

Series 4

Steve Austin $6.00

Chyna $6.00

Triple H $6.00

X-Pac $6.00

Road Dogg $6.00

Bad Ass $6.00

Signature Series
Series 1

Triple H $6.00

LOD Animal $6.00

LOD Hawk $6.00

Mankind $6.00
Goldust $6.00

Steve Austin $12.00

Series 2

Billy Gunn $6.00
Road Dogg $6.00

Kane $6.00
Undertaker $6.00

Shawn Michaels $6.00
Dude Love $6.00

Series 3

Steve Austin $10.00
The Rock $8.00

Edge $6.00
Triple H $8.00

Undertaker $8.00
Jackie $6.00

Slammers
Series 1

Steve Austin $12.00
Bret Hart $6.00
Goldust $6.00
Mankind $6.00
Undertaker $6.00
Farooq $6.00

Series 2

Taka Michinoku $6.00
Brian Pillman $6.00
Shawn Michaels $6.00
Dude Love $6.00
Kane $10.00
Patriot $10.00

Ringside
Series 1

Sable $10.00
Sunny $10.00
Referee $25.00
Vince McMahon $10.00

Series 2

Vince McMahon $12.00
Referee $12.00
Jim Ross $8.00

Jim Cornette $8.00
Honky Tonk Man $10.00
Sgt. Slaughter $8.00

Tag Teams

Legion of Doom $12.00

Godwinns $12.00

New Blackjacks $12.00

Headbangers $12.00

Manager 2-Packs Series 1

Bob Backlund/Sultan . .$10.00

Clarence Mason/Crush $10.00

Paul Bearer/Mankind . .$10.00

Sable/Marc Mero $10.00

Special Edition Tag Teams

Al Snow/Mankind $12.00

D-Lo Brown/ Mark Henry $12.00

Headbangers $12.00

KB Special Edition Series 1

Ahmed Johnson $8.00

British Bulldog $8.00

Sunny $10.00

The Rock $10.00

Undertaker $10.00

Vader $8.00

Yokozuna $25.00

Series 2

Farooq $8.00

Goldust $8.00

Triple H $8.00

Sable $8.00

Savio Vega $8.00

Steve Austin $12.00

Yokozuna $25.00

Series 3

LOD Hawk $8.00

LOD Animal $8.00

Dan Severn $8.00

Triple H $8.00

Ken Shamrock $8.00

Marc Mero $8.00

Series 4

Steve Austin $16.00

Mankind $8.00

Undertaker $8.00

Chyna $8.00

Road Dogg $8.00

Bad Ass Billy Gunn $8.00

Series 5

X-Pac $8.00

Edge $8.00

Val Venis $8.00

Al Snow $8.00

Ken Shamrock $8.00

Mark Henry $8.00

Don't Trust Anybody Series 1

Kane $8.00

Dude Love $8.00

Shawn Michaels $8.00
Faarooq $8.00
Chainz $8.00
8-Ball $8.00
Vader $8.00
Triple H $8.00

Series 2
Al Snow $10.00
Blue Blazer $30.00
Edge $10.00
Jeff Jarrett $8.00
Steve Blackman $8.00
Undertaker $12.00

Wrestlemania 14
Mosh $6.00
Trasher $6.00
Triple H $6.00
Shawn Michaels $10.00
Steve Austin $20.00
The Rock $10.00

Livewire Series 1
Undertaker $6.00
Chyna $10.00
Ken Shamrock $6.00
Steve Austin $30.00
Mankind $6.00
Vader $6.00

Series 2

Shawn Michaels $8.00
Marc Mero $6.00

Mark Henry $6.00
X-Pac $12.00

Val Venis $8.00
The Rock $12.00

Shotgun Saturday Night Series 1
Steve Austin $20.00
Hawk $6.00
Animal $6.00
The Rock $8.00
Henry Godwinn $6.00
Phineas Godwinn $6.00
Undertaker $12.00
Savio Vega $6.00

Series 2
Shawn Michaels $6.00
Jeff Jarrett $6.00
Sable $10.00
Kane $6.00
Road Dogg $6.00
Billy Gunn $6.00

Fully Loaded Series 1

Al Snow $6.00
Triple H $8.00

Road Dogg $6.00
Billy Gunn $6.00
Kane $6.00
The Rock $6.00

Series 2

Steve Austin $6.00
The Rock $6.00

Shane McMahon $6.00
Test $6.00

Road Dogg $6.00
X-Pac $6.00

Maximum Sweat Series 1

Undertaker $10.00
Steve Austin $10.00

Triple H $10.00
Shawn Michaels $10.00

The Rock $10.00
Kane $10.00

Series 2

Steve Austin $10.00
Undertaker $10.00

Road Dogg $10.00
Mr. Ass $10.00

Edge $10.00
Ken Shamrock $10.00

Series 3

Big Show $10.00
Gangrel $10.00

The Rock $10.00
Steve Austin $10.00

Big Bossman $10.00
Mankind $10.00

Series 4

Kane $10.00
Steve Austin $10.00

Mr. Ass $10.00
Road Dogg $10.00

Droz $10.00

Best of 1997 Series 1

Ahmed Johnson $6.00
Bret Hart $10.00
British Bulldog $8.00
Owen Hart $10.00
Steve Austin $12.00
Undertaker $10.00

Series 2

Crush $6.00
Goldust $6.00
Triple H $10.00
Ken Shamrock $6.00
Marc Mero $10.00
Shawn Michaels $6.00
The Rock $6.00
Undertaker $6.00

Best of 1998
Series 1

Steve Austin $10.00
Shawn Michaels $10.00
Brian Christopher $10.00
Chyna $10.00
Vader $10.00
Bradshaw $6.00

Series 2

Dan Severn $8.00
Dude Love $8.00
Triple H $8.00
Jeff Jarrett $8.00
Ken Shamrock $8.00
Mark Henry $8.00
Steve Austin $10.00
Undertaker $8.00

Tag Teams

New Age Outlaws $12.00
Headbangers $12.00
Legion of Doom $12.00

2-Packs

Bret Hart vs. Owen Hart $30.00
British Bulldog vs. Sid $12.00
Triple H vs. Owen Hart $12.00
Ken Shamrock vs. Dan Severn $12.00
Luna vs. Sable $12.00
Mark Henry vs. Vader $12.00
Razor Ramon vs. Diesel $100.00
Road Dogg vs. Al Snow $12.00
Shawn Michaels vs. Triple H $12.00
Shawn Michaels vs. Vader $12.00
Steve Blackman vs. Marc Mero $12.00
Steve Austin vs. Shawn Michaels $12.00
Steve Austin vs. Vince McMahon $12.00
Taka Michinoku vs. Brian Christopher $12.00
Undertaker vs. Kane $12.00
X-Pac vs. Jeff Jarrett $12.00

Sunday Night Heat

Bad Ass Billy Gunn $6.00
Road Dogg $6.00
Sable $6.00
Undertaker $6.00

Raw is War

Steve Austin $6.00
Mankind $6.00
Undertaker $6.00
The Rock $6.00

Deadly Games

Steve Austin $6.00
Droz $6.00

Road Dogg $6.00
Kurrgan $6.00

Triple H $6.00
Edge $6.00

Breakdown

Steve Austin $8.00
Droz $8.00

D-Lo Brown $6.00

Goldust $8.00

Mankind $10.00

X-Pac $8.00

Road Rage

Godfather $8.00

Hardcore Holly $6.00

The Rock $6.00

Mankind $6.00

Test $6.00

Al Snow $6.00

Jakk'd Up

Steve Austin $6.00

Undertaker $6.00

Kane $6.00

Sable $6.00

Federation Fighters 12-inch Figures

Undertaker $15.00

The Rock $15.00

Kane $15.00

Steve Austin No. 1 . . . .$15.00

Steve Austin No. 2 . . . .$15.00

Back Talkin' Crushers 9-Inch Figures
Series 1

Steve Austin $15.00

The Rock $15.00

The Undertaker $15.00

The Big Show $15.00

Rumble Gear
Series 1

Austin (Camo Gear) $8.00

Undertaker (Lord of Darkness & Survivor Series Versions) $8.00

Referee $8.00

Multi-Packs
Survivor Series

Ahmed Johnson, Shawn Michaels, Ultimate Warrior, Goldust $60.00

King of the Ring

Ahmed Johnson, Referee, Bret Hart, Steve Austin $40.00

Buried Alive

Mankind, Paul Bearer, The Executioner, Undertaker $65.00

Raw is War

Bret Hart, Sunny, Vince McMahon, Sid $30.00

Triple Threat

Ahmed Johnson, Marc Mero, Yokozuna $35.00

Nation of Domination

Clarence Mason, Crush, Farooq, Savio Vega . . .$25.00

Wrestlemania 14
Triple H, Shawn Michaels, Steve Austin, Undertaker $30.00

Faces of Foley
Cactus Jack, Dude Love, Mankind $25.00

Attitude
LOD 2000, Steve Austin, Shawn Michaels $25.00

No Holds Barred
Cactus Jack, Kane, Steve Austin $25.00

Degeneration X
Road Dogg, Triple H, Chyna, Billy Gunn $25.00

Badd Blood
Kane, Paul Bearer, Steve Austin, Undertaker . . .$40.00

Off The Mat
Billy Gunn, Road Dogg, Steve Austin, Undertaker $25.00

Shotgun Saturday Night
Kane, Shawn Michaels, Steve Austin, The Rock $25.00

Go Mental
Dude Love, Triple H, Steve Austin, Undertaker . . .$25.00

Fully Loaded
Billy Gunn, Road Dogg, Steve Austin, Undertaker $25.00

Legends Past & Present
Andre the Giant, Steve Austin, Undertaker . . .$25.00

Over The Edge
Triple H, Kane, Steve Austin, The Rock $25.00

Judgment Day
Steve Austin, Undertaker, Vince McMahon $25.00

3-Pack Special Collections
Steve Austin $25.00
Undertaker $25.00

Bad To the Bonz 3-Pack
Steve Austin $25.00

Titan Tron Live 3-Pack
Austin, Kane, X-Pac . . .$25.00

Survivor Series 4-Pack
Austin, Rock, Kane, Undertaker $25.00

Championship Title
Austin, Rock, X-Pac, Kane $25.00

Perfect 10
Big Show, Kane, Rock, Steve Austin, Undertaker, Billy Gunn, Mankind, X-Pac, Triple H, Road Dogg $75.00

Survivor Series 3-Pack
Steve Austin, Rock, Billy Gunn $25.00

Camo Carnage
Steve Austin, Triple H, Billy Gunn $25.00

Last Man Standing
Steve Austin, The Rock, Shane McMahon, Vince McMahon $30.00

Raw is War No. 2
Mankind, Austin, Rock, Undertaker $30.00

No Chance
Austin, Vince McMahon, Paul Wight $25.00

Hardcore Match
Al Snow, Mankind, Bob Holly, Boss Man . .$30.00

Misc.
K-Mart Steve Austin (gift set No. 1) $15.00
K-Mart Steve Austin (gift set No. 2) $15.00
K-Mart The Rock (gift set No. 1) $15.00
KB Toys Steve Austin .$15.00
Toyfare Undertaker . . .$20.00

Toyfare Steve Austin . .$20.00

Whites Guide Sable . . .$20.00

Whites Guide Undertaker $20.00

Jakks Steve Austin 1-in-40 Contest $25.00

KB Toys Austin Signature belt w/fig $25.00

Wrestlemania 3-Packs

Triple H, Shawn Michaels, Thrasher $25.00

Steve Austin, Mosh, Undertaker $25.00

Fantasy Warfare

Steve Austin vs. Andre the Giant $20.00

Mankind vs. Undertaker .$15.00

Jakks Ripped & Ruthless Series 1

Goldust $10.00

Mankind $10.00

Steve Austin $15.00

Undertaker $10.00

Series 2

Triple H $10.00

Kane $40.00

Sable $10.00

Shawn Michaels $10.00

Legends

Andre the Giant $15.00

Capt. Lou Albano $10.00

Freddie Blassie $10.00

Jimmy Snuka $10.00

Jakks Mini Figures

Wrestlemania $30.00

Raw is War $25.00

Royal Rumble $25.00

King of the Ring $25.00

No Mercy $20.00

Sudden Threat $20.00

Playmates Heroes of Wrestling

Undertaker (14 inch) . .$40.00

Undertaker (9 inch) . . .$10.00

Sid (9 inch) $10.00

Playmates Ringmasters

Bret Hart $8.00

Goldust $5.00

Shawn Michaels $5.00

Sid $5.00

Undertaker $5.00

Yokozuna $8.00

Playmates Grudge Match Mini Figures 2-Packs

Steve Austin vs. Bret Hart $15.00

Ahmed Johnson vs. Yokozuna $15.00

Owen Hart vs. Shawn Michaels $15.00

Sid vs. Vader $15.00

Mankind vs. Undertaker .$15.00

Savio Vega vs. Goldust .$15.00

Playmates Stretch'ums

Bret Hart $10.00

Sid $10.00

Undertaker $10.00

Shawn Michaels $10.00

Playmates, WWF Thumb Wrestlers 1997

Owen Hart vs. Steve Austin $10.00

Undertaker vs. Shawn Michaels $10.00

Mankind vs. Triple H ..$10.00

British Bulldog vs. Ken Shamrock $10.00

Galoob, WCW 1993

Ric Flair $20.00

Arn Anderson $20.00

Barry Windham $20.00

Sid Vicious $20.00

Sting $20.00

Lex Lugar $20.00

Ron Simmons $20.00

Butch Reed $20.00

Rick Steiner $20.00

Scott Steiner $20.00

Brian Pillman $20.00

Tom Zenk $20.00

United Kingdom releases

Ric Flair (red) $25.00

Arn Anderson (red) ...$25.00

Barry Windham (blue) .$25.00

Sid Vicious (pink) $25.00

Lex Lugar (green) $25.00

Lex Lugar (robe) $85.00

Ron Simmons (blue/striped) $60.00

Rick Steiner (green) ...$30.00

Scott Steiner (pink) ...$25.00

Brian Pillman (blue) ...$25.00

Sting (coat) $85.00

Dustin Rhodes $100.00

Michael Hayes $60.00

Jimmy Garvin $60.00

Big Josh $100.00

El Gigante $75.00

Galoob, WCW 14-inch

Sid $100.00

Sting $100.00

Ric Flair $100.00

Lex Lugar $100.00

JusToys, WCW Bendies 1992

Ric Flair $15.00

Arn Anderson $20.00

Barry Windham $15.00

Sid Vicious $15.00

Sting $15.00

Lex Lugar $15.00

Ron Simmons $20.00

Butch Reed $20.00

Rick Steiner $20.00

Scott Steiner $20.00

Brian Pillman $15.00

Tom Zenk $15.00

Original San Francisco Toymakers, WCW 1994-1998 Series 1

Ric Flair $8.00

Vader $8.00

Johnny B. Badd $8.00

Hulk Hogan $12.00

Sting $8.00

Jimmy Hart $8.00

Brian Knobs $8.00

Jerry Sags $8.00

Kevin Sullivan $8.00

Series 2

Ric Flair $15.00

Vader (re-release) $15.00

Johnny B. Badd $15.00

Hulk Hogan (re-release)$15.00

Sting (pink) $15.00

Sting (green) $15.00

Jimmy Hart $15.00

Kevin Sullivan $15.00

Macho Man $20.00

Tag Teams

Nasty Boys $20.00

Hulk Hogan & Sting . . .$20.00

Booker T. & Stevie Ray $20.00

Series 3

Ric Flair $12.00

Hulk Hogan $12.00

Sting $12.00

Macho Man $12.00

Alex Wright $12.00

Big Bubba Rogers $12.00

Craig Pittman $12.00

The Giant $12.00

Booker T. $12.00

Stevie Ray $12.00

Figures Inc. Exclusive Tag Teams

Blue Bloods $30.00

Hulk Hogan & Macho Man $25.00

Harlem Heat $25.00

Nasty Boys $25.00

Nitro (vibrating)

Kevin Nash $8.00

Scott Hall $8.00

Chris Benoit $8.00

The Giant $8.00

Hollywood Hogan $8.00

Sting $8.00

Kevin Sullivan $8.00

Lex Lugar $8.00

Tag Team Two Packs

Sting & Lex Lugar $30.00

Scott Hall & Kevin Nash .$30.00

Nitro (non-vibrating)

The Giant $8.00

Booker T. $6.00

Stevie Ray $6.00

Hollywood Hogan $8.00

Ric Flair $8.00

Brian Knobs $6.00

Jerry Sags $6.00

Kevin Sullivan $6.00

Macho Man $8.00

Lex Lugar $10.00

Sting $10.00

Sting (2 Pack) $20.00

WCW/NWO Hard Plastic Series 1

Kevin Nash $8.00

Sting (White) $8.00

The Giant $8.00

Ric Flair $8.00

Raven (Black) $8.00

Diamond Dallas Page . .$8.00

PPV Match-Ups

Scott Hall vs. Lex Lugar .$25.00

Hulk Hogan vs. Sting . .$30.00

Kevin Nash vs. The Giant $25.00

Kevin Nash vs. DDP . . .$25.00

Series 2

Hulk Hogan $8.00

Scott Hall $8.00

Randy Savage $8.00

Curt Hennig $8.00

Lex Lugar $8.00

Bret Hart (wings) $8.00

Series 3

Goldberg $8.00

Sting (Red) $8.00

Rey Mysterio Jr. $8.00

Buff Bagwell $8.00

Scott Steiner $8.00

Chris Benoit $8.00

K-Mart Exclusive Ring

With Sting and jacket .$30.00

4-Packs

Thunder Champions

Goldberg, Bret Hart, Scott Hall, The Giant (w/belts) $25.00

Fearsome Foursome

Ric Flair, Chris Beniot, Dallas Page, Goldberg $25.00

NWO Hollywood

Buff Bagwell, Hollywood Hogan, Scott Steiner, The Giant $25.00

NWO Wolfpack

Sting, Kevin Nash, Randy Savage, Lex Lugar $25.00

4.5-inch Mini Figures

Hollywood Hogan $6.00

Macho Man $6.00

Scott Hall $6.00

Scott Steiner $10.00

Kevin Nash $6.00

Rick Steiner $6.00

The Giant $6.00

Lex Lugar $6.00

Sting $6.00

Ric Flair $6.00

Goldberg $10.00

12-inch Figures

Goldberg $30.00

Hollywood Hogan $25.00

Macho Man $25.00

Sting (white) $25.00

Sting (red) $25.00

Belt Buckle 1/2-inch Figures

Hulk Hogan & Sting . . .$15.00

Outsiders vs. Nasty Boys $15.00

2-Pack

Hollywood Hogan/ Dennis Rodman $20.00

ToyBiz, WCW 1997-current
Slam 'N Crunch
Series 1

Buff Bagwell $10

Konnan $10

Kevin Nash $10

Sting $10

Smash 'N Slam
Series 1

Diamond Dallas Page $10

Sting $10

The Giant w/Rey Mysterio Jr. $13

Lex Luger $10

Series 2

Hollywood Hogan $10

Kevin Nash $10

Macho Man $8

Scott Hall $10

Goldberg w/masked wrestler $12

Ring Fighters

Bret Hart $8

Chris Benoit $8

Booker T $8

Big Poppa Pump $8

Ring Masters
Series 1

Chris Jericho $12

Goldberg $10

Lex Luger $10

Bret Hart $10

Collector Twin Packs
Series 1

Macho Man & Elizabeth . .$15

Sting & Hollywood Hogan .$15

Giant & Kevin Nash $15

Grip & Flip
Series 1

Raven vs. Diamond Dallas Page $15

Goldberg vs. Hollywood Hogan $15

Chris Jericho vs. Dean Malenko $15

Series 2

Sting vs. Lex Luger $15

Kevin Nash vs. Bret Hart .$15

Scott Steiner vs. Rick Steiner $15

Road Wild Wrestlers
Series 1

Goldberg $10

Sting $10

Kevin Nash $10

Brawlin' Bikers

Diamond Dallas Page $10

Goldberg $10

Sting $10

Bend 'N' Flex 5-inch Wrestlers
Series 1

Goldberg $7

Sting $7

Scott Hall $7

Kevin Nash $7

Series 2

Diamond Dallas Page $7

Bret Hart $7

Booker T $7

Scott Steiner $7

IV Horsemen Set

Ric Flair, Chris Benoit,
Dean Malenko,
Steve McMichael $25

Tuff Talkin' 12-inch Figures
Series 1

Diamond Dallas
Page & Sting $20

Goldberg & Kevin Nash . .$20

Series 2

Konnan $15

Buff Bagwell $15

Randy Savage $15

Scott Steiner $15

Rumble 'N' Roar Wrestlers

Goldberg $15

Sting $15

Bruisers
Series 1

Kidman $10

Rey Mysterio Jr. $10

Disco Inferno $8

Raven $8

Stevie Ray $8

PowerSlam
Series 1

Goldberg $8

Hak $10

Sid Vicious $8

Hollywood Hogan $8

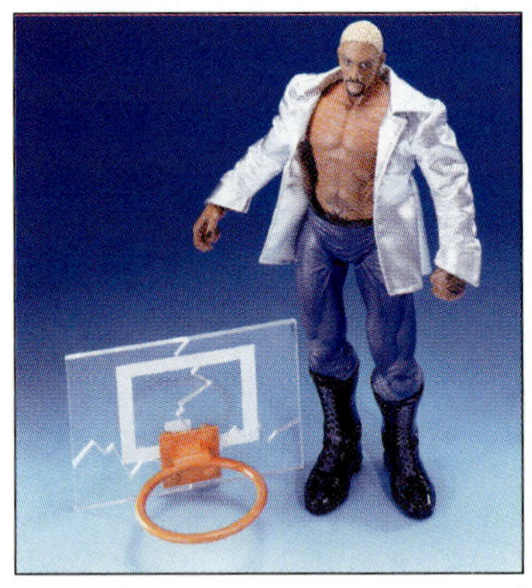

Dennis Rodman $10

Series 2

Roddy Piper $7

Buff Bagwell $7

Kevin Nash $7

Sting $7

Thunderslam 2-Packs

Sting vs. Bret Hart $15

Kevin Nash vs. Scott Hall . $15

Goldberg vs. Bam Bam Bigelow $15

Evolution of Sting Six-pack $45.00

Original San Francisco Toymakers, ECW 1999 Series 1

Taz $6.00

Rob Van Dam $6.00

Sabu $6.00

Shane Douglas $6.00

Chris Candido $6.00

Justin Credible $6.00

Series 2

Tommy Dreamer $6.00

Lance Storm $6.00

New Jack $6.00

D-Von Dudley $6.00

Bubba Ray Dudley $6.00

Hyper Heroes, New Japan Pro Wrestling 1998-current

Masa Chono $25

Riki Chosyu $25

Shinya Hashimoto $25

Kensuke Sasaki $25

The Great Muta # 1 (black) .$25

The Great Muta # 2 (red) .$25

The Great Muta # 3 (nWo) .$25

Hiroyoshi Tenzan $25

Antonio Inoki (red) $25

Antonio Inoki (blue) $25

Jushin Thunder Liger $25

Tatsumi Fujinami $25

Manabu Nakanishi $25

Kendoh Ka-Shin $25

Kazuo Yamazaki $25

El Samurai $25

Masa Saito $25

Satoshi Kojima $25

Koji Kanemoto $25
Shinjiro Ohanti $25

Special releases

Great Muta & Masa Chono $60.00
Special Antonio Inoki (red) $40.00
Keiji Muto & Masa Chono (nWo) $60.00
Atsushi Onita & Akira Maeda $45

All Japan Pro Wrestling, 1998

Jun Akiyama $20
Mitsuhara Misawa $20
Kenta Kobashi $20
Giant Baba $20
Takashi Kawada $20
Akira Taue $20

Original San Francisco Toy Makers, CMLL 1992

Satanico $10.00
Atlantis $10.00
Brazo de Plata $10.00
Vampario Canadiense .$10.00
Blue Demon $10.00
Lizmark $10.00
Sangre Chicana $10.00
Pierroth $10.00
El Brazo $10.00
Ultimo Dragon $10.00
Brazo de Oro $10.00
Rayo de Jalisco $10.00

Kelian (Mexico), AAA

Octagon $20
Blue Panther $20
Hijo Del Santo $20
Fuerza Guerrera $20
Cien Caras $20
Konnan $20
La Parka $20
Mascara Sagrada $20
Psicosis $20
Heavy Metal $20
Perro Aguayo $20
Rey Mysterio Jr. $20

Special Issues
Jesse Ventura, 1998-current

Governor $20.00

Navy SEAL $30.00

Football Coach $20.00

Sideshow Toys, Jesse Ventura 3.5-inch Dolls, 1999

Governor $15.00

Coach $15.00

Navy SEAL $15.00

Hasbro, G.I. Joe 1989

Sgt. Slaughter $35.00

Phoenix Toys, Rocky III 1983

Thunderlips
(Hulk Hogan) $25.00

Figures Inc., Heroes of Wrestling, 1999
Series 1

King Kong Bundy $8.00

King Kong Bundy
(bloody) $8.00

Series 2

Abdullah the Butcher . .$8.00

Abdullah the Butcher
(bloody) $8.00

Series 3

Killer Kowalski $8.00

chapter 5 Card Collecting and Knickknacks

Wrestling cards are a special part of the wrestling-collectibles market. For many fans, it is their first foray into the sport. That's because wrestling cards are perhaps the one item that connects the wrestling world to the rest of sports-memorabilia collecting.

Nowadays, fans can go to any local comic book store or tobacco shop and find the latest issue of wrestling collector cards—full color, glossy and embossed cards that are true artifacts that should be kept and cherished for many years to come. But the truth is, wrestling cards are not new. In fact, the history of wrestling cards dates back to when the very first sports cards were ever made.

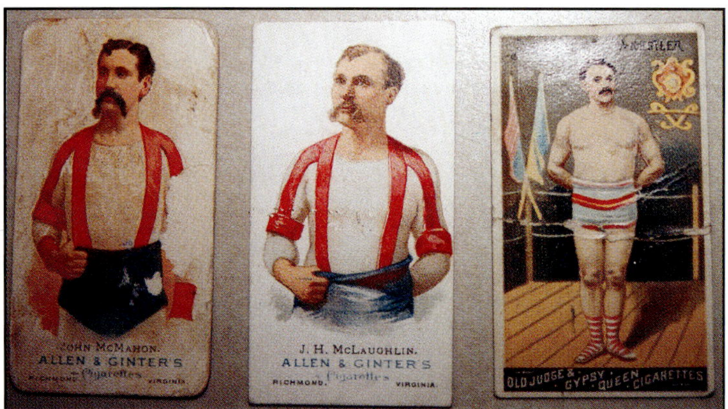

Allen and Ginters Cigarettes (left and center) and Gypsy Queen Cigarettes (right), $150.

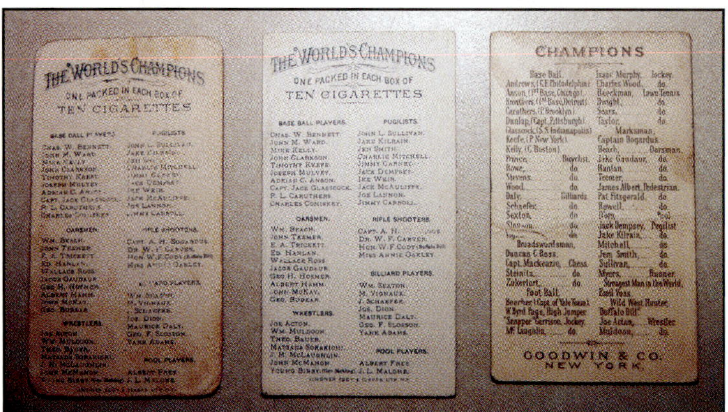

Cigarette cards (reverse).

In the late 1800s, it was common for wrestling to be featured as classic tobacco cards. In 1887, the Allen & Ginters Tobacco Company released a set of seven wrestlers as part of a sports-card set. This, by all accounts, was the very first sports card set ever produced. Who would have thought that alongside the greats of baseball and boxing of the day would stand professional wrestlers. Today, one can't imagine The Rock being offered in a set with the likes of Michael Jordan or Randy Moss. But in the latter part of the 19th century, wrestling stars were considered the cream of the crop of pro athletes.

Through much of the early 1900s, many cigarette cards, which graced pictures of old-time grapplers, were produced in the United States and abroad. But it wasn't until the 1950s that the first all-wrestling set of collector cards was produced. In 1948, the Topps Company issued a 25-card set called the Magic Photo Cards. These postage stamp-sized cards had one blank side that "developed" a picture when it was moistened. Then, from 1954 to 1956, the Parkhurst Company in Canada, issued two complete sets of wrestling's first superstars. With stars like Buddy Rogers, Lou Thesz and Gorgeous George, this set today, complete and in superior condition, can fetch as much as $1,000 on the current market.

Fans had to wait nearly 30 years before the next full set of wrestling cards became available. In 1982, Norman Kietzer's Pro Wrestling Enterprises issued four sets of his wrestling superstars line that included stars from the regional territories like the American Wrestling Association and the National Wrestling Alliance. For new fans, this set is

FRANK GOTCH.
Champion Wrestler

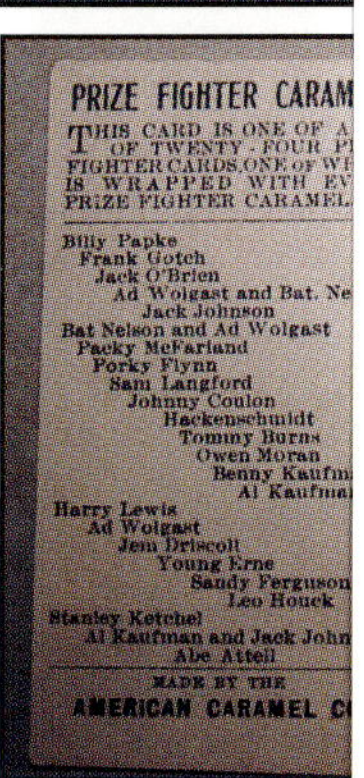

S. Zbys

Stanislaus Z
Miner's T

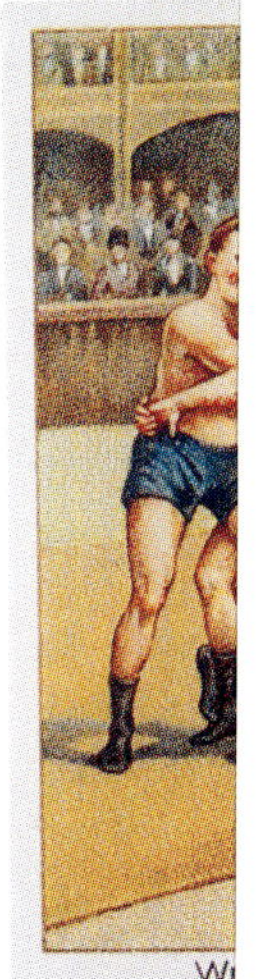

Turf Cigaret

Pro Wrestlin

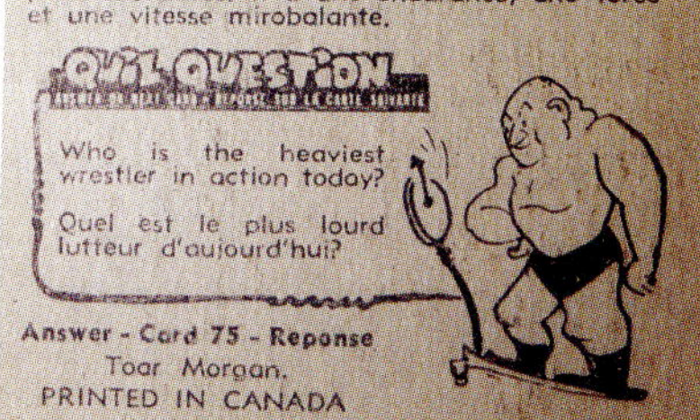

Champion Lou Thesz — THE PERFECT WRESTLER

Lou is recognized as Heavyweight Champion of the World by the N.W.A. He has not been defeated since 1948 and has been beaten two times in the last 12 years. Taught by several old-timers, Lou is now managed by former champion, Ed "Strangler" Lewis. Thesz is 6 feet, 1 inch tall, weighs 230 lbs. He has tremendous speed, strength and endurance and is familiar with every hold and counter.

LE LUTTEUR PARFAIT

Le N.W.A. reconnait Lou comme le Champion Poids-lourd mondial. Il ne perdit aucun combat depuis 1948, et ne fut battu que trois fois depuis ces douze dernières années. Entrainé par plusieurs anciens champions, Lou est maintenant sous les ordres de l'ancien champion Ed "l'Etrangleur" Lewis. Thesz mesure 6'1" et pèse 230 livres. Il a une endurance, une force et une vitesse mirobolante.

QUIZ QUESTION

Who is the heaviest wrestler in action today?

Quel est le plus lourd lutteur d'aujourd'hui?

Answer - Card 75 - Reponse
Toar Morgan.
PRINTED IN CANADA

Reverse of the Lou Thesz card.

Parkhurst, Lou Thesz card, $95.

sentimental for many reasons, the most important being these are the stars who got them interested in wrestling to begin with. Whole sets of this type are rare, but are still floating around. No one can dispute the quality, as the card backs were loaded with information.

When the World Wrestling Federation took its promotional efforts national in 1984 and exposed pro wrestling to a mass audience, it issued the first set of WWF cards which are some of the most popular for fans today. In 1985, the O-Pee-Chee company released a duel French-American set of cards that are widely considered the most rare to find. Released in Canada, the cards are written in both English and French. Collectors "druell" over this set because of one card: No. 70. That card is the very first WWF-released Jesse "The Body" Ventura card (his first card is No. 20 of the 1982 Pro Wrestling Enterprises line). That same year, Topps released an English set in the United States. "The Body" is included in this set as well, and his card has skyrocketed in value since his appointment as Governor of Minnesota.

In 1986, Monty Gum produced a wrestling superstars line that is a mixture of old NWA and WWF grapplers. Then, in 1987, Topps produced its second WWF set and it is considered a superior-quality card when compared with the earlier release. Three years passed before Classic Cards produced a WWF set which includes wrestlers such as the Ultimate Warrior and Shawn Michaels. In 1988, the NWA put out a line from Wonderama, and WCW's first venture into collector cards came in 1991 when Championship Marketing released a widely available set.

Through the years, especially since wrestling's boom period in the mid-'80s, fans have been treated to food cards. These are the cards that were included in ice cream bars or cookies and snacks. Though they are hard to find, fans are always on the look out, trying to recapture their enthusiasm for wrestling they had as a youth.

Parkhurst, Pat O'Connor card, $100.

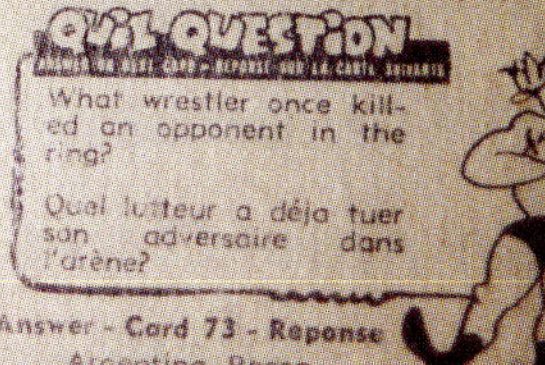

Pat O'Connor — NEW ZEALAND FLASH

Born in Raetihi, N.Z. in 1926, O'Connor won the N.Z. Heavyweight title 4 times and the B.E. title once.. He was discovered by old pros Butch Levy and Joe Pazandak who brought him along until he now rates among the top ten grapplers. His best hold is the Airplane spin. Pat stands 6 feet, 1½ inches tall, and weighs around 230 lbs. He has a degree in Agriculture from Massey College, N.Z.

LUMIERE DE LA NOUVELLE ZELANDE

Né à Raetihi, N. Z. en 1926, O'Connor gagna 4 fois le titre Poids-lourd de N. Z. et une fois le titre de l'E.B. Il fut découvert par Butch Levy et Joe Pazandak qui l'entrainèrent jusqu'à ce qu'il devint un des dix meilleurs lutteurs. Sa meilleure tactique est la vrille d'avion. Pat mesure 6 pieds et 1 pouce et demi et pèse environs 230 livres. Il reçut un degré en Agriculture du Collège Massey, N. Z.

QUIZ QUESTION

What wrestler once killed an opponent in the ring?

Quel lutteur a déja tuer son adversaire dans l'arène?

Answer - Card 73 - Reponse
Argentina Rocca
PRINTED IN CANADA

O'Connor card (reverse).

WREST

1948 Top

1954 Par

1955 Par

1982 Pro

1983 Pro

1985 WV
Stars . .

1985 WV
Wrestlin

1986 Mo
Wrestlin

1987 WV

1987 WV

1988 NV
Superca

1990 WV

1991 WV
Stickers

1991 WV

1991 WC

1991 Im

1991 WV

1991 WC

1992 WV

1994 WV

1995 WV

1995 WV

1997 Ja

1997 WCW Chromium Card $30.00

1997 WWF Trivia Card Game $15.00

1998 WWF Magazine Trading Card $10.00

1998 WWF Trivia Card Game $10.00

1998 WCW/NWO Up Front Sports $20.00
Pop Up Card

Food Cards

1986 Carnation Major League Wrestling .$50.00

1987 WWF Hostess $40.00

1987 WWF Stuart Wrestling $50.00

1987 WWF Circle-K/Coca Cola Supermatch $35.00

1988 WWF Hostess $25.00

1988 WWF Ice Cream Bar Collector Cards
(Series 1) $60.00

1989 WWF Ice Cream Bar Collector Cards
(Series 2) $30.00

1990 WWF Ice Cream Bar Collector Cards
(Series 3) $30.00

1991 WWF Ice Cream Bar Collector Cards
(Series 4) $30.00

1992 WWF Ice Cream Bar Collector Cards
(Series 5) $30.00

1993 WWF Ice Cream Bar Collector Cards
(Series 6) $30.00

1994 WWF Ice Cream Bar Collector Cards
(Series 7) $30.00

1995 WWF Ice Cream Bar Collector Cards
(Series 8) $30.00

1996 WWF Ice Cream Bar Collector Cards
(Series 9) $30.00

1997 WWF Ice Cream Bar Collector Cards
(Series 10) $30.00

Parkhurst, Buddy Rogers, 1955, $150.

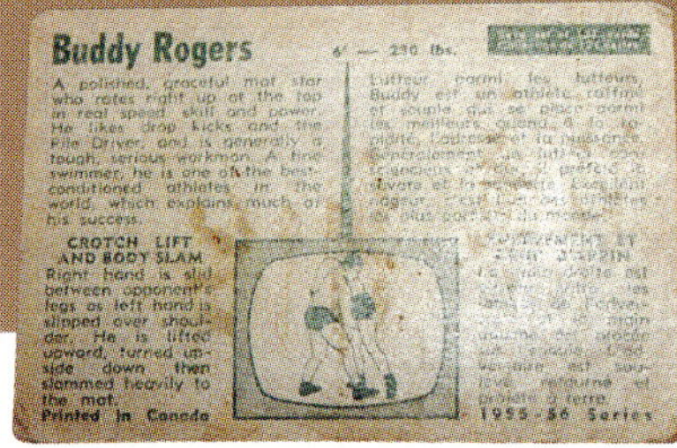

Buddy Rogers' card (reverse).

T.C.G. Ringside card of Antonino Rocca, $75.

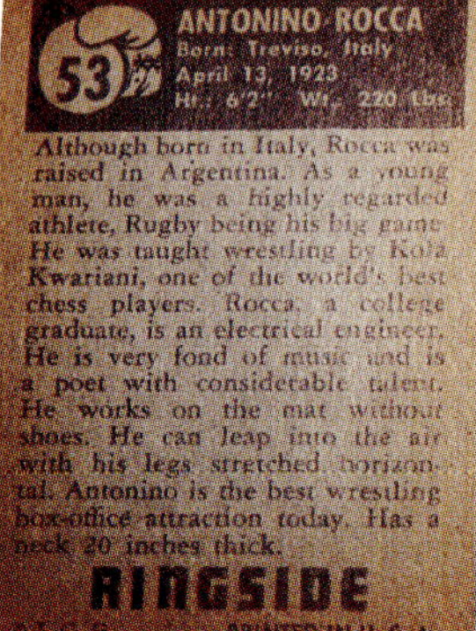

T.C.G. Antonino Rocca card (reverse).

Buddy Rogers card, $35.

Bruno Sammartino, Focus on Sports, 1978, $25.

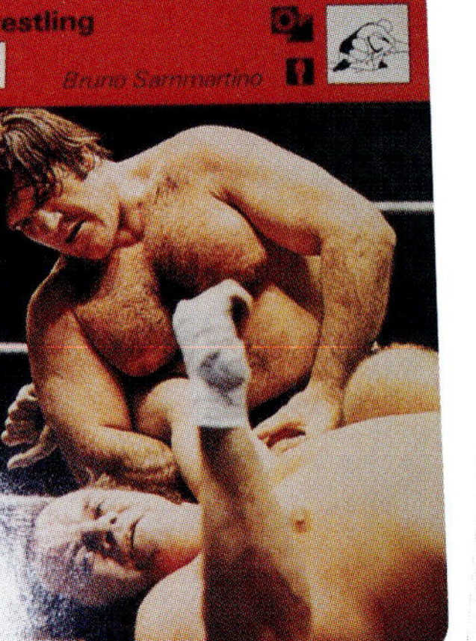

Bruno Sammartino card (reverse).

1998 WWF Ice Cream Bar Collector Cards (Series 11) $30.00

1999 WWF Ice Cream Bar Collector Cards (Series 12) $30.00

1999 WCW/NWO Little Caesar's $15.00

1999 WWF Poster Puzzle $10.00

KNICKKNACKS

Comic Images, WWF Mini Beanie Bears, 1998
Series 1: Steve Austin, Undertaker, Godfather, Kane, Mankind, Sable, Ken Shamrock, New Age Outlaws, the set $75.00

Racing Champs WCW/nWo Beanie Bears, 1998
Kevin Nash, Four Horsemen, Sting, Diamond Dallas Page, Hollywood Hogan, Goldberg, Nitro Girls, Wolfpack, Konnan, the set .$70.00

Toy Island, WWF Attitude Racers 1999
Series 1, 1/64: Steve Austin, Undertaker, Triple H, Ken Shamrock, Nation of Domination, The Rock, each $10.00
Grudge Packs, Series 1, 1/64: The Rock vs. Triple H, Mankind vs. Kane, Steve Austin vs. Undertaker, each $10.00
Series 1, 1/24: Chyna, Triple H, Nation of Domination, each $10.00

Talking Monster Trucks, International Promotions, 1999
Series 1: Steve Austin, Undertaker, Legion of Doom, each $20.00

Mini Monster Trucks

Series 1: Steve Austin, The Rock, Undertaker, each $20.00

Remote Control Monster Trucks

Series 1: Steve Austin, Undertaker, The Rock, each $20.00

Danbury Mint, WWF 24K Trading Cards 1998 . . . .$25.00

DIC Animations, Hulk Hogan Rock & Wrestling Videos, 1985
Hulk Hogan All-Time Champ, Ghost Wrestlers, Four-Legged Pickpocket, The Last Resort, each $15.00

WWF Bean Bag Bangers, 1999

Series 1
Triple H, Undertaker, Dude Love, Undertaker,each $10.00

Series 2
The Rock, Kane, Sable, Steve Austin, Road Dogg, Billy Gunn, each $10.00

WWF Punching Bags, 1999
Steve Austin, Kane, each $10.00

WWF Squirt Heads, 1992
Hulk Hogan, Hawk, Animal, Shawn Micheals, Marty Janetty, Million Dollar Man, Big Bossman, Butch, Luke, Jake Roberts, Ultimate Warrior, Randy Savage, each $8.00

ToyBiz, WCW Bobbing Heads, 1998
Sting, Goldberg, Diamond Dallas Page, Hollywood Hogan, each $15.00

WWF Attitude Beanie Bears, Comic Images 1999
Series 1

Val Venis (Hello Ladies) $10.00

Sable (Hands Down Winner) $10.00

Stone Cold Steve Austin (That's the bottom line) $18.00

Stone Cold Steve Austin (100% Pure Whoop Ass) $18.00

The Rock (Smell what the Rock is Cooking) $10.00

D-Generation X (Suck It) $10.00

Kane (No Kane, No Pain) $10.00

Undertaker (The Lord of Darkness) $10.00

Series 2

Stone Cold Steve Austin (SCU) $18.00

Steve Austin (Class 3:16) $18.00

Mr. McMahon (Don't Cross the Boss) . .$10.00

Al Snow with Head (J.O.B. Squad) $10.00

Mankind with Socko (Have a Nice Day) $10.00

The Rock (Know Your Role) $10.00

Road Dogg Jesse James
(Roll the Dogg a Bone) $10.00

Cesar Inc., WWF Full Head Masks, 1997

Steve Austin $25.00

Kane $35.00

Kane (mask only) $8.00

Bret Hart $35.00

Shane Michaels $35.00

Sycho Sid $25.00

Goldust $35.00

Undertaker $35.00

Mankind $35.00

Rock $25.00

Vince McMahon $25.00

Sable $35.00

WCW postage stamps from St. Vincent in the Caribbean, 1999 . . . .$30.00

Advanced Graphics, WWF Life-size Standups, 1997

Austin, Rock, Undertaker,
Shawn Michaels $30.00

Classic Collectible Products, WCW Commemorative Tickets 1998

Kevin Nash, Goldberg $25.00

Future Toys (Mexico), CMLL Wrestling Buddies 1993

Vampario Canadiense $25.00

Atlantis $25.00

Tinieblas $25.00

Ace Novelty Company, WWF Stuffed Dolls 1991

Hulk Hogan (2-foot) $25.00

Hulk Hogan (3-foot) $50.00

Diamond Publishing, WWF Hulk Hogan's Rock & Wrestling Sticker Album, 1986 . . . . .$10.00

Ultimate Creations, Ultimate warrior Comic Book, 1996 Issues 1 through 5 . . . .$10.00

Checkerboard Press, WWF Poster Books, 1991 . . . .$10.00

Marvel Comics, WCW Comic Books, 1992 Issues 1-12 . . . .$10.00

CHAOS Comics, Steve Austin, Mankind, Undertaker Comic Books, 1998-99 . . . . .$5.00

BBM, Japanese Pro Wrestling Cards, 1997, 8 cards in set $20.00

Jakks, WWF Vince McMahon Microphone, 1998 . . . .$15.00

Jakks, WWF title belt, Stone Cold Skull belt, 1998 . . . .$15.00

A complete collection of 12 NWA Mello Yellow cans features Flair, Rhodes, Windham, Sting, Animal, Hawk, Magnum T.A. and others, $35. Photo courtesy of Dr. Bob Bryla.

A pre-prohibition beer ad, $25. Photo courtesy of Dr. Bob Bryla.

Dr. David Schultz's license plate, $200. Photo courtesy of Dr. Bob Bryla.

A Billy Watson Whipper soda bottle from Canada; very rare, $175. Photo courtesy of Dr. Bob Bryla.

Bob "Dr. Wrestling" Bryla, surrounded by some of his wrestling collectibles. Photo courtesy of Dr. Bob Bryla.

MEMBERSHIP CARD
Pat O'Connor Fan Club
Mrs. Winifred Hilkert
is a lifetime member
president

A Pat O'Connor fan-club medal from the 1950s, $15. Photo courtesy of Dr. Bob Bryla.

Plush toys in the image of some of Japan's female wrestlers, $25 each.

Boxing and All the Leading Sports

The National Police Gazette

The Leading Illustrated Sporting Journal in the World

WRESTLING IS A POPULAR SPORT.

A page from the Police Gazette, $5. Photo courtesy of Mike Chapman.

NWA calendars from 1954, 1955 and 1957, $45 each. Photos courtesy of Mike Chapman.

A "peep show" ad, $55.
Photo courtesy of Mike Chapman.

Original photos of George Hackenschmidt, $35.
Photo courtesy of Mike Chapman.

A souvenir photo of The Sheik, $15.
Photo courtesy of Norman Kietzer.

Abe Lincoln comic, $45.
Photo courtesy of Mike Chapman.

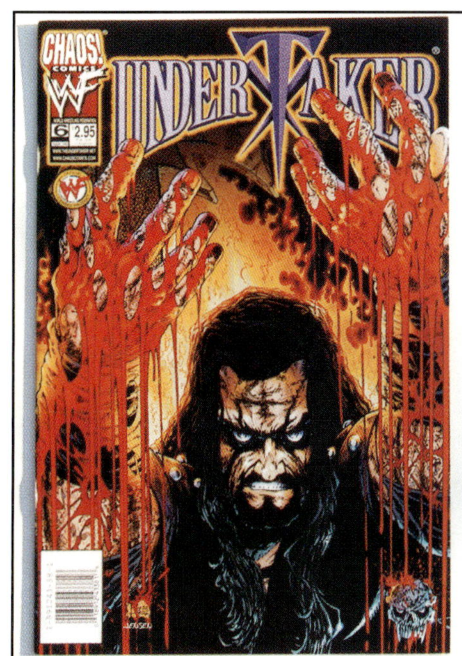

Undertaker comics 5 and 6, $5 each.

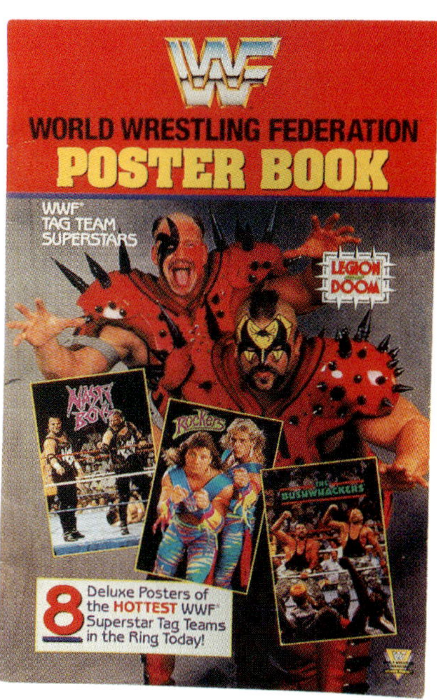

WWF posterbook 2, $10.

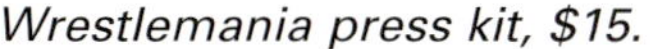
Wrestlemania press kit, $15.

Undertaker and Mankind comics, $5 each.

Nick Bockwinkel plaque, $45.
Photo courtesy of Mick Karch.

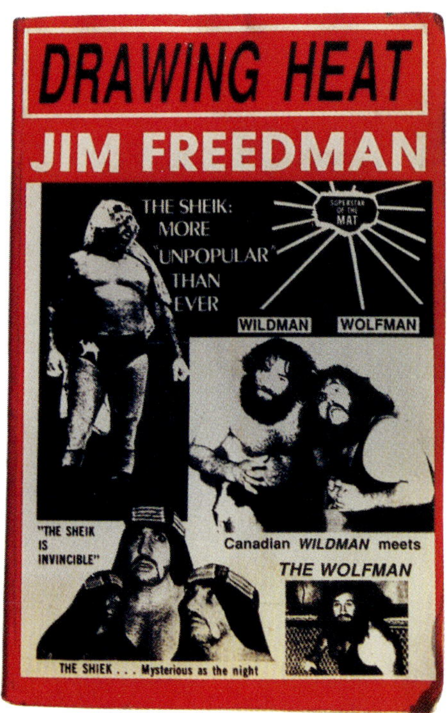

Drawing Heat, $10.

DESIGNERS & MANUFACTURERS OF

OFFICIAL

WRESTLING WEAR

K&H ORIGINALS

FOR THE DISCRIMINATING PROFESSIONAL

PHONE:
Area Code 614
855-1535

P.O. Box 447
JOHNSTOWN, OHIO
43031

K&H gear catalog, circa 1960s, $15.
Photo courtesy of Mick Karch.

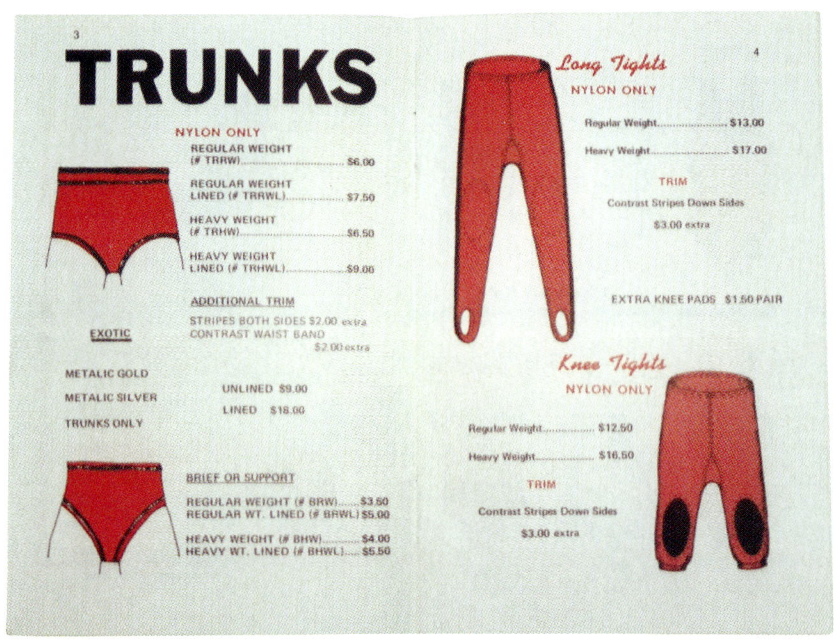

3

TRUNKS

NYLON ONLY

REGULAR WEIGHT (# TRRW) $6.00

REGULAR WEIGHT LINED (# TRRWL) $7.50

HEAVY WEIGHT (# TRHW) $6.50

HEAVY WEIGHT LINED (# TRHWL) $9.00

ADDITIONAL TRIM

STRIPES BOTH SIDES $2.00 extra
CONTRAST WAIST BAND $2.00 extra

EXOTIC

METALIC GOLD
METALIC SILVER
TRUNKS ONLY

UNLINED $9.00
LINED $18.00

BRIEF OR SUPPORT

REGULAR WEIGHT (# BRW) $3.50
REGULAR WT. LINED (# BRWL) $5.00

HEAVY WEIGHT (# BHW) $4.00
HEAVY WT. LINED (# BHWL) $5.50

4

Long Tights

NYLON ONLY

Regular Weight $13.00

Heavy Weight $17.00

TRIM

Contrast Stripes Down Sides
$3.00 extra

EXTRA KNEE PADS $1.50 PAIR

Knee Tights

NYLON ONLY

Regular Weight $12.50

Heavy Weight $16.50

TRIM

Contrast Stripes Down Sides
$3.00 extra

A page from the K&H gear catalog, circa 1960s.
Photo courtesy of Mick Karch.

A Fred Beell postcard, $10.

A Franklin Mint coin of Jake "The Snake" Roberts, $45.

An NWA mailing envelope showing women pro wrestlers from Japan, $15. Photo courtesy of Mick Karch.

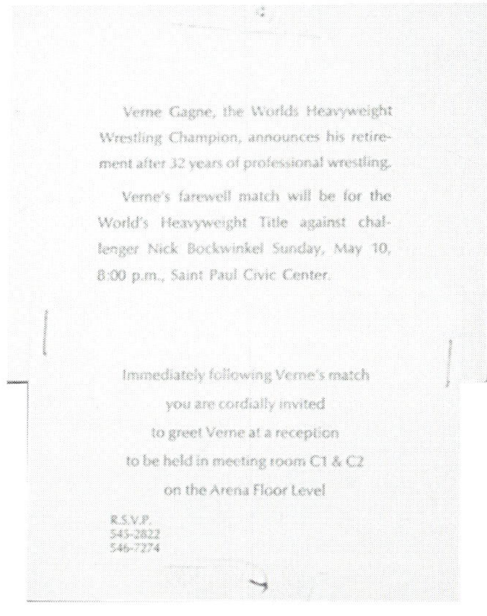
Verne Gagne, the Worlds Heavyweight Wrestling Champion, announces his retirement after 32 years of professional wrestling.

Verne's farewell match will be for the World's Heavyweight Title against challenger Nick Bockwinkel Sunday, May 10, 8:00 p.m., Saint Paul Civic Center.

Immediately following Verne's match
you are cordially invited
to greet Verne at a reception
to be held in meeting room C1 & C2
on the Arena Floor Level

R.S.V.P.
545-2822
546-7274

An invitation for Verne Gagne's retirement, $25. Photo courtesy of Mick Karch.

Original and extremely rare drawings done by Jerry "The King" Lawler. The cartoon is $100 and the illustration of Jackie Fargo is worth $300 because it is signed.

A Universal Wrestling Superstars Heavyweight Title Belt worn by VWS champs Big Boss Man, Jimmy Snuka, Ax, Greg Valentine, Jake "The Snake" Roberts, Paul Orndorff, Tito Santana, Rick Mattel, Tony Atlas, Hacksaw Duggan, Hercules Hernandez and others, $800. Photo courtesy of Dr. Bob Bryla.

Stone Cold Steve Austin and Undertaker comics, No. 1, $5 each.

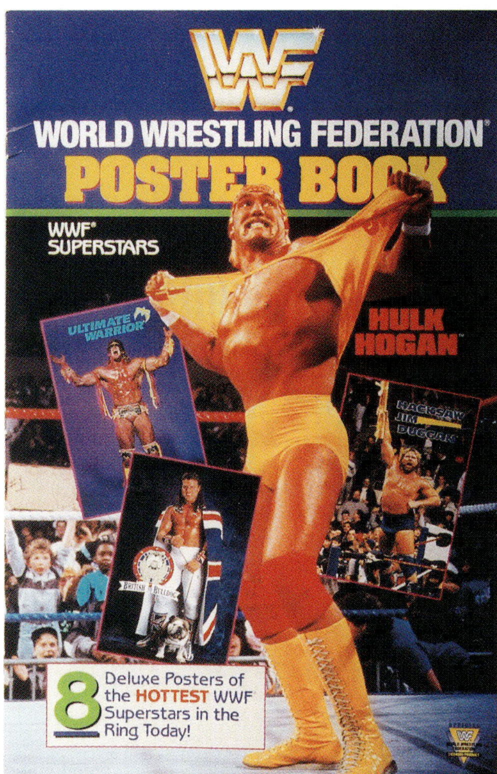

WWF posterbook, $10.

A Verne Gagne trivia game, $60. Photo courtesy of Mike Chapman.

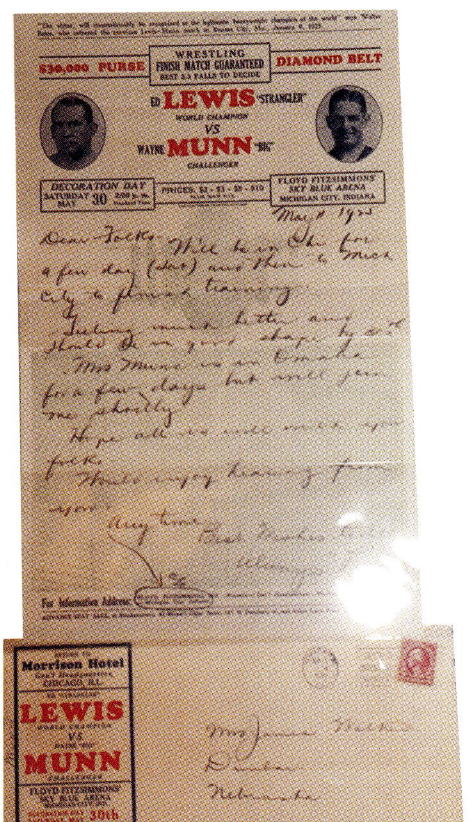

$30,000 PURSE

WRESTLING
FINISH MATCH GUARANTEED
BEST 2-3 FALLS TO DECIDE

DIAMOND BELT

ED LEWIS "STRANGLER"
WORLD CHAMPION
VS
WAYNE MUNN "BIG"
CHALLENGER

DECORATION DAY
SATURDAY MAY 30

FLOYD FITZSIMMONS'
SKY BLUE ARENA
MICHIGAN CITY, INDIANA

May 1925

Dear Folks:
Will be in Chi for a few days (Sat) and then to Mich City to finish training.
Feeling much better and should be in good shape by 30th.
Mrs Munn is in Omaha for a few days but will join me shortly.
Hope all is well with you folks.
Would enjoy hearing from you anytime.
Best wishes to all,
Always

For Information Address:

Morrison Hotel
CHICAGO, ILL.
LEWIS
WORLD CHAMPION
VS
MUNN
CHALLENGER
FLOYD FITZSIMMONS'
SKY BLUE ARENA
DECORATION DAY
SATURDAY, MAY 30th

Dunbar
Nebraska

IWIM induction poster from 1998, $5. Photo courtesy of Mike Chapman.

A letter from Wayne "Big" Munn, 1925, $150. The stationery advertises an upcoming bout with Strangler Lewis. Photo courtesy of Dr. Bob Bryla.

Shawn Michaels' autographed WMXII plaque, along with a piece of the ring mat, $60. Photo courtesy Chris Perry.

A cartoon cel from "Hulk Hogan's Rock 'n' Wrestling" cartoon show that aired on CBS, $115. Photo courtesy of Dr. Bob Bryla.

A 12" Frank Sexton bust.
Photo courtesy of Dr. Bob Bryla.

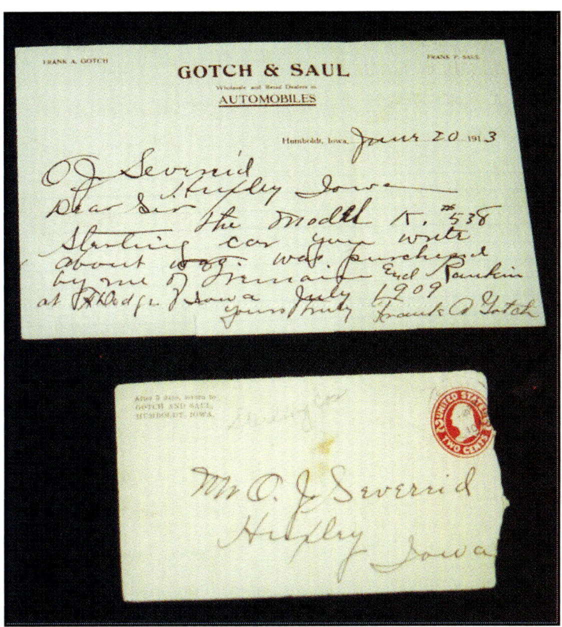

GOTCH & SAUL

AUTOMOBILES

Humboldt, Iowa, June 20 1913

O J Severid
Hurley Iowa
Dear Sir The Model K. #538
Starting car you write
about was purchased
by me of Armour and Rankin
at Ft Dodge Iowa July 1909
Yours truly Frank A Gotch

Mr O. J. Severid
Hurley Iowa

A Frank Gotch letter/autograph from 1931,
$75. Photo courtesy of Mike Chapman.

Lucca Brazzi, $10. Photo
courtesy of Mick Karch.

A Gotch-Hackenschmidt ad, $10. Photo courtesy of Mike Chapman.

chapter 6

The Wrestling Museum

When fans of any sport think of Hall of Fames, they think of Cooperstown, New York or Camden, Ohio. It is there the greats of baseball and football are enshrined into the histories of their respective sports. While most of the general populous is naïve, professional-wrestling fans have always known that the history of their favorite sport is just as, if not more, vast and meaningful than the big sports.

Until now, pro wrestling has never had a real home for the artifacts and history that make up the last 100 or so years of the sport. That's why, when Mike Chapman of Newton, Iowa, had a dream to see his favorite sport with a home of its own, the long-time editor, publisher and wrestling fanatic decided to take it upon himself to build a house for pro wrestling.

That was three years ago—and when all was said and done, Chapman finally opened the doors to the International Wrestling Institute and Museum. The building is part of an old hotel and gathering hall. But through hard work and never letting go of his dream, Chapman turned that rickety old building into an 8,000-square foot, wonderful, magical hall dedicated to the sport of wrestling. About a four-hour drive from the Minneapolis-St. Paul area, one hour from Des Moines and about six hours from Chicago, this wrestling Mecca is a must-see event for all fans of the sport. And for collectors, well, this is your place.

Chapman, an enthusiast of wrestling like you've never seen, began the IWIM with one purpose. After writing numerous books on his childhood idols like Lou Thesz and Frank Gotch, Chapman saw that those athletic icons were not justly honored. Here were Olympic medalists, world champions and modern-day entertainers being ignored by the mainstream. The non-profit IWIM's mission is to preserve the heritage of the sport, and there is no finer candidate to do that than Chapman. In fact, Chapman, the museum's curator, has loaded the museum with pieces from his private collection.

Amateurs who went pro.

When the IWIM opened in the fall of 1998, six past Olympic champions, various pro-wrestling legends, including Lou Thesz, and nearly 2,500 fans and collectors attended the gala event in Newton. It is fitting that the museum is situated in Iowa, the birthplace of many of the greatest wrestlers who ever lived: Classic grappler Farmer Burns (as well as dozens of pros of all eras), one of the most celebrated athletes of any era, Frank Gotch and super coach Dan Gable, were all born and successful in Iowa. Another Iowan, Earl Caddock, was the first great amateur champion to become a professional champion. Even today, Iowa is the wrestling center of the world.

The first-ever NCAA wrestling championships in 1928 were held in Ames, Iowa. In 1997, more than 90,000 attended a three-day NCAA tournament at the University of Northern Iowa. The state also holds the record for the largest crowd to attend a dual meet. The event was held at the University of Iowa and was attended by 15,890. That is due, in large part, to the success of the recently retired Gable. He is easily the most honored and recognizable figure in the history of collegiate wrestling. His on-the-mat coaching accomplishments are unparalleled. As Gotch and Burns did in the early parts of the century, Gable has kept Iowa's name in the headlines regarding wrestling in the 1970s and 1980s.

It's no shock that even a pro-wrestling museum honors the likes of Gable, Gotch and Burns. The museum gives a visual, walking history of the sport from its infancy to the present. Upon first entering the IWIM, one can see how the sport was born.

The Verne Gagne section at the museum.

On loan from the National Geographic Society are various mementos from the very first Olympic Games. The Olympic Pavilion pays homage to the great amateur wrestling champions of the past 100 years. The Lou Thesz/George Tragos wing has become home to pro-wrestling's Hall of Fame. Ed "Strangler" Lewis, Verne Gagne, Frank Gotch and Tragos himself were inducted in the museum's first class.

Civil War veteran William Muldoon is proudly featured as the world's first real professional and first real superstar. After the war, Muldoon joined the New York police department. To earn extra money on weekends, he would wrestle all comers in taverns. Shortly after, he realized he could earn more money wrestling full time and became one the first athletes to jump on the merchandising bandwagon. In 1887, he was featured on trading cards by Allen & Ginters. He caromed that into opening a chain of health clubs. Later, he trained boxing legend John L. Sullivan and in the 1930s was featured in cigarette advertising campaigns.

Literally every inch of the museum is dedicated to displaying such treasures. Many Iowans cherish the amateur displays and collectors from all corners of the world have stood in awe of the George Tragos/Lou Thesz Hall of Fame area dedicated to the pros that, for the most part, were standout amateurs as well. Posters, tickets and more are displayed in the hall. There is a replica wrestling ring and the pulley and punching bag once used by Joe Stecher. Also featured are a shop-worn AWA belt once worn by Verne Gagne, an AWA tag-team belt, Lou Thesz' robe and boots, a jacket worn by the unbeatable Light Heavyweight Champion Danny Hodge, a poster of the French Angel, a poster from Madison Square Garden advertising the epic battle between Bruno Sammartino and Gorilla Monsoon, and hundreds of inspirational mementos. A fabulous painting by Hal Bruntsch of the Leo Nomellini-Lou Thesz 1953 clash in displayed and on loan by Lou and Charlie Thesz.

Certainly no wrestling museum would be complete without depicting the phenomenal accomplishments of Jesse Ventura. Also prominently displayed is a wrestler who took politics a bit farther than Minnesota's governor—Abraham Lincoln. Another worldly dignitary, Henry VIII, made famous by Herman's Hermits' early 1960s' rock chart buster, was also an accomplished grap-

Frank Gotch's traveling trunk.

pler. Collectibles of either are considered to be priceless. But they are featured here. Speaking of Lincoln, the museum has an entire section dedicated to the wrestling president in what is titled, The "Sport of Lincoln."

Chapman has many items that can't be found anywhere else on the planet. Two items come immediately to mind: the original Strangler Lewis "headlock machine" and an original trunk used by Gotch. The Lewis machine, on loan to the IWIM, is a solid walnut wood carving of a human head that Lewis used to practice squeezing his dreaded "headlock" maneuver on. While there were several of the machines made, the one here is the first one and dates back to the 1920s. The Gotch trunk is a classic piece that Gotch traveled with all around the world. The piece was donated to Chapman's museum. Another trinket are two figures of a referee and wrestler that for many years stood proud on the desk of Chicago promoter Fred Kohler. The museum also has a section dedicated to pro wrestlers and movies.

Iowa Public Television is a major sponsor of the IWIM. It has helped put together the Institute's "wrestling theater." Its clippings of the 1920 Madison Square Garden clash between Joe Stecher and Earl Caddock are shown. To help guarantee the museum's future, it has established a Golden Ring Club and is tax deductible. Members of the club are given color prints of Thesz signed by the artist Don Smith and the former champion, as well as a copy of Jack and Carole Bender's print of an 1831 match between Jack Armstrong and Abraham Lincoln.

For more information, check out the website at www.wrestlingmuseum.org or contact Andre Gibson at P.O. Box 794, Newton, Iowa, 50208; or call (515) 791-1517. Adult admission is only $3.

Strangler Lewis' headlock machine.

Lou Thesz's World Title belt.

A John Pesek poster.

All photos in this chapter are courtesy of Mike Chapman

"Wrestling as show."

Wrestling cards.

Rocky Marciano memorial.

AWA tag-team belt.

The real champion—Old Abe.

Painting from San Francisco.

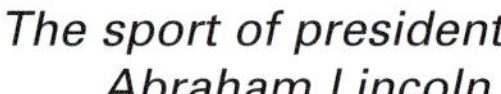

The sport of president Abraham Lincoln.

Jim Browning, Jim Landos and Don George cards.

Wall of Fame.

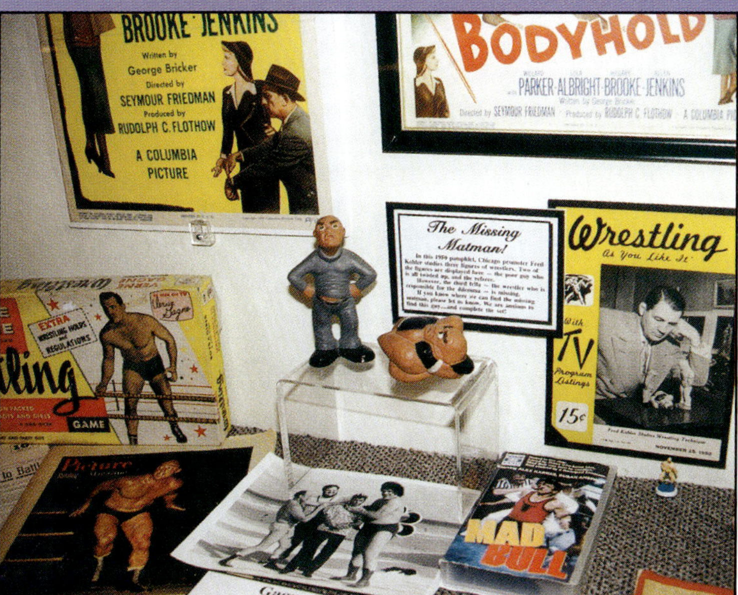

Fred Kohler trinkets.

"The Wrestler" movie poster.

George Tragos.

chapter 7 Programs, Magazines and Books

Drive into Mankato, Minnesota on any given day and you are not likely to see many people driving or waiting around downtown. You'll come across mom-and-pop restaurants, barber shops, the local city hall and virtually all your standard small-town USA landmarks.

But hidden away in this two-horse town is one of the finest collections of wrestling history found anywhere in the world. On Main Street, in a small office building next to a local watering hole, sits the head offices of more than 40 years of wrestling memories. It's home to Norman Kietzer, founder and editor and publisher of the popular wrestling magazine the *Wrestling News*.

"Oh yeah, it's all here," said Kietzer, while on a recent visit to the vaults of vicious tempers. Stacked away neatly in binders are every issue of the *Wrestling News* and *Ring Wrestling*, which Kietzer recently acquired. The magazines are the icon of virtually every wrestling fan's connection to the sport.

Why? Because for those 40-plus years, Kietzer's publications were used as the official programs for wrestling's most famous promotions and territories. Throughout his career, Kietzer provided first-run color programs for the AWA, NWA, WWF and Mid South groups. Throughout that time,

Norman Kietzer, right, with Bill Watts.

Kietzer accumulated the largest collection of wrestling photographs not in the possession of Stanley Weston or Bill Apter.

"Sure I've done a lot in wrestling," he said. "I worked with all the big promoters. Vince McMahon Sr., Bill Watts, Bob Geigel, Paul Boesch, Verne Gagne and the Crocketts. But I was no big shot. I did a job."

Most people will remember Kietzer's famous mug shot with the dark-rimmed glasses on his monthly column "As I See It." Old-time fans will be happy to know that Kietzer has changed little since those days. Today, Kietzer still publishes the *Wrestling News* about four times a year. Before wrestling burst into the information age, Kietzer's magazines provided the best place for news and gossip. Before the advent of cable television, fans only saw their local wrestling programs. They were eager to hear about goings on from other parts of the country and the *Wrestling News* was one of only a few publications that catered to the fans. Way back when, the only way to get educated about the new wrestler who was coming to your home town was by reading Kietzer's magazines.

His programs were the ones sold at some epic battles of the past. The legendary Bruno Sammartino versus Larry Zbyszko fight at Shea Stadium in New York and Bruno's subsequent retirement at the Meadowlands were two shows in particular that Kietzer was summoned to write programs for. Bill Watts' Louisiana Superdome shows were also shows where Kietzer was the man on call. Through his career, Kietzer's mags were sold at such hallowed grounds as Madison Square Garden, the San Francisco Cow Palace and the St. Paul Civic Center. Thousands of wrestlers graced the covers of his publications: Ric Flair, Hulk Hogan and Bruno, just to name a few.

By the mid-1980s, as promotions were closing

up due to the WWF's successes, Kietzer's network went with it. When McMahon Jr. asked Kietzer to be his exclusive supplier of programs, Kietzer declined. He continued to supply Gagne with programs, but that relationship ended by 1990. That was around the time that the *Wrestling News*, as fans knew it, came to an end.

But the legacy continues. Out of Kietzer's magazine came a wealth of knowledge, lifelong pen pals and an underground of information, which was the precursor to "underground sheets" like the *Wrestling Observer*. In many ways, Kietzer was a power broker of talent. Those who got started in wrestling through the network laid by Kietzer's work reads like a who's who. Tully Blanchard was a correspondent. Dr. Tom Pritchard, who went on to headline in Smoky Mountain Wrestling and now trains future WWF stars, started as a columnist for Kietzer. Rick Patterson, who became Japan's Leatherface, was also said to be a columnist at one point. Jerry "the King" Lawler sent his caricatures to Norman's magazines.

Jim Cornette, who became perhaps the greatest manager of all time and is now a promoter and booking agent, sent his photos in regularly. "Cornette had an amazing talent as a photographer," recalled Kietzer recently. "He sent me an up close of Lawler that couldn't have been done better by a $500-an-hour professional." Wrestlers Eddie and Doug Gilbert were also correspondents. "But I can't take credit for their careers," he said. "It was in their lineage. Their father wrestled."

Paul Heyman built up quite a following as wrestling's roving photographer. As a teen, he stuck to wrestlers like white on rice and came away with more than a handful of great shots. His snapshot of the Freebirds in Confederate war paint remains one of the greatest shots ever. Needless to say, Paul did a fine job as manager Paul E. Dangerously and against all odds became the head of ECW, a third major US promotion.

Other correspondents have included Ron Hutchinson (trainer and wrestler in Canada), Bruce Hart (Calgary trainer and promoter), the late Brian Hildebrand (who refereed in WCW and was heavily involved in Cornette's Smoky Mountain group), Don Laible (wrestling author), George Napalitano (one of the sports' more celebrated photographers), Jimmy Hart, Tom Burke (a top collector in the world), and a cast of other talent.

A vital part of Kietzer's publications offered fans the opportunity to sell their wares and post pen-pal messages. Many of the top news hounds of the sport today benefited by networking through his pages. When reminded that his magazines put together great talent and gave many their first start in wrestling, Kietzer said, "Everyone starts somewhere."

After Kietzer stopped publication, the WWF and WCW were publishing their programs at full steam. The WWF had its own publishing house and WCW relied on magazine editor Dennis Brent for many years as the main supplier of programs in that territory. Some of the modern-day classic programs come from what promoters called "Supercards." These shows, like Wrestlemania, Starrcade, Summerslam, and the Great American Bash, became trendy in the '80s. Now, they are staples of the wrestling business.

Programs like the first *Wrestlemania* program, or from Starrcade, are getting $30 to $50 on the open market. Most collectors determine the worth of a program with a few criteria: who is on the cover, how relevant was the card, and what condition it's in. The *Wrestlemania II* program is quite a find for $35 because the artwork inside is all original, airbrushed drawings of the WWF wrestlers. In preceding years, no program could touch the quality that was seen in the WWF's works. The color and graphics are superior.

Aside from the big "Supercards," programs are hard to attach values to. For the better part of 20 years, before McMahon's WWF took wrestling into directions that no one had before, most programs were four-page booklets that included an insert lineup for the specified town. Some collectors, like Mick Karch of Minneapolis, prefer this format because it is what they grew up with. The programs told the stories behind why the matches were happening, or what feuds were brewing. Programs from the '50s and '60s are hard to come by, but in good shape, they can bring close to $20 each. If they are autographed, depending on whose signature it is, that price can double.

Programs like Kietzer's were popular because they added the new with the old. The writing and correspondence was "old school" but the photos were shot in color. Certainly, with the big promotions publishing their own programs, the days of editors like Kietzer probably will never be seen again.

Nowadays, Kietzer runs a shop that sells karaoke compact discs and also publishes a catalog selling old spaghetti western movies. He even adds a few pages devoted to wrestling. But for the most part, Kietzer knows the wrestling business today is much different than when he was active.

He's seen the world, covered major conventions and historic main events and rubbed shoulders with the greatest stars of our time. He had a major part in wrestling's history. Today he remains a passionate fan, exemplary storyteller and seems to have put the wrestling chapter of his life to rest. Kietzer hears some praise offered by a journalist and he smiles humbly. Kietzer acknowledges his past, but cherishes his present and future, as he sells a karaoke CD and looks to the mailbox for his weekly wrestling newsletter.

Dallas Wrestling

Wild Irish vs. Mad Japanese!

Irish Danny McShane

The Great Yamato

Dallas Wrestling, 1953; McShane-Yamamoto, $10.

10c PER COPY

SPORTS FACTS

NOMELLINI BATTLES SHIBUYA

AT MINNEAPOLIS AUDITORIUM

ARMORY NEXT WEEK

LEO WANTS TAG TITLE

BOXING THURS., JUNE 2 FLANAGAN VS. DAVIS

LADIES FREE!

WRESTLING NEXT TUESDAY at the MPLS. ARMORY

Sports Facts, Minneapolis, Minn., 1955; Nomellini-Shibuya, $10.

"SPORTS FACTS"

MINNEAPOLIS BOXING & WRESTLING CLUB

BATTLE of the BRUISERS . . .

STAN VS. GENE

TINY MILLS vs. JOE SCARPELLO

ON TONIGHT'S PRO WRESTLING BOUT

STAN KOWALSKI vs. GENE KINISKI

Sports Facts, Minneapolis, Minn., 1960; Kiniski-Kowalski, $10.

"SPORTS FACTS"

Published by MINNEAPOLIS BOXING & WRESTLING CLUB

605 DYCKMAN HOTEL — MINNEAPOLIS 2, MINNESOTA

PENALTY BOX COMES BACK IN TAG TEAM MATCH TONIGHT!

Frank TOWNSEND & Haystack CALHOUN

vs.

TINY MILLS & Krusher KOWALSKI

ALL WRESTLING BOUTS FOR THE REMAINDER OF THE YEAR AT MINNEAPOLIS AUDITORIUM

PLENTY OF CHOICE SEATS!

Photos on this and the previous page are courtesy of Mike Karch

Sports Facts, Minneapolis, Minn., 1959; Mills-Kowalski, $10.

"SPORTS FACTS"

Published by MINNEAPOLIS BOXING & WRESTLING CLUB

605 DYCKMAN HOTEL — MINNEAPOLIS 2, MINNESOTA

SCHMIDT vs. CAMPBELL

CAN GERMAN MOVE A MOUNTAIN?

FACTS — ON TONIGHT'S PRO WRESTLING BOUT

Sports Facts, Minneapolis, Minn., 1960; Schmidt-Campbell, $10.

MINNEAPOLIS (Complete Card — Page 3)

SPORTS FACTS

KOWALSKI TO MEET RAINES!

Dirty Dick Gets Last Laugh!

Stecher Picks Top Mat Talent

Sports Facts, Minneapolis, Minn., 1950; Raines-Kowalski, $10.

MINNEAPOLIS (Complete Card — Page 1)

SPORTS FACTS

NAG THIRD MAN!

RAINES-KASHEY REMATCH SET FOR MONDAY MAY 15

What's Happened In Past Matches

Keep Rules or "Blue Monday"

Sports Facts, Minneapolis, Minn., 1950; Kashey-Raines, with Nagurski as the referee, $15.

RASSLIN'

SPORTATORIUM — Cadiz & Industrial — DALLAS

June 27, 1961 — Dallas Wrestling Club — 15c

VON ERICH VS. BOCKWINKLE!

Two Tigers Tangle!!

Young Stars Lock Horns In Big Main Event Assignment For Both!

Promoter Ed McLemore Contacting Champion Pat O'Connor For Date!

GOMEZ & DIXON vs. IRON MIKE & CYCLOPS!

page 2

Rasslin', Dallas, 1961; Bockwinkel-Von Erich, $12.

AWA Superstar Billy Graham, $10.

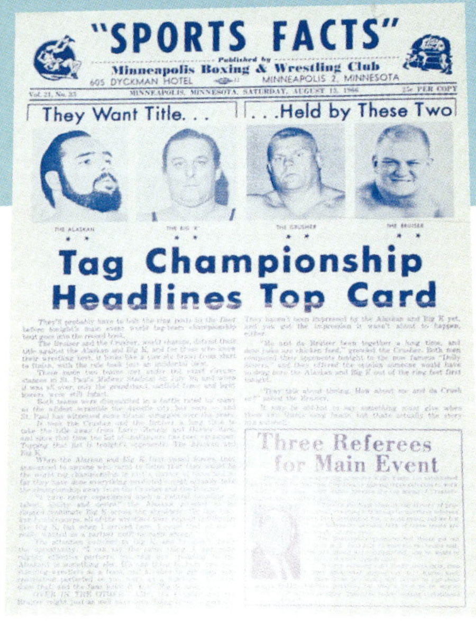
"SPORTS FACTS"

Published by Minneapolis Boxing & Wrestling Club

605 DYCKMAN HOTEL — MINNEAPOLIS 2, MINNESOTA

They Want Title. . . | . . .Held by These Two

THE ALASKAN — THE BIG K — THE CRUSHER — THE BRUISER

Tag Championship Headlines Top Card

Three Referees for Main Event

Sports Facts, Minneapolis, Minn., 1966; Crusher/Bruiser-Big K/Alaskan, $10. Photos this page courtesy of Mike Karch.

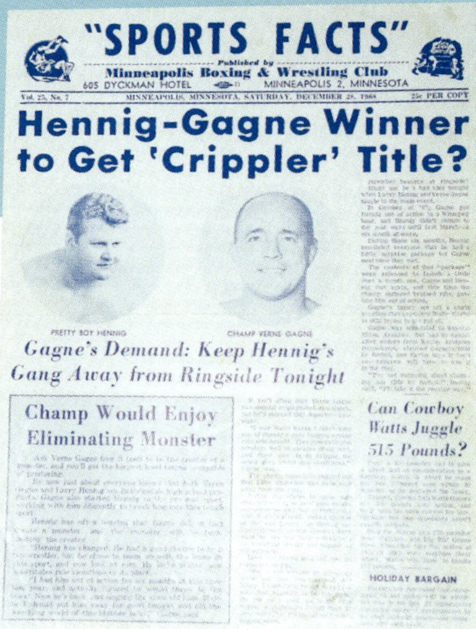
"SPORTS FACTS"

Published by Minneapolis Boxing & Wrestling Club

605 DYCKMAN HOTEL — MINNEAPOLIS 2, MINNESOTA

Hennig-Gagne Winner to Get 'Crippler' Title?

PRETTY BOY HENNIG — CHAMP VERNE GAGNE

Gagne's Demand: Keep Hennig's Gang Away from Ringside Tonight

Champ Would Enjoy Eliminating Monster

Can Cowboy Watts Juggle 515 Pounds?

HOLIDAY BARGAIN

Sports Facts, Minneapolis, Minn., 1968; Hennig-Gagne, $10.

THE LEGENDS OF SLAMBOREE '94

OLE ANDERSON — KILLER KOWALSKI — THE ASSASSIN — ERNIE LADD — PENNY BANNER — CRUSHER — RED BASTIEN — WAHOO McDANIEL — TULLY BLANCHARD — ANGELO MOSCA — DON CURTIS — DUSTY RHODES — TERRY FUNK — RAY STEVENS — GREG GAGNE — LOU THESZ — VERNE GAGNE — JOHNNY WEAVER — MIKE GRAHAM — MR. WRESTLING II — HARD-BOILED HAGGERTY — TOMMY YOUNG — LARRY HENNIG

WCW Slamboree 1994, inside shot of wrestlers' autographs, $500.

"SPORTS FACTS"

Published by Minneapolis Boxing & Wrestling Club

605 DYCKMAN HOTEL — MINNEAPOLIS 2, MINNESOTA

Who Will Be the 'Best Dressed' Man Tonight?

HANDSOME HARLEY . . . to Wear Dress?

"Greatest Injustice in Ring History" Claims MD Vachone

Other Wrestlers Are Interested in Watching the Fun

BLOODY AND IRATE CRUSHER

SIX BIG BOUTS FEATURED ON TONIGHT'S PRO WRESTLING CARD

Autographed copy of Sports Facts, Minneapolis, Minn., 1965; Crusher-Race, $125.

★ Wrestling Program ★

GULF ATHLETIC CLUB — PAUL BOESCH, PROMOTER

NO. 6078 — SUNDAY, MAY 29, 1977 — HOUSTON, TEXAS — PHONE 659-7793 — PRICE 50¢

WELCOME TO THE SUMMIT

THE SUMMIT

Jimmy Snuka Risks His Texas State Title! Faces Bruiser Brody in Coliseum Friday!

BRUISER BRODY

TICKET SALES FOR NEXT FRIDAY'S COLISEUM CARD START MONDAY!

Wrestling Program, Houston, 1977; Snuka-Brody, $25.

"SPORTS FACTS"

Published by Minneapolis Boxing & Wrestling Club

605 DYCKMAN HOTEL — MINNEAPOLIS 2, MINNESOTA

Crusher vs. Miller

DEATH MATCH TONITE!!

Big Bill Miller

Sports Facts, Minneapolis, Minn., 1964; Crusher-Mr. M., $10.

WCW Hulk Hogan, 1993, $50. Photo courtesy of Mike Karch.

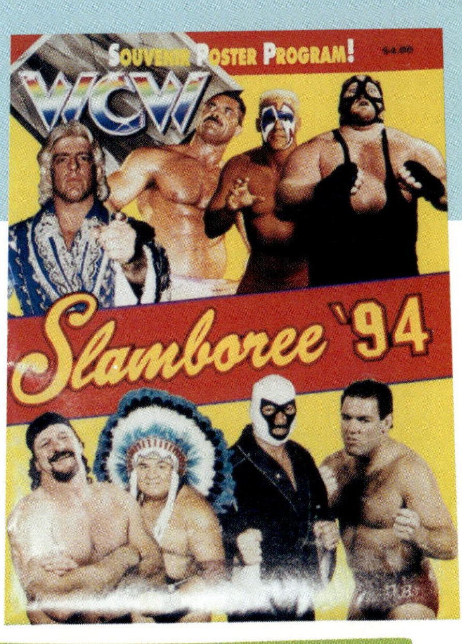

WCW Slamboree 1994, $25.

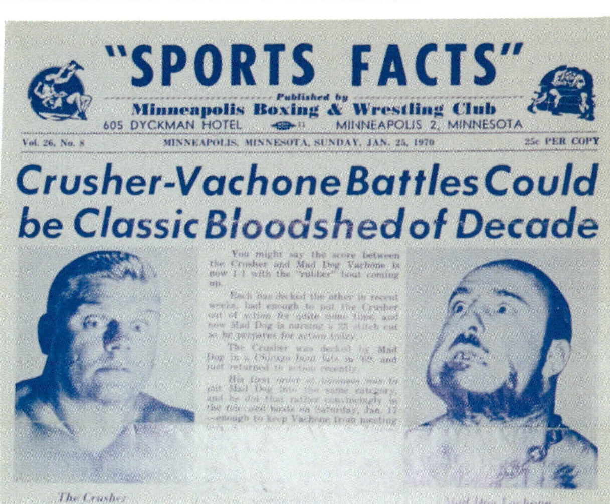

"SPORTS FACTS"

Published by
Minneapolis Boxing & Wrestling Club
605 DYCKMAN HOTEL — MINNEAPOLIS 2, MINNESOTA

Vol. 26, No. 8 — MINNEAPOLIS, MINNESOTA, SUNDAY, JAN. 25, 1970 — 25c PER COPY

Crusher-Vachone Battles Could be Classic Bloodshed of Decade

You might say the score between the Crusher and Mad Dog Vachone is now 1-1 with the "rubber" bout coming up.

Each has decked the other in recent weeks, bad enough to put the Crusher out of action for quite some time, and now Mad Dog is nursing a 25 stitch cut as he prepares for action today.

The Crusher was decked by Mad Dog in a Chicago bout late in '69, and just returned to action recently.

His first order of business was to put Mad Dog into the same category, and he did that rather convincingly in the televised bouts on Saturday, Jan. 17 —enough to keep Vachone from meeting

The Crusher

Mad Dog Vachone

Sports Facts, Minneapolis, Minn., 1970; Crusher-Mad Dog, $10. Photo courtesy of Mike Karch.

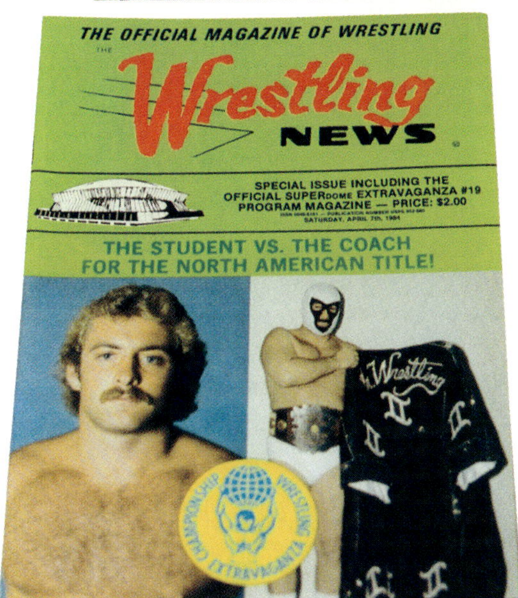

Wrestling News, 1984; Mr. Wrestling-Magnum T.A., $8.

Mid-South Christmas Show, 1978, $8. Photo courtesy of Mike Karch.

Wrestling News, 1982; Junkyard Dog-Ernie Ladd, $8.

AWA Wrestling, 1985; Road Warriors, $8.

Major League Wrestling, 1983; WWF Mascaras-Stevens, $10.

Mid-South show, 1982; Reed-Duggan, $8.

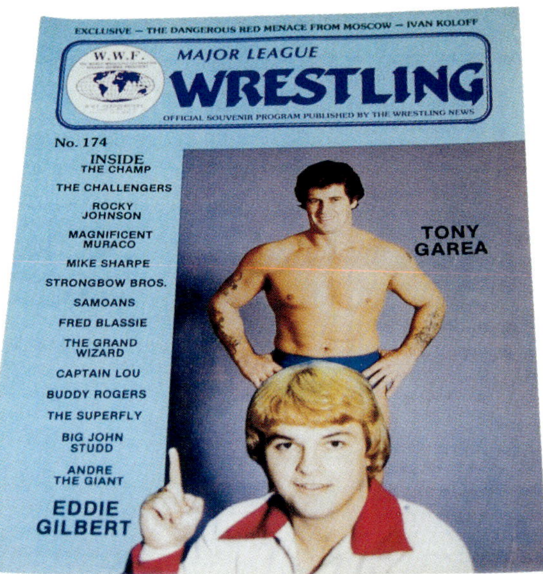

WWF, Gilbert-Garea, $8.

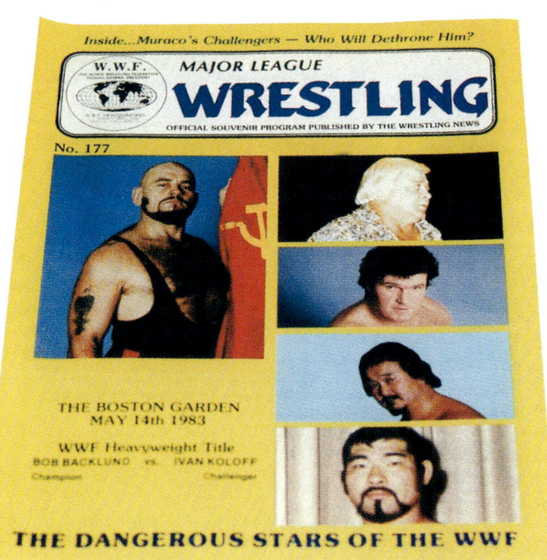

WWF Backlund-Koloff, 1983, $12.

NWA, 1985, Dusty Rhodes, $10.

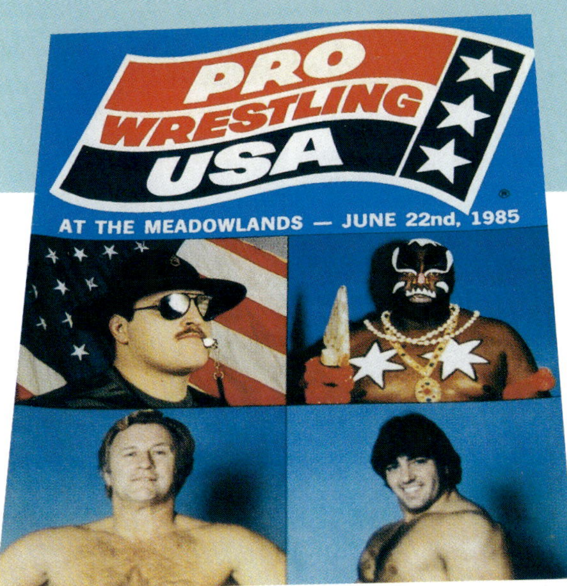

Pro Wrestling USA, 1985; Slaughter-Kimala, $5.

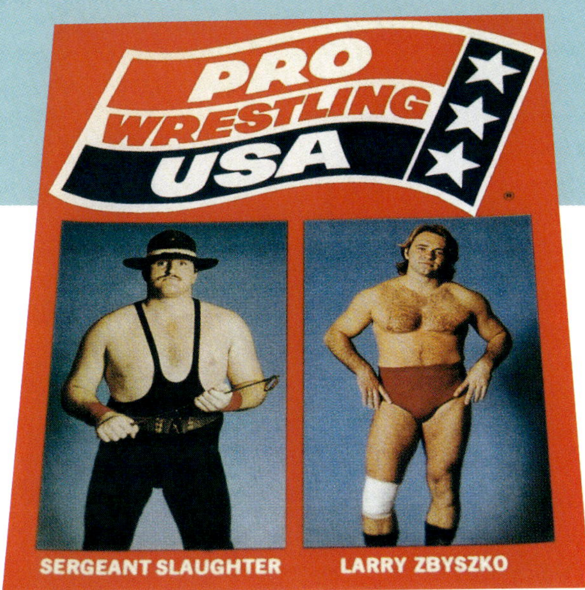

Pro Wrestling USA, 1985; Slaughter-Zbyszko, $5.

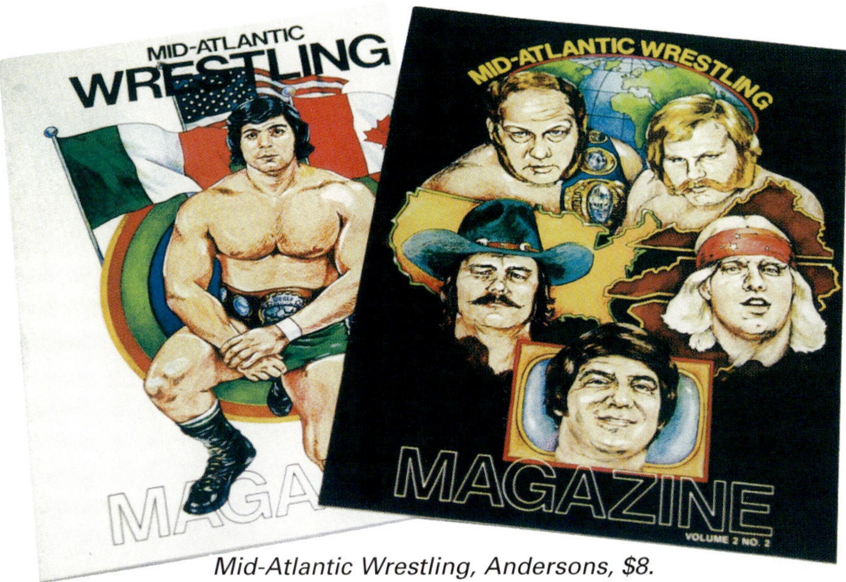

Mid-Atlantic Wrestling, Andersons, $8.

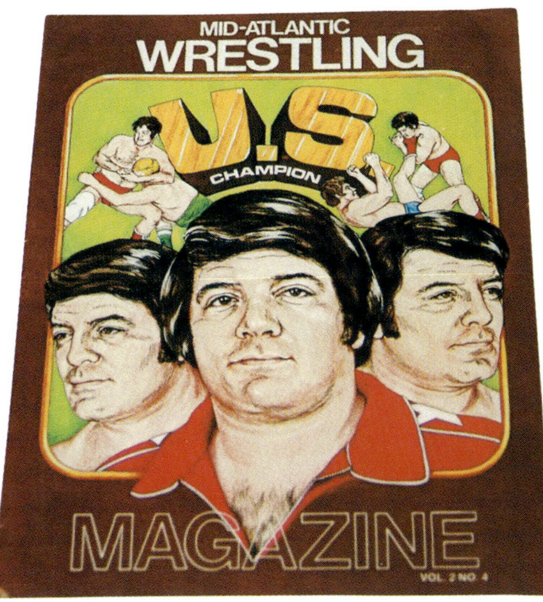

Mid-Atlantic Wrestling, Paul Jones, $8.

Mid-Atlantic, magazine issue, 1982, $8.

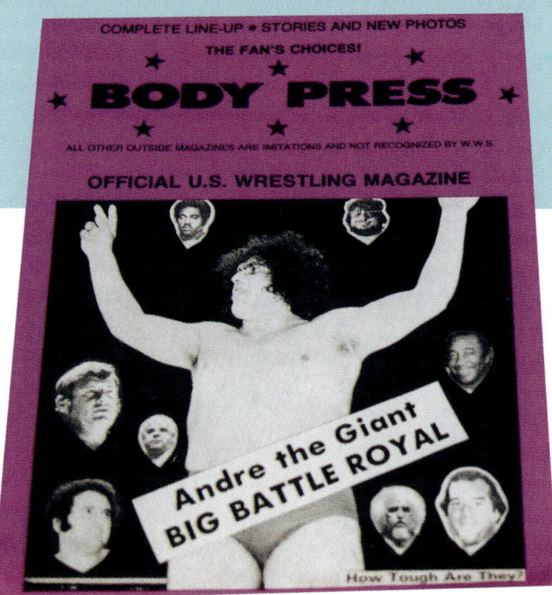

Body Press, Detroit, Andre the Giant, $7.

Mid-Atlantic, Blackjack Mulligan, $8.

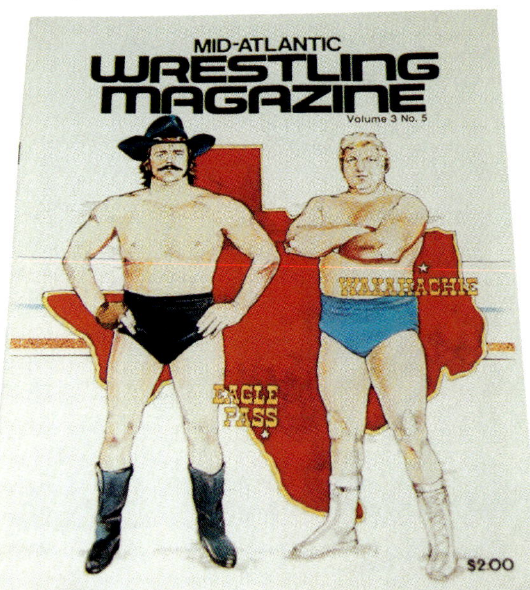

Mid-Atlantic, Mulligan-Murdoch, $8.

Mid-Atlantic, Mighty Igor, $5.

Mid-Atlantic, Wahoo McDaniel, $7.

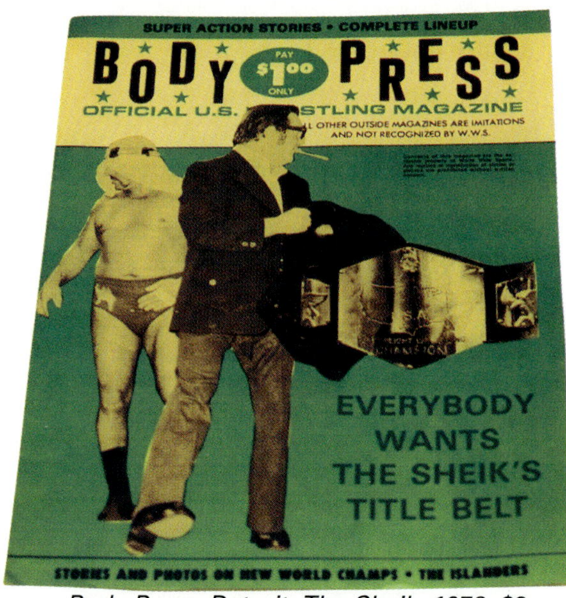

Body Press, Detroit, The Sheik, 1978, $8.

Body Press, Detroit, The Sheik, 1978, $8.

Wrestling News' WWWF edition, Strongbow-White Wolf, 1977, $10.

Wrestling News, Mid-South, Junkyard Dog-DiBiase, 1982, $8.

Wrestling News, Billy White Wolf, 1978, $8.

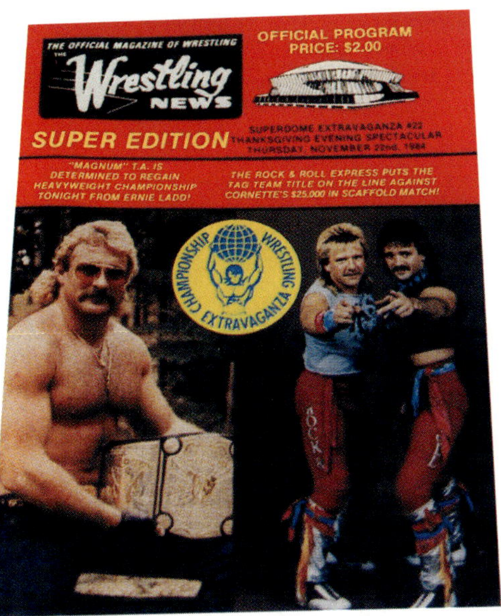

Wrestling News, Mid-South, Magnum T.A.-Rock & Roll Express, 1984, $8.

Wrestling News, Junkyard Dog-Mr. Olympian, 1983, $8.

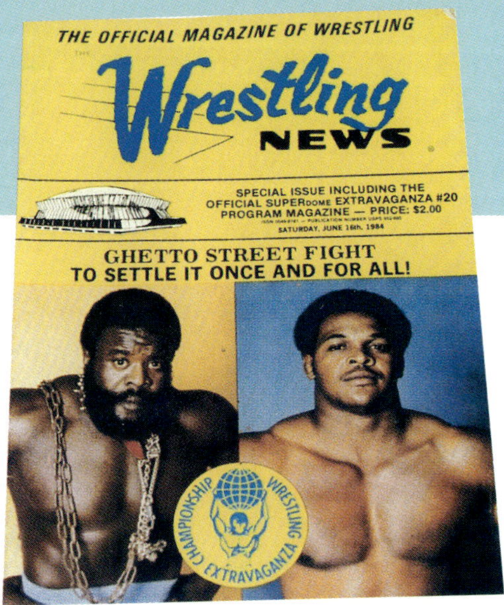

Wrestling News, Junkyard Dog-Reed, 1984, $8.

Wrestling, Paul Boesch issue, $7.

WWF Farewell to Bruno Sammartino, 1981, $75.

Wrestling News, AWA edition
featuring Jim Brunzell, 1976, $5.

Wrestling News, Gulas, Yamamoto,
Jarrett, Fargo; 1977, $7.

WWF Photo Album
Program, $15.

SummerSlam 1992; Royal Rumble 1992, $12 each.

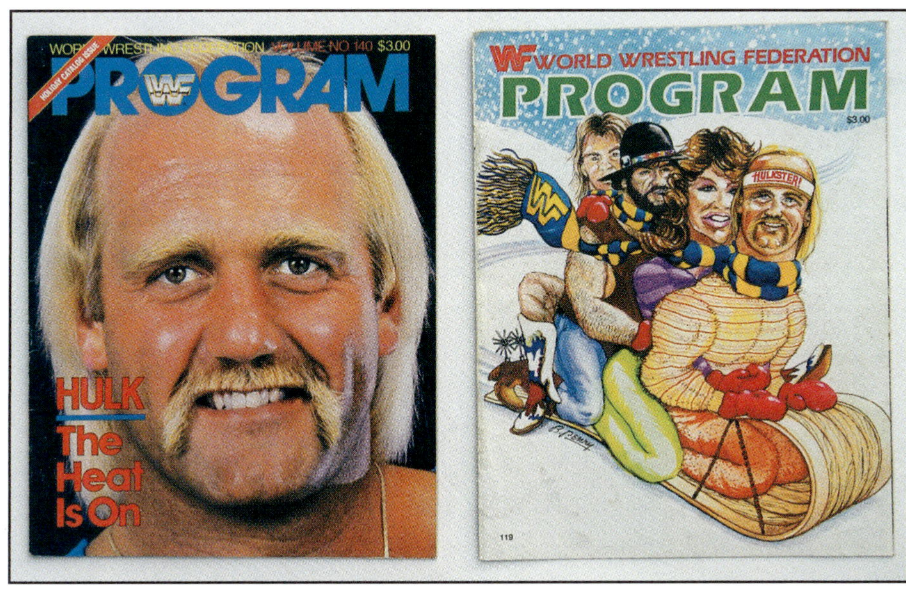

WWF Program, 1984-85, $15.

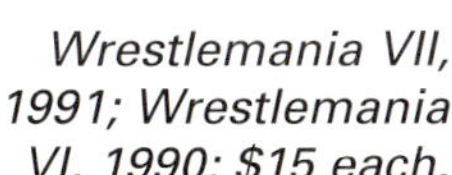
Wrestlemania VII, 1991; Wrestlemania VI, 1990; $15 each.

AWA Super Clash III, 1988; NWA Bunkhouse Stampede, 1987; $10 each.

Wrestlemania 2, 1986, left, $25; and Wrestlemania 1, 1985, $30.

SummerSlam, 1989; Survivor Series, 1987; $15 each.

WWF Program, Hulk Hogan, #184; WWF Program, Von Erich, #182; $8 each.

WWF Program, Jimmy Snuka, #117; WWF Program, Ultimate Warrior, #179; $8 each.

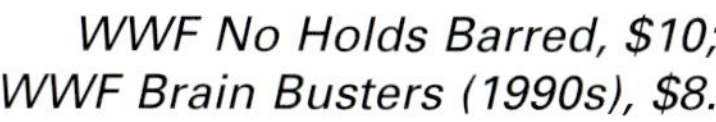
WWF No Holds Barred, $10; WWF Brain Busters (1990s), $8.

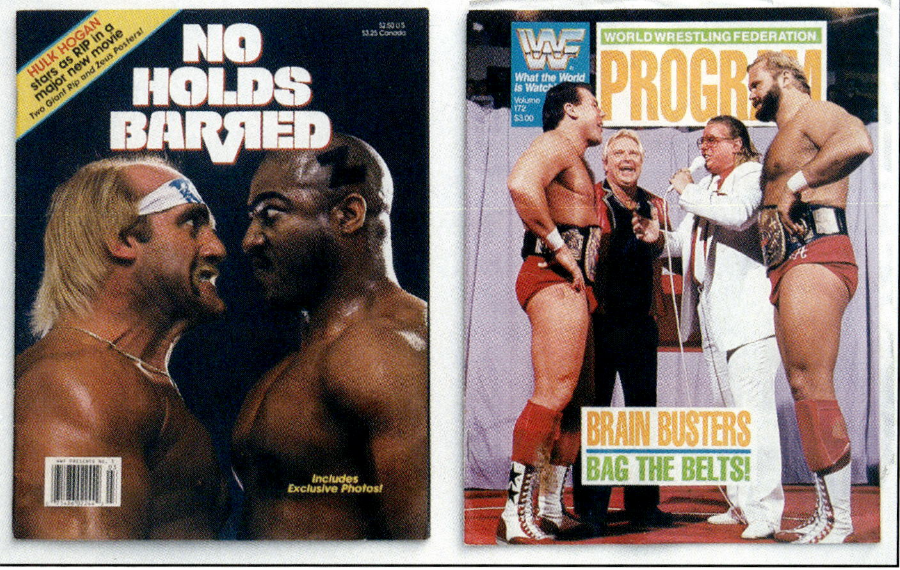

SUNDAY, JULY 19th, 1981 — ST. PAUL, MINNESOTA

TONIGHT'S OFFICIAL LINE-UP

The Main Event for the World's Tag Team Championship

GREG GAGNE Mound, Minnesota and "JUMPING" JIM BRUNZELL White Bear Lake, Minnesota "Champions"	vs.	JESSE "THE BODY" VENTURA San Diego, California and "GOLDEN BOY" ADRIAN ADONIS New York City "Challengers"

Winner To Get Title Match With Nick Bockwinkel

TITO SANTANA Mission, Texas	vs.	SHEIK ADNANN EL KAISSEY Bagdad, Iraq
BRAD RHEINGANS Appleton, Minnesota	vs.	JERRY BLACKWELL Stone Mountain, Georgia
BARON VON RASCHKE Germany	vs.	RAY "THE CRIPPLER" STEVENS San Francisco, California
"ROCK & ROLL" BUCK ZUM HOFE Honolulu, Hawaii	vs.	"Opponent To Be Named"
LAURENT SOUCIE Milwaukee, Wisconsin	vs.	KENNY "SOD BUSTER" JAY Cleveland, Ohio

THE NEXT TWIN CITY WRESTLING MATCHES SUNDAY, AUGUST 9th, IN MINNEAPOLIS

WATCH ALL STAR WRESTLING ON TELEVISION EVERY SUNDAY FROM 11 A.M. TO 12 NOON ON KMSP-TV - CHANNEL 9 - IN LIVING COLOR

DON'T FORGET ABOUT THE 24 HOUR WRESTLING HOTLINE - JUST DIAL 545-9376

WWF, The History of WrestleMania, 1989, $10; AWA lineup, champions Greg Gagne and "Jumping" Jim Brunzell vs. challengers Jesse "The Body" Ventura and "Golden Boy" Adrian Adonis, 1981, $8.

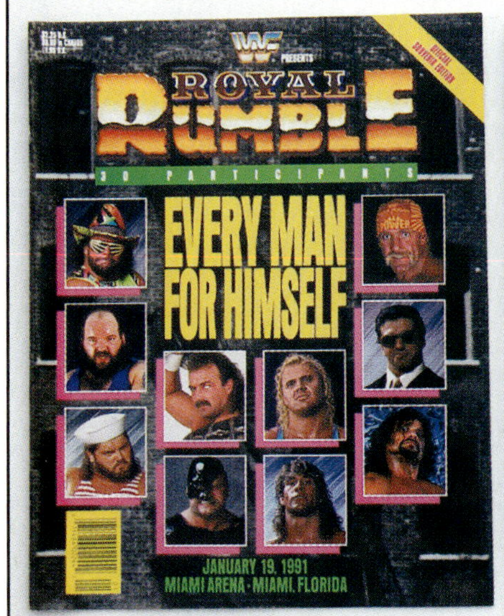

WWF Royal Rumble, 1992; Survivor Series, 1990; $10 each.

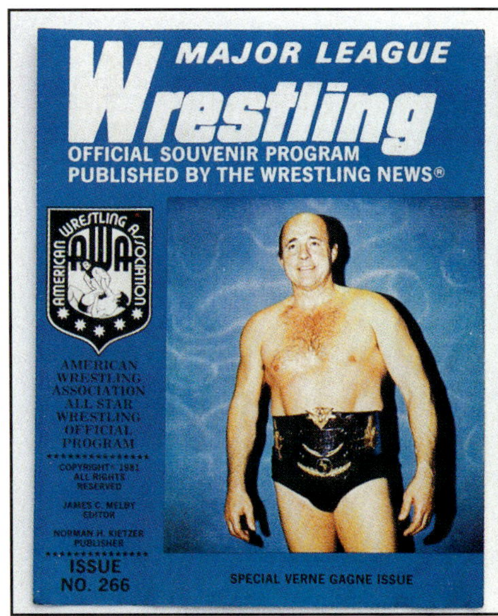

Two Major League Wrestling souvenir programs, #266 and #277, from 1981; $10 each.

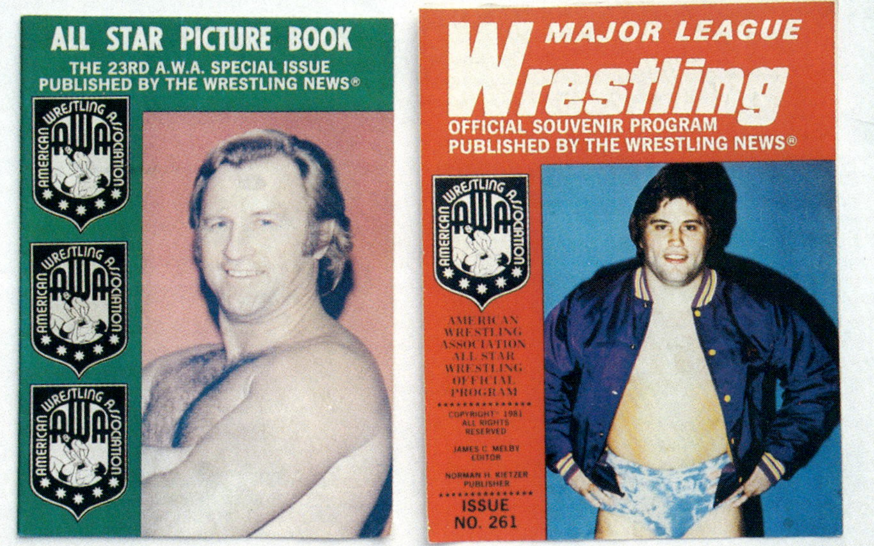

All Star Picture Book and Major League Wrestling issue #261; $10 each.

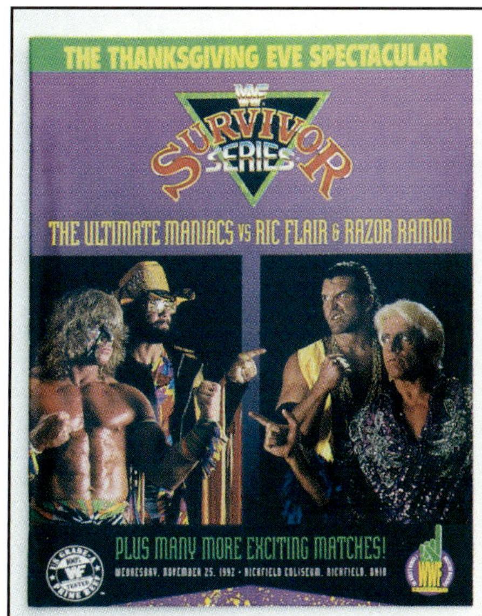

Survivor Series, 1992, left; Survivor Series 1991; $10 each.

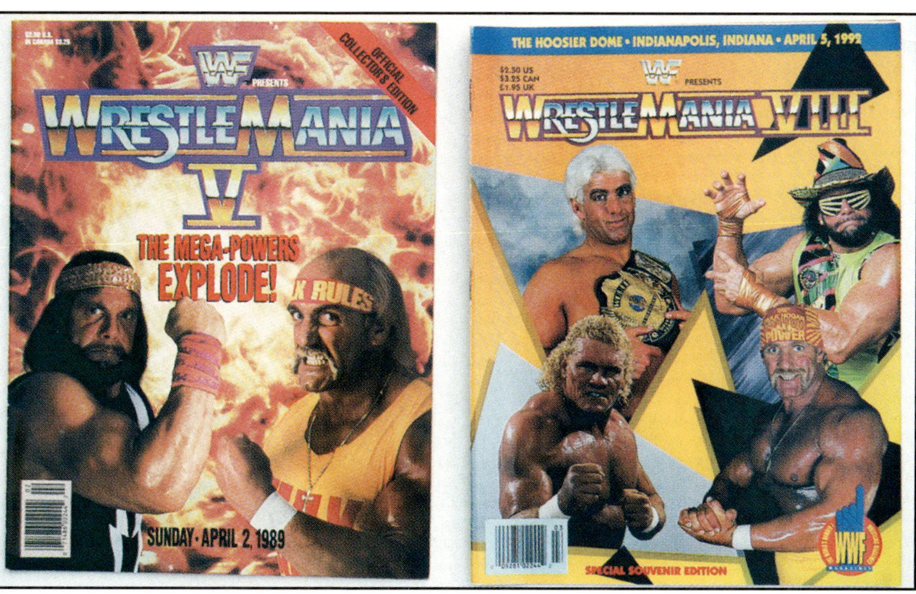

WrestleMania V, 1989; WrestleMania VIII, 1992; $15 each.

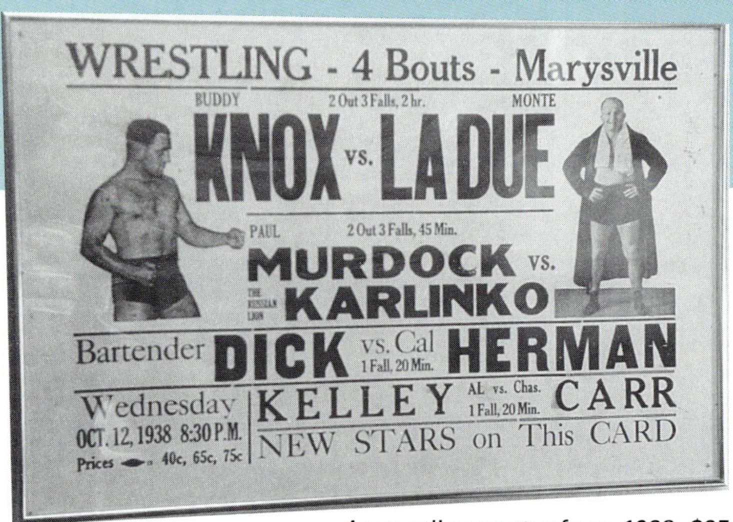

A wrestling poster from 1938, $25.
Photo courtesy Dr. Bob Bryla.

Large poster from New Zealand, Detroit Big Time, 1970s, $35. Photo courtesy Dr. Bob Bryla.

SummerSlam 1990; SummerSlam 1991; $12 each.

Race and Hennig tag-team match in St. Peter, Minn. $15.

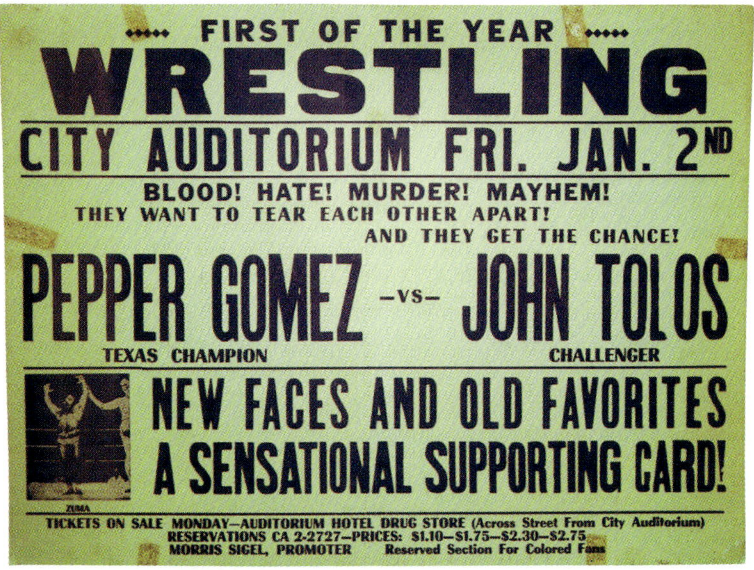

A poster from Texas touting the match between Pepper Gomez and John Tolos, $15.

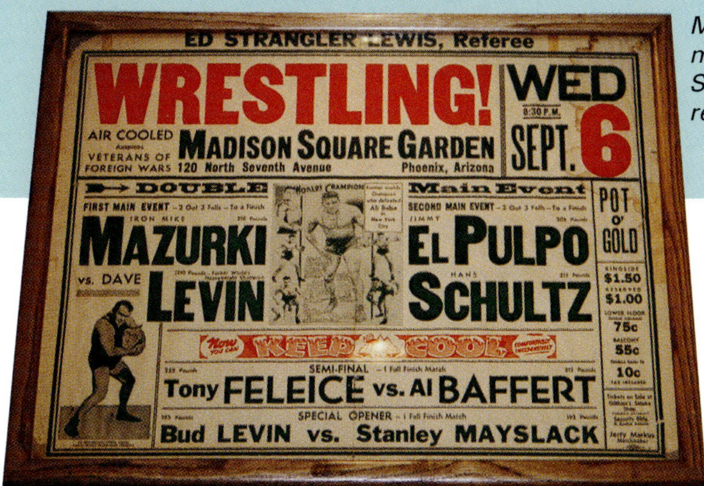

Madison Square Garden match, featuring Ed Strangler Lewis as the referee; $15.

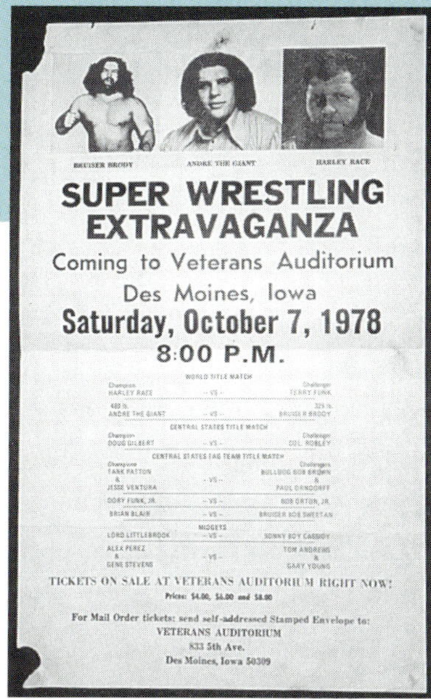

A double header in Des Moines, Iowa, featuring Race vs. Funk and Brody vs.Andre; $12.

A French poster; $12.

Madison Square Garden, Blassie vs. Sammartino; $22.

Movie poster for "Alias the Champ"; $35.

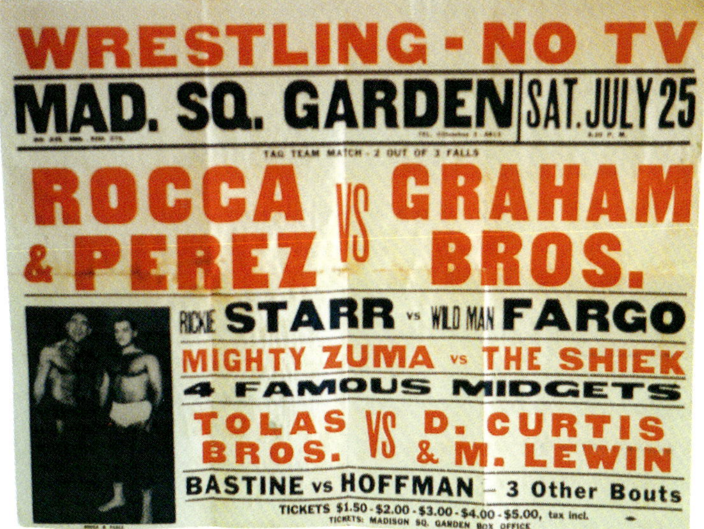

WWWF, Madison Square Garden, 1970s, $45. Photo courtesy of Dr. Bob Bryla.

Magazines

Most fans have come into contact with a magazine or two during their days as a wrestling fanatic. Older fans will look fondly at *Ring Wrestling* magazine, while today's fans will think of *Pro Wrestling Illustrated*. There is no question, though, that magazines are a popular source of collecting for fans all around the world.

The most collectable magazines are determined by age, cover art, and condition. Another plus are finding first issues of different magazines. The original *Ring Wrestling* is worth about $75. Lots of magazines that had connections with boxing—such as *Boxing* and *Wrestling and Boxing Illustrated,* and *Wrestling News* are highly collectible because boxing enthusiasts put a high premium on them.

In the '50s and '60s, fans regularly read *Wrestling Life*, a small tabloid-like magazine. Later on, *Wrestling Revue* and *Wrestling Illustrated* were highly successful. Copies with cover art that depicted a world title change are worth more than others. Copies of *Wrestling Revue* and *Wrestling Illustrated* range between $30-$50; cover stories of world-title wins bump the price up by about $5.

More contemporary magazines include the WWF in-house magazine *WWF Magazine* and *Pro Wrestling Illustrated*. The early copies of *WWF Magazine*, worth around $15-$20, are collectible because at that time, it was the only place to get great photos of the WWF stars, as no other magazine photographers, other than the WWF's own, were allowed to shoot at ringside. Times have gotten a little better for editor and journalists since that greedy time. The most current titles like *WOW* Magazine will have to wait a while before collectors are seeking them out at inflated prices.

Special editions from any era are keepers plain and simple because they were usually short-run issues, meaning not a lot of them were printed. Any autographed magazine is worth a pretty penny, especially depending on which wrestler autographed it. Prices are pretty much whatever the market will pay.

NWA Wrestling, 1951; $30.

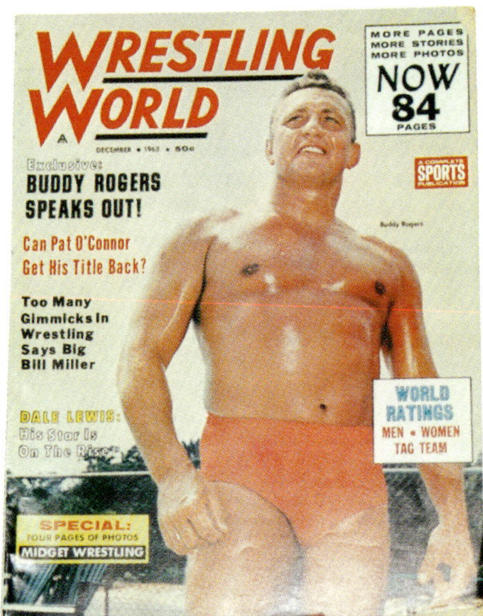

Wrestling World, 1963; $25.

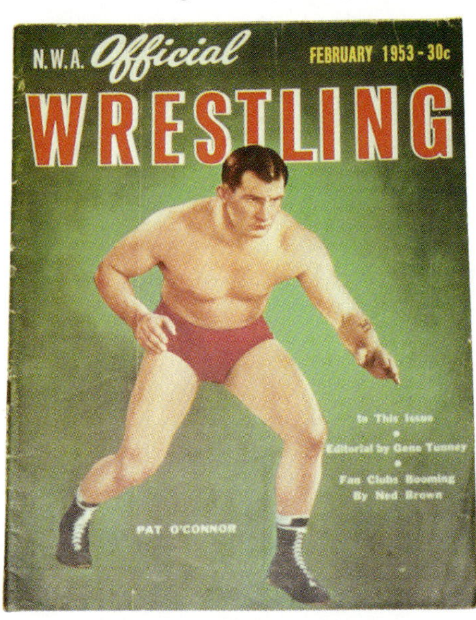

NWA Wrestling, 1953; $30.

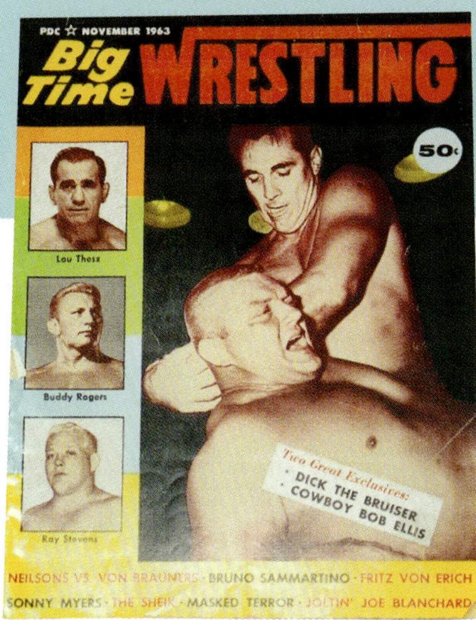

Big Time Wrestling, 1963; $25.

Wrestling Life, Wrestling as You Like It, 1953, and Wrestling Life, 1964; $30 each.

MAD Magazine wrestling special, 1999; $10.

WWF Magazine, 1998; $8.

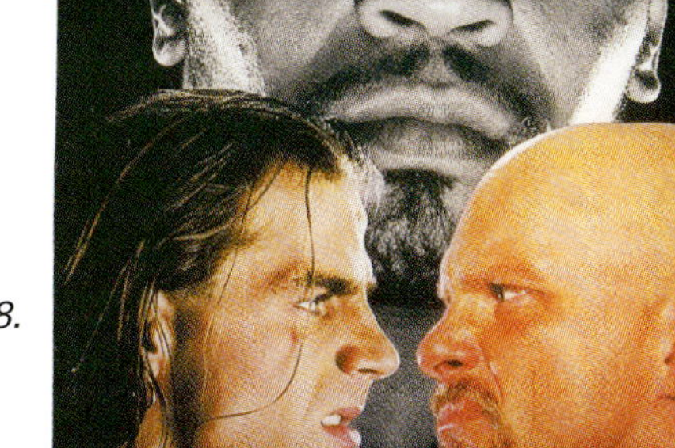

Japan magazines, Gong and Weekly Pro Wrestling; $10 each.

Gong (Japan); $10.

TV Guide, Dec. 5-11, 1999, featuring The Undertaker on one cover and Stone Cold Steve Austin on another; $5 each.

Newsweek, October 1999; $8.

Time, November 1998, featuring Minnesota governor-elect Jesse "The Body" Ventura; $8.

Americana '99, Japan; $10.

Wrestling Revue, Issue 1, 1959; $30.

Books from Japan, 1999; $10 each.

Weekly Pro Wrestling, Japan, Baba issue, 1999; $20.

Weekly Pro Wrestling, Goldberg-Fujinami, 1999; $15.

Sports Illustrated, Danny Hodge, 1957; $55.

New Japan Special, 1984; $10.

A magazine from Japan featuring Tiger Mask, 1987; $10.

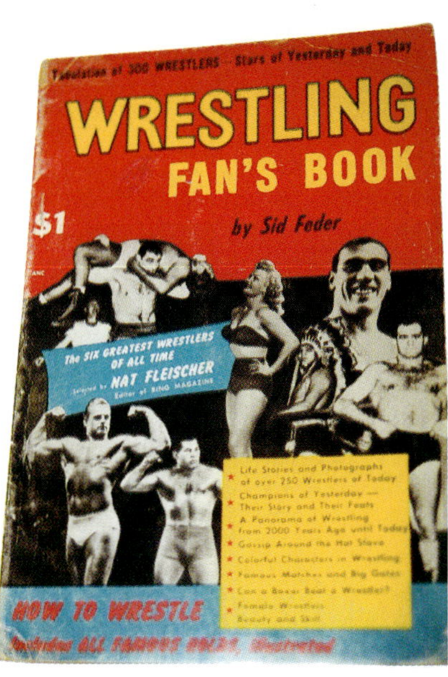

Wrestling Fan's Book; $15.

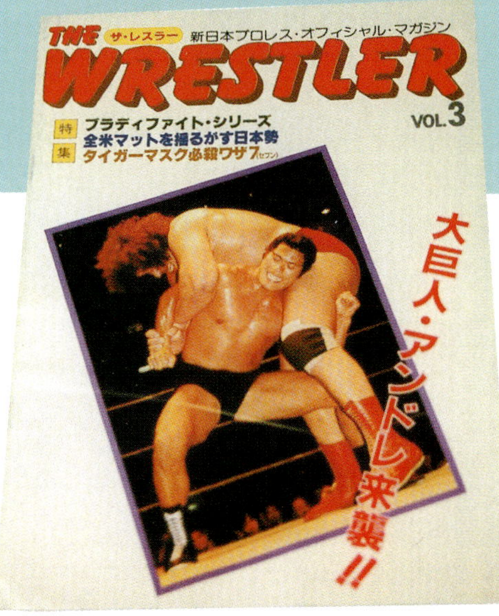

The Wrestler, Andre-Inoki; $15.

UWF, Japan; $8.

New Japan Special; $8.

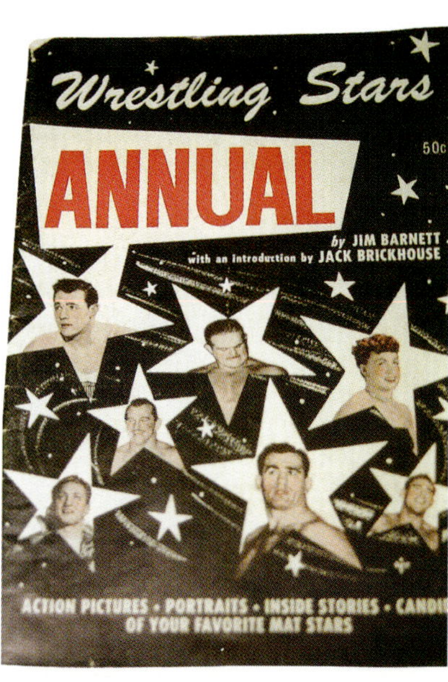

Wrestling Stars Annual; $10.

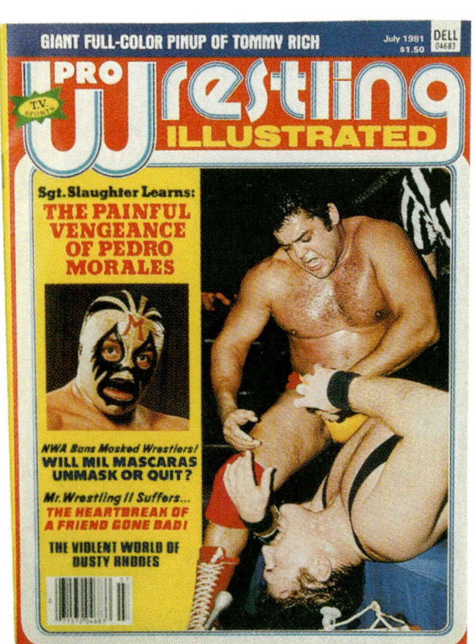

Pro Wrestling Illustrated, Morales-Mascaras, 1981; $10.

Pro Wrestling Illustrated, 1991; $10.

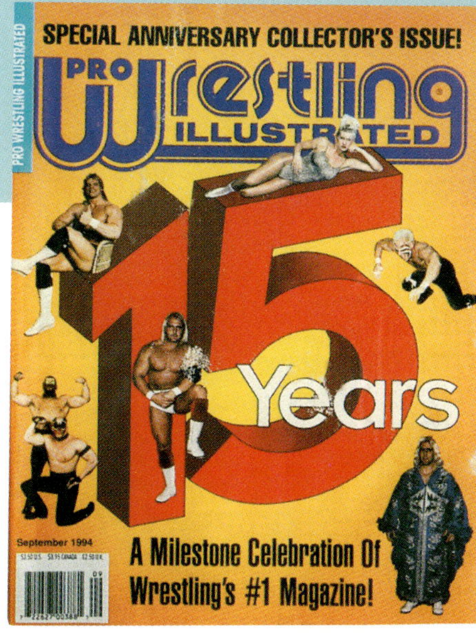

Pro Wrestling Illustrated, 1994; $10.

Premiere issue of WOW, 1999; $8.

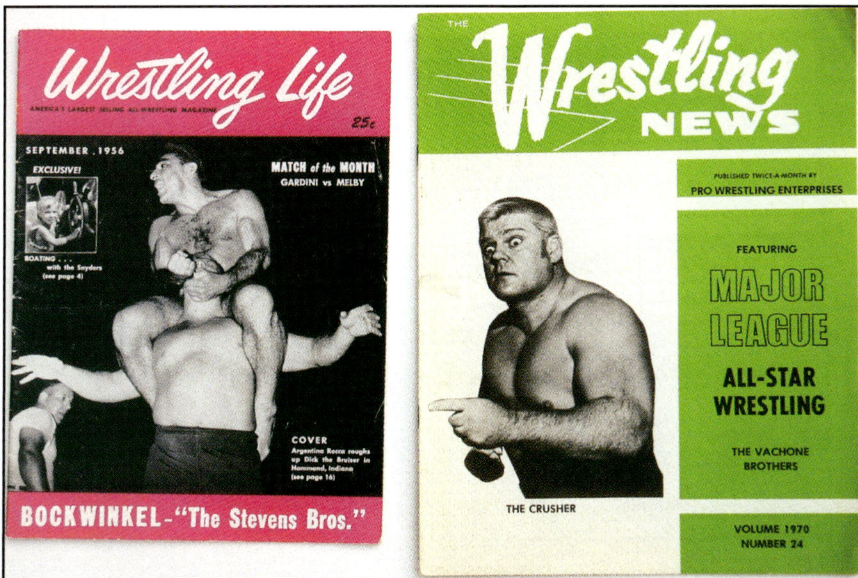

Wrestling Life, 1956, $30; Wrestling News, 1970; $15.

Wrestling World, Lou Thesz, 1963; $25.

Wrestling Revue, 1961; $25.

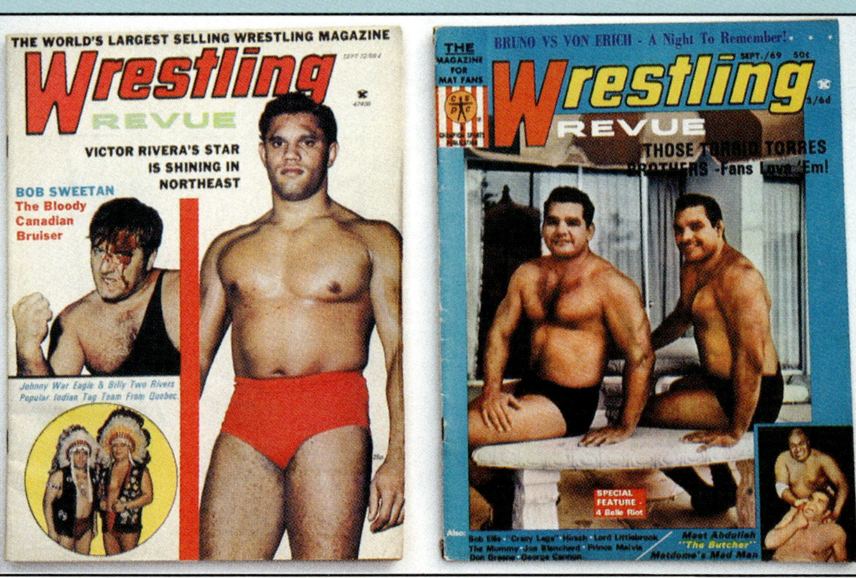

Wrestling Revue, 1972, left, and 1969; $15 each.

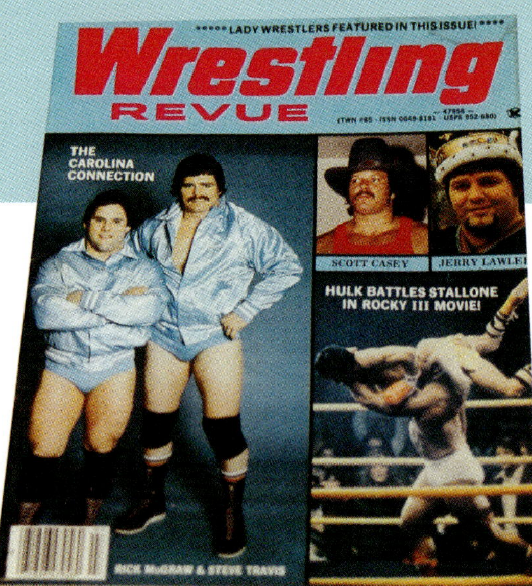

Wrestling Revue, Stallone-Hogan-Lawler, 1984; $15.

Official Wrestling, 1964, $25; and AWA Yearbook, 1972; $15.

Wrestling Revue, Hulk Hogan, 1983; $15.

Wrestling Life, 1955, $30; and Wrestling Illustrated, 1965; $25.

Books

Once upon a time, New York publishing houses treated professional wrestling like a cancer. From 1920 to 1980, there were less than fifty books published about one of the world's top grossing spectator sports.

Therefore, those who fill gaps of pro-wrestling history with Internet services, newsletters and title histories provide a valuable resource to those interested in wrestling's history.

When the boom of the mid-'80s exploded, publishers caught onto wrestling. Many picture and photos books with little or no journalistic merit were released.

Roberta Morgan, George Napalitano and Jim Melby put together the best of these books. Because none of them made any money, publishers retreated to their moral high ground once again and didn't want anything to do with the sport.

These three authors, during our pre-computer era, spent thousands of hours compiling a pro-wrestling encyclopedia. Professional agents who pitched the book were shamefully told, "Sorry fellas, the bosses in New York think wrestling fans can't read."

Fast forward to 1999. It was a year where not only one, but two, pro wrestlers wrote autobiographies that broke the charts of the *New York Times* Best Seller list. Wrestler-turned-politician Jesse Ventura hit it big with *Ain't Got Time to Bleed*.

Publishers said the book had only limited appeal and it sold simply because of Ventura's political upset in Minnesota. Ventura captured the interest of America and the book tour took him everywhere, from the "Montel Williams Show" to a head-to-head interview with Barbara Walters.

When Mick Foley's *Have a Nice Day: A Tale of Blood and Sweatsocks* reached No. 2, everyone was shocked. Insiders said the only reason it didn't start at No. 1 was because there weren't enough copies made. The following week, the book hit No. 1 on the *New York Times* list. Now several books in the same vain are sure to follow, including The Rock's autobiography, which even topped Foley's success.

Despite the fact that very few books about wrestling were ever written, there are some good reads floating around if you can find them. Mike Chapman's books have been well researched and are worthy of putting on your bookshelf. *Two Guys Named Dan*, Chapman's book about amateur wrestling coach Dan Gable and wrestling great Dan Hodge, is an excellent selection. Chapman's written a dozen books and plans to write more. Most of his work is available at the International Wrestling Institute in Iowa and can be purchased through his website.

One of the most popular books about pro wrestling is, *What Ever Happened to Gorgeous George?* It is a book that fills the reader in on what various wrestlers did after they retired. It's hard to find and hopefully one day it will be reissued. In the late '80s, Canadian professor Jim Friedman put his academics aside to write an amazing book titled *Drawing Heat*. Friedman put about a year of his life on hold to travel and study with renegade promoter Dave "The Canadian Wolfman" McKigney. The professor gives readers an inside look at virtually every element of promoting wrestling. *Drawing Heat* is a captivating book. Many will want to read it in one or two sittings. Friedman fully understands the passion of fans, promoters' struggles and the wrestlers' dreams. Much is also written about the

Original Sheik.

Ted DiBiase and Arn Anderson published biographies in the mid-'90s. DiBiase focuses on his faith in God, as well as his wrestling escapades, in *Every Man Has His Price*. Anderson sticks to wrestling in his book *Arn Anderson 4 Ever* and as one would expect, he is a straight shooter. The Dynamite Kid recently published a book. It will one day be a collector's item. The Kid turned pro as a teen in his homeland of England. WWF books about Steve Austin and others will soon be on the market. WCW is said to be countering with biographies of Diamond Dallas Page and Bill Goldberg.

Lou Thesz' book *Hooker*, $20, is very hot with collectors. It bridges eras of days gone by with the NWA of the '70s and even covers his travails in Japan. Tiger Mask's book was a hot seller in Japan, too.

Some fans avoid the big publishing houses and self-publish their own works because of the devotion they have to the sport. Writer Gary Will and publisher Royal Duncan have spent what seems like a lifetime compiling the book, *World Title Histories*. The book sells for $55 and is a must-own for fans and collectors. Will and Duncan have put together the only piece of history ever published about wrestling history of world title wins and losses. Hundreds of promoters are featured. Every group, from the WWWF to the extremely weird is listed. The book itself is quite large and is a spectacle to behold.

Some books to consider putting on your shelf

Arn Anderson 4 Ever: A Look Behind The Curtain, by Arn Anderson (1997)

Bill Goldberg, by Kyle Alexander (1999)

Black Stars of Professional Wrestling, by Julian L.D. Shabazz (1999)

The Complete Idiot's Guide to Pro Wrestling, by Lou Albano (1999)

The Composite Guide to Wrestling, by Jim Gallagher (1998)

Every Man Has His Price: The Story of Ted DiBiase, by Ted DiBiase (1997)

Inside the Lion's Den: The Life of Ken Shamrock, by Ken Shamrock (1998)

I Was A Teenage Professional Wrestler, by Ted Lewin (1994)

Jesse Ventura: The Story of the Wrestler They Call "The Body," by Matt Hunter Published (1999)

Professional Wrestling: Sport and Spectacle (Performance Studies Series), by Sharon Mazer (1998)

The Professional Wrestling Trivia Book, by Robert Myers and Adolph Caso (1999)

Slammin': Wrestling's Greatest Heroes and Villains, by David Hofstede (1999)

Steve Austin: The Story of the Wrestler They Call "Stone Cold," by Dan Ross (1999)

Superstars of Men's Pro Wrestling, by Matt Hunter (1998)

Theater in a Squared Circle, by Jeff Archer (1998)

Undertaker, by Dan Ross (1999)

World of Wrestling: Best of WWF, WCW, ECW, by Mike Morris (1999)

Wrestling Madness: A Ringside Look at Wrestling Superstars, by Matt Hunter (1999)

Wrestling Renegades: An In-Depth Look at Today's Superstars of Pro Wrestling, by Dan Cohen (1999)

Biographical Dictionary of Professional Wrestling, by Harris M. Lentz III (1997)

Pure Dynamite, by Tom Billington (1999)

Encyclopedia of American Wrestling, by Mike Chapman (1989)

Have a Nice Day: A Tale of Blood and Sweatsocks, by Mick Foley (Mankind) (1999)

A History of Wrestling in Iowa: From Gotch to Gable, by Mike Chapman (1981)

Leaping Lanny: Wrestling With Rhyme, by Lanny Poffo (1998)

Professional Wrestling As Ritual Drama in American Popular Culture, by Michael R. Ball (1990)

This is Wrestling!: Today's Stars, Tomorrow's Legends, by George Napolitano (1993)

TV Wrestlers Specials No. 1; The Beauties of Wrestling (1998)

Wrestling Superstars (1985)

Wrestling Superstars II, by Dan Cohen (1986)

Wrestling: Heroes and Villains (1987)

All About WWF Super Stars, by Larry Humber

Andre the Giant, by Don Ward

Awesome!: An Inside Guide to Wrestling Superstars, by Joe Bosko

Bruno Sammartino: An Autobiography of Wrestling's Living Legend, by Bruno Sammartino and Bob Michelucci

Championship Wrestling, by George Napolitano

Drawing Heat, by Jim Friedman

Dusty Rhodes, by Dan Zadra

Gordon Solie: Master of the Ring, by Gordon Solie

Hulk Hogan, by Dan Zadra

Hulkamania: The Official Biography of Hulk Hogan, by the World Wrestling Federation

Hulkamania!: Hulk Hogan America's Hero, by Abbot Neil

Inside Wrestling, by Tom Valentine

Main Event: The World of Professional Wrestling, by Roberta Morgan

Mat Wars, by Verne Gagne and Jim Melby

A Pictorial History of Wrestling, by George Napolitano

The Pictorial History of Wrestling: The Good, the Bad and the Ugly, by Bert Sugar, George Napolitano

Pro Wrestling Confidential: How Some of Your Favorite Pro Wrestlers Were Put in a Headlock of Violence, Intrigue and Drugs, by John T. Arezzi

The Road Warriors, by Dan Zadra

Rowdy Roddy: The Official Biography of Rowdy Roddy Piper, by the World Wrestling Federation

Trouble in Paradise: Behind the Scenes of Amateur and Professional Wrestling—Behind the Cameras of Network Television, by Irwin Wilbur Stanton

The Von Erichs: A Family Album: Tragedies and Triumphs of America's First Family of Wrestling, by Kirk Dooley

Whatever Happened to Gorgeous George?, by Joseph Frank, Jares

The Who's Who of Wrestling, by Joe D'Orazio

Wrestlin': Pro Wrestling Close Up, by Raeanne Rubenstein and Alan Green

Wrestling the Greatest Stars: Bashers and Beauties, by George Napolitano

Wrestling's Great Grudge Matches: Battles and Feuds, by Bert Sugar, George Napolitano

WWF Presents All About Tag Teams Fact Book, by Larry Humber

WWF Presents All About Ultimate Warrior Fact Book, Larry Humber

WWF: The Official Book, by Ed Ricciuti

chapter 8

Wrestlers and the Silver Screen

There have been well more than 200 television programs and movies that have incorporated pro wrestling since the first reel film graced the silver screen. A most recent movie, released in theaters in April, was "Ready to Rumble." This WCW comedy is "Wayne's World" meets "Encino Man." The star (David Arquette) is mad his favorite wrestler, Jimmy King, is fired by an evil promoter. Goldberg, Dallas Page, Sting, Saturn and Bam Bam Bigelow appear. Unfortunately, other than biographies and a few gems, most movies with wrestling ties have been virtually un-watchable.

One such gem well worth watching was The Rock's performance on "Saturday Night Live," which he hosted in March, and was game enough to send up his macho image by wearing a dress and big blonde wig for one skit.

While a wrestler's appearance on a television show virtually guarantees a ratings' boost, most of the movies have been flops at the box office. That is not to say all of the wrestlers who have dabbled in films have done poorly. But clearly, Hollywood has failed to capitalize on wrestling's drama on a consistent basis. With the WWF going public in 1999, it says it will enter the film world. Hopefully, it'll capture the magic that so many wrestling fans feel each and every week watching wrestling television shows.

Long a star in the ring, Stone Cold Steve Austin has also tackled acting. His performances on the CBS TV show "Nash Bridges" were the most watched of that series in 1998.

Hollywood tends to want wrestlers to "act." Renowned movie and wrestling critic Pat Hollis has an opinion about wrestlers appearing in movies. "There is inherently a problem with that," Hollis analyzed. "Wrestler are already actors when they wrestle. Nobody pays to see Terry Bollea act. They want Hulk Hogan. And certainly, nobody in Minnesota voted for Jim Janos. They voted for Jesse Ventura. Hollywood's ego seems to get in the way. Movies which try to capitalize on a wrestler of wrestling as a whole are in trouble."

But hey, this book isn't designed to critique the merits of a wrestler's ability to act in Hollywood. We're concerned about the collectibility, right?

Through the history of film and wrestling, several big-name wrestlers had gotten their opportunity to become stars on the big screen. Vivian Vachone's "Wrestling Queen" was a camp thriller that can be found at second-tier video stores. "The Wrestler," starring Verne Gagne and Ed Asner, was a 1972 film wrestling fans hoped would capture some of the sports' mystique. Although it was about wrestling, it failed to be a commercial or critical success. When it was first released on videocassette in the mid-'80s, it was rare and hard to find. At one point, even dubs of "The Wrestler" netted collectors up to $100. Today, it has been re-released with numerous cover designs and is worth only about $20. Only the hardcore collectors can see the value in the movie's first pressing. Had it reached the success

Jerry "The King" Lawler once "broke" Comedian Andy Kaufman's neck during an infamous wrestling match.

that no wrestling movie ever had, (into the hearts of fans), it could have been a true classic. Although most collectors want to own it, the film's artistic value is close to nil.

Other wrestlers have had minor roles in some very popular films. Harold Sakata, an Olympic silver medalist weight lifter wrested as Tosh Togo. Even more attention getting than his Olympic medal is his role as Odd Job in the James Bond 1964 hit, "Goldfinger." The video itself is worth $20, but Sakata's role is priceless. In 1972, wrestler Len Montana became the character Lucca Brazzi in the epic film, "The Godfather." The role was memorable and a pivotal one for Montana. Eight-by-ten glossy photos of Montana as Brazzi can sell for up to $30—double that if autographed. In the '80s, Billy Crystal's "Princess Bride" was a huge hit that co-starred Andre the Giant. Again, anything and everything available about wrestling's connection with Hollywood has value to some wrestling fan.

"I like to Hurt People" is a semi-biographical look at the insane Sheik, Ed Farhat. Because Sheik's matches were, more often than not, blood baths, they have always had a cult appeal. Sheik's best matches were pre-video era, which makes "I Like to Hurt People" even more precious. At one point, it was worth about $50 to $60, but because of its many re-issues and availability, don't expect to fetch that much at an auction. It may only sell for about $20. Real wrestling fans wouldn't think of parting with it, anyway.

Lenny Montana found some Hollywood fame after appearing as Lucca Brazzi in "The Godfather."

Comedian Andy Kaufman's foray into professional wrestling was insane. Though many consider Kaufman to be on the talent level of a genius, most of the public could not figure out what he was doing when he ventured into the world of wrestling. For nearly a year, he went on television programs pinning women out of the audience. Tapes of him doing so on "Saturday Night Live" are collectibles that sell for $20 to $40. He then took his act to Memphis, where Jerry "The King" Lawler made mincemeat out of him. As part of the storyline, Lawler broke Kaufman's neck in a match and then the two performers banged heads on the "David Lettermen Show." Homemade, good quality tapes that cover the Lawler vs. Kaufman feud are worth about $40. Anything less is a bargain. Before his death, Kaufman made one last film in 1983, which to wrestling fans is a real classic and keeper. Kaufman invited manager Fred Blassie, who had some mainstream appeal himself after recording the popular hit "Pencil Necked Geek," to a local restaurant in Los Angeles. The two ordered breakfast and chatted about life and even threw barbs with fellow patrons of the restaurant. What resulted was a real-time film that was titled, "My Breakfast With Blassie." It's $25 and hard to find, but if you do see it, grab it. You won't forget it.

"A Day in the Life of Nord Barbarian," released

in 1988, saw star wrestler John Nord (The Berzerker from WWF fame) on top of the world. Through his "barbarian" television ads, he had become a Midwest cult hero. The ads boosted his father's car dealership to record sales and he had been the late Bruiser Brody's hand-picked successor. At the top of his career, Nord agreed to make this unmistakably classic film short. The 15-minute video is hilarious as Nord, adorned in his "barbarian" outfit, goes to the bank, shops and slams bystanders through windshields—you know, all the daily rigors of a barbarian. Since then, the car dealership has folded and Nord's career has been in limbo. But those who have seen this well-produced mini-movie see wrestling writing and comic appeal at its finest. The video has long been out of print. Dubs are worth $15 to $20 and originals are valued at twice that price. Autographed copies or posters advertising the video are worth about $50.

Movies from Mexico are also popular amongst collectors. Mexico's "Night of the Bloody Apes" is a classic that nets only $20-$30 on the collectibles scene. But this wacky horror flick is worth that and then some. The plot revolves around a masked grappler whose heart gives out in the ring. A mad doctor replaces his heart with an ape's and all goes to, previously unforeseen, wacky heights. "Samson Versus the Vampire Women" is considered by many to be the ultimate in wrestling fun. Dubbed "Samson," first pressing copies are worth about $50. However, as time goes on, expect these films to increase in value.

With more than 200 films and programs available, an entire book could be written on the appeal of wrestling film collecting itself. Meanwhile, if you are a new collector, here are just some of our favorites that should be considered must-sees for any collector:

- "Around the World in a Daze" (1961). A Three-Stooges comedy, where Larry Fine and Moe Howard push Joe De Rita into wrestling his way to hijinx. The video is worth about $20, while posters can be found for $40.
- "Alias the Champ" (1949). This is a film about, and starring, Gorgeous George, the wonderful star of the 1940s and 1950s. Posters in mint condition range from $50 to $100, while ragged versions can be found for $20. The video, $25 new, is hard to find in catalogs, but with wrestling's popularity, it's sure to be re-released. Tor Johnson, "The Swedish Angel," is one of the many storied characters in the movie.
- "Arena" (1991). This one is for the whacked-out collector only. Paul Satterfield III stars as Steve Armstrong, who has to battle an intergalactic monster in the ring. Valued at $25.
- "Beyond the Mat" (1999). The masterpiece of wrestling fan-turned-filmaker Barry Blaustein, this documentary ventures into the secret inner sanctum of pro wrestling. Starring Mick Foley, Terry Funk and Jake Roberts. Cameos by The Rock, Steve Austin, Droz, Mike Modest and more.
- "Body Hold" (1949), $25. Bodybuilder Tommy Jones is upset when he realizes wrestling may just be crooked.
- "Body Slam" (1987), $25. A highly watchable cable hit, with Roddy Piper and Tonga Kid shilling for the "good" promoter.
- "Ferocious Freedom Fighters" (1982), $25. This is a campy escapade that focuses on a female wrestler who wants to quit, but her ex-wrestling man wants her to get an operation. An Elvis impersonator who throws karate kicks also stars.
- "Gable" (1999). This is a documentary about the fabled amateur champion and coach Dan Gable. It's valued at around $35.

Woody Strode was one of wrestling's first cross-over stars and appeared in more than 60 movies.

- "Go to Hell" (1999), $25. Dario Dare is an ex-wrestling manager who reports for tabloids and finds out a supernatural freak is out to kill a Vatican cardinal.
- "Grunt! The Wrestling Movie" (1985). A quintessential B-grade movie, this is a mock-documentary about a wrestler who disappears after killing an opponent. It's camp at its finest. Stars wrestlers Adrian Street, Dick Murdoch and Billy Varga, and also pre-Rush Limbaugh political mouthpiece Wally George. Worth about $30.
- "I'm From Hollywood" (1992), $25. Documentary about Andy Kaufman and his wrestling adventures. Announcer Lance Russell is seen in rare form, as is the "King" Jerry Lawler. Comedian Robin Williams is also interviewed.
- "Night and the City" (1950), $25. Richard Widmark gives a five-star performance as Harry Fabian, a despicable but likable character from London, who sets out to be a wrestling promoter. A classic performance by a true legend that tells the oldest wrestling tale of them all...you can fool some of the people some of the time, but the only real fool is you. Widmark loses out big time. Robert DeNiro stars in the remake, which replaced wrestling with boxing.
- "One and Only" (1978), $25. This is a movie where Henry Winkler of "Happy Days" fame stars as a failed thespian, who turns to wrestling to make a living. It's almost watchable, but collectors can find this on shelves below listed value. The same can be said about Alex Karras' "Mad Bull," $25. More could be expected from Karras, an NFL player turned wrestler turned actor, but the likable lunkhead just didn't have the material to pull it off.
- "Requiem for a Heavyweight" (1962), $25. This is very well one of the greatest movies of all time. It's consistently gut-wrenching and passionate. What else can be expected from a Rod Serling script? The film is an essay on broken dreams and broken hearts. In short, washed up, punch-drunk boxer Mountain Rivera (Anthony Quinn) is forced to wrestle as "Big Chief Rivera" to pay his own bills, and the bills of those who turned on him. The movie has a young Cassius Clay in textbook form. Maybe he should have watched this film a few more times. Jackie Gleason co-stars. The play, which was seen during television's black-and-white glory days, chillingly starred Jack Palance. "Requiem" shows deeply how real life is often scarier than fiction.
- "Wrestling With Shadows" (1998), $20. The documentaries on wrestling have always done well. This film chronicled WWF star Bret "Hitman" Hart and his match at the 1997 Survivor Series. It's a detailed look at the life of a wrestler behind the scenes and shows that the on-screen product is not always what it seems. A must-see.

The Cross-over Stars

Some of the individuals who have the largest followings in the collectible circuit are those who have done more than just wrestle. These "cross-over stars" have included wrestlers appearing in

Hulk Hogan in full regalia as "Thunderlips" in "Rocky III." United Artists Corporation.

movies and boxers and football players who wind up grappling. Artifacts from these films rate high with collectors. The publicity photos, press kits, movie posters and other memorabilia about wrestling films are highly collectible items.

Some cross-over stars had more notoriety in films than in wrestling. Take Woody Strode. Strode appeared in more than 60 films and was, without a doubt, wrestling's first crossover to films. He was honored by many critics, starred or co-starred in more than a dozen films and even appeared in several top spaghetti westerns. Roderick Toombs, otherwise known as "Rowdy" Roddy Piper (who is still going strong—artificial hip and all), was another cross-over star. After "Body Slam" in 1987, Piper hit the big screen in John Carpenter's 1988 science-fiction thriller, "They Live." Here, the mad Scotsman proved to Hollywood that wrestlers could indeed be bankable stars. Piper is a natural as a homeless hero battling aliens. Full-length movie posters of the film are valued at $60. The video is still readily available at rental stores. The success of the movie catapulted Piper to appear in dozens of other films and television programs. There are those who collect everything they can about Piper. His mid-1990s action picture, "Back in Action," $15, is a novelty for collectors, as it co-stars Tae Bo kingpin, Billy Blanks.

Terry Funk, here with another wrestling great, Lou Thesz, appeared on both the silver and small screens.

The most widely known cross-over star is also the man who claims to have "taken wrestling to where it is today," Hulk Hogan. Terry Bollea (his real name) has appeared in more than 15 movies and televised programs. Ironically, he could never capture his persona, that so many love, on the big screen. Despite being the most-noted wrestler of the 1980s, his movies were terrible flops. He did well in "Rocky III" as Thunderlips in a role that changed his life forever. Between his appearance in "Rocky" and his main events in the AWA at the same time, Hogan became a bigger-than-life star. For most Hogan videos, search the bargain bin. Placards and glossies of Hogan in "Rocky III" are worth up to $30 and his cartoon series "Hulk Hogan and His Wrestling Friends" ($10 for each episode) are sure to be worth ten times their cover price in future years.

Hardcore legend Terry Funk has appeared in many movies and television series. Copies of the 1985 "Wildside," where he stars as a Western-styled tough guy, are very rare. They have never been released commercially and Funk fanatics have been known to pay $50 for the four "Wildside" episodes that he appeared in. In 1992, he appeared in the short-lived "Tequila and Bonetti," which also was never released commercially. Tapes of that series are worth something only to the fan who absolutely has to have everything Funk appeared in. Funk's best role was that

With the all of the flamboyancy he exibited as a wrestler, it's no wonder Jesse "The Body" Ventura (here with Fred Blassie, another wrestling legend), also found fame in the movies, starring in many action roles.

of Frankie the Thumper in 1978's "Paradise Alley." Because "Paradise Alley" is written by, and stars, Sylvester Stallone, anything to do with the movie is of some value. The movie itself is good fun and marks one of Armand Assanti's first roles. Glossies of Funk arm wrestling as Frankie are found for $35.

Tor Johnson, the "Swedish Angel," began a film career in 1934 that lasted until 1961. He appears as himself in "Alias the Champ," the 1949 film starring Gorgeous George. In 1958, Johnson appeared as Inspector Daniel Clay in Ed Wood's immortal "Plan 9 From Outer Space." "Plan 9" memorabilia is worth more to sci-fi than wrestling fans. Many of Tor's films are grade-B and C-level, but are worth seeing. Because of his freakish oversized body parts, he was a cult hero to movie and wrestling fans. The items he appeared in can be a bit pricey.

Jesse "The Body" Ventura hit pay dirt in many big-time flicks, including "Predator," "Batman & Robin" and the "Running Man." While The Body should probably thank Arnold for the big payoffs, Ventura created a niche for himself in bit parts. Remember, most of Ventura's roles are recent, so don't pay for more than the cover price.

More than 30 other wrestlers—men and women—have gone on to appear in movies. Most of them were character actors. Some like Pepper Martin, Hard Boiled Haggerty, Gene LeBell, Wild Bill Montana, Mike Mazurki, Count Billy Varga and Strode probably made more money on the screen than they did in the ring. Zeus, a.k.a. Tiny Lister, had a phenomenal run in the WWF in the late 1980s against Hulk Hogan in the ring and in the film "No Holds Barred." Lister is the first man to have started in films and later became a wrestler. At 6-foot-9, 300-plus pounds, he has found it quite easy to stay busy in the movie world. "Between the Ropes" was a short-lived series about a wrestling teacher that starred the late NFL star, Lyle Alzado. Again, these comedies have never been commercially released. But if one had every episode on tape, collectors would make a bid for it. The show often featured NWA wrestlers like Road Warriors and Steiner Brothers. Japanese legend Antonio Inoki has dozens of collectibles made on his behalf. But he'd probably rather forget his appearance in "Bad News Bears Go to Japan." This one is barely worth the cover price of $20.

The Mexican Wrestling Legends

When we talk about cross-over stars, the greatest cross-over star never appeared in an American movie. But still, no wrestler made more films than El Santo. The masked Mexican superhero began wrestling in 1942. On July 26 of that year, he entered the ring and won his first match,

Mil Mascaras in a still from the movie, "Los Campeones Justicieros."

a battle royal in Mexico City. In 1958, he made his first of more than 50 movies. Between his first bout in 1942 and the time he became a hero on the silver screen, he won virtually every major title in Mexico's world of wrestling. He was the national welterweight champion, national middleweight champ (four times), won the NWA world welterweight title (twice), the national light heavyweight title and he also held the national tag team title on two occasions.

El Santo, a.k.a. the Saint, had numerous episodic battles in and out of the ring, but also went on to save the world from the Mummy, Dracula, Frankenstein, sorcerers, mobsters and even martians. If there was an evil face, El Santo beat it. If there was any genre of film, be it music, comedy or western, he did that too. Most of El Santo's films are available for the basic cover price of the video. However, his rarest videos may be worth around $100.

El Santo was also the first mass-marketed wrestler. He was the first since the 1920s to be featured on action figures, pop bottles, games and comic books. Although Hulk Hogan likes to believe the movie and wrestling marriage was one that he pioneered, El Santo did all the Hulkster did and then some, years before Terry Bollea became a wrestler. His replica masks are valued at $35 to $70, depending on the quality, workmanship and era.

Relying on the mass appeal of Santo, marketers chose bodybuilder Aaron Rodriguez to star as Mil Mascaras, who became the 1970s answer to El Santo in movies and comics. Original posters featuring the Saint star may be worth $200 or more to some collectors, while Mascaras posters sell for around $100.

According to Hollis, stars like El Santo are the roots to another special place in wrestling-collectibles history: the mask. The wrestling movie expert says that the Mexican Lucha Libre wrestling masks are worth more than any other replica collectibles anywhere. Although modern-day fans may see Tiger Mask or Justin Liger as their favorite masked stars, hardened collectors have Mexican stars El Santo and Mil Mascaras on their list. Both grapplers are true legends of professional wrestling, even though their successes were found south of the border. The masks which they wore made them, and all Mexican wrestlers who wore them, bigger than life. Sometimes, in the case of El Santo and Mascaras, the country adopted them as their own son. Wrestling fans in Mexico cherished them as performers and athletes and even non-wrestling fans respected the appeal of characters like El Santo.

The masked wrestlers of Mexico became the world's first cross-over stars during the 1960s. The real claim to fame for masked wrestlers was not necessarily their in-ring performances—it was what they did on the silver screen that helped them become mainstream successes. Originally, wrestlers would be asked to do a movie or two. Eventually, after witnessing the monstrous success of El Santo, savvy Mexican mass-marketers developed a character first and then simply found a man to fit the slot.

The masked wrestlers were diverse if nothing else. Long before Arnold tried to crack jokes or Stallone tried to sing "Rhinestone Cowboy," the Mexican superheroes did it all. Masked wrestlers from the mystical lands of Mexico, starred in spy movies, did comedy routines on talk shows, starred in westerns, fought in jungles like Indiana Jones and even sang. They appeared in every aspect of entertainment. Because of their immense cross-over talent and broad appeal, they became bigger-than-life megastars. Because it was taboo to be filmed or televised without their masks, the general public never saw them outside their characters. That fact added to their mystique and popularity.

Because of the mask's popularity, many wrestler's careers were built around the "hood." Feuds were often settled by having classic "Mask vs. Mask" battles. Standing-room-only crowds would pay to see these epic wars where the loser would have to be unmasked and stripped of his identity. Those bouts in which someone is unmasked are $30 to $100 among collectors.

In the 1960s, the mask phenomenon made its way to the United States. Legit tough-guy veteran, Dr. Bill Miller, was a main event star as "Mr. M." Later, former AAU standout Dick Beyer was a headliner as "Dr. X," or as he liked to call himself, "The Intelligent Sensational Destroyer." As the Destroyer, Beyer's wars against Freddie Blassie were said to be gory with a capital "G." He also became one of Japan's top stars.

Tim Woods found a niche as Mr. Wrestling and the Irwin brothers later had success as the Super Destroyers. John Studd and Killer Kowalski had some top matches as the Executioners in the WWWF and regional acts like the Interns (L.A.), the Assassins (Carolinas), and others did well as masked men. But not since the '60s has any U.S. wrestler seen superstardom using a mask. Is the legend of the mask complete?

If you're looking for an authentic Mexican Lucha Libre mask, expect to pay from $30 to $150 each. The higher-quality masks, and ones with great detail, are seen for sale for about $250. For authentic masks worn by the top grapplers themselves (Tiger Mask, El Santo, etc.) $1,000 would not be unreasonable. Even today, Dr. X and Destroyer masks can still be found for about $20.

But if it's the movie that you're after, here is a list of some of the movies that starred El Santo and can be found on the market new for around $20-$30. These, of course, are the translated titles:

"Brain of Evil," 1958

"Santo vs. the Infernal Men," 1958

"Invasion of the Zombies," 1961

"Santo vs. the Diabolical Brain," 1961

"Santo in the Hotel of Death," 1961

"Santo vs. the Vampire Women," 1962

"Santo vs. the Strangler," 1963

"Santo vs. the Ghost of the Strangler," 1963

"The Diabolical Axe," 1964

"Santo vs. Baron Brakola," 1965

"Santo the Silver-Masked One vs. the Martian Invasion," 1966

"Santo in the Treasure of Dracula," 1968

"Santo and Blue Demon vs. the Monsters," 1969. Also starring Blue Demon.

"Santo vs. the Head Hunters," 1969

"Santo in the Vengeance of the Vampire Women," 1970

"Santo in the Vengeance of the Mummy," 1970

"Santo vs. the Daughter of Frankenstein," 1971

"Killers from Other Worlds," 1971

"The Royal Eagle," 1971

"The Mummies of Guanajuato," 1971. Also starring Blue Demon and Mil Mascaras.

"Santo and Blue Demon vs. Dracula and the Wolfman," 1972. Also starring Blue Demon.

"Santo and Blue Demon vs. Dr. Frankenstein," 1973. Also stars Blue Demon.

"The Vengeance of the Crying Woman," 1974

"Mystery in Bermuda," 1975. Also starring Blue Demon and Mil Mascaras.

"Santo on the Border of Terror," 1979

"Santo vs. the Television Killer," 1981.

chapter 9

The Rock & Wrestling Connection

In the mid-1980s, when famed wrestling manager Captain Lou Albano appeared in Cyndi Lauper's video for her upcoming hit "Girls Just Wanna Have Fun," a new era of rock and wrestling was under way. The video, one of the first to be a mini-movie, helped not only make Lauper an overnight sensation, but helped mold a generation of video nuts. Call it luck, call it timing or call it a stroke of genius, but Lauper and Albano were at the cusp of an explosion that would forever change how we looked at music. Though the "Girls Just Wanna have Fun" video was but a small part of the MTV Generation, it was a part, nonetheless.

For the sport of professional wrestling and its fans, the video also played a part in how wrestling would be viewed by the general populous. It also helped bring the sport into an era where wrestling would outgrow anyone's dreams. Truth be known, even Vince McMahon's.

At the time, MTV was a fledgling cable station seen in about 30 percent of America's homes. It was also a time when McMahon's WWF was transforming from a regional promotion into one with worldwide recognition. Other promoters folded their businesses in a rapid pace. On the surface, the WWF grew by leaps and bounds. Lauper was everywhere and even had a stint as Wendi Richter's manager. MTV and NBC aired high-profile wrestling cards and matches. The "Rock & Wrestling" connection was born. Or was it?

Rock 'n' roll and professional wrestling share many unique characteristics. Rock 'n' roll was formed as a crossbreed of church music, field hollers and country rhythms, while being embraced by an underground core of fans. Eventually, rock 'n' roll ruled the nation, but it had always had a cult following. Wrestling grew side by side during the same years as rock 'n' roll. To be a fan, you had to go against the norm. After all, rock 'n' roll was considered to be the devil's music and pro wrestling was considered "fake." Both garnered little acceptance by the mainstream. But through hard work, a whole lot of talent and television stations having a need for product, both rock 'n' roll and professional wrestling found an audience by the early '60s. Each major city had its own wrestling promotion and its own rock stars.

Musicians and wrestlers have always lived a paralleled existence. Both enjoy performing, seek fame, bust their tails before a few or a few thousand, and both hold the dream of one day "making it." Not all wrestlers, nor did all rockers, get the connection at first, but many did.

Over the course of history, many wrestlers were closet rockers and vice versa. One-time artist and Memphis dee jay, Jerry Lawler, was once urged by wrestling manager Sam Bass that he would be a natural as a wrestler. By the late 1970s, Lawler became the area's second "King" and became instrumental in being part of some of the sport's most memorable moments. Many of the stars Lawler promoted or fought stayed close to the

Sputnik Monroe was a regular member of Sun Studios' coffee club in the 1950s, witnessing Charlie Rich, Howlin' Wolf, Johnny Cash, Jerry Lee Lewis, Carl Perkins and Elvis Presley lay down some of the greatest rock music ever cut.

Jerry Lawler and "Mouth of the South" Jimmy Hart, former lead singer of The Gentrys, sing "Act Naturally."

rock 'n' roll theme. Ricky Morton and Robert Gibson became the Rock 'n' roll Express and danced their way to stardom. Steve Keirn & Stan Lane were struggling mid-card wrestlers when Lawler suggested a new gimmick for them. In Memphis, Lane & Keirn did a music video to the tune of ZZ Top's "Sharp Dressed Man" and the legendary tag team, the Fabulous Ones, was born. Other tag teams in Memphis added rock, heavy metal or rap genres to their acts and became bigger hits than they were prior to adding music to their repertoire.

During the WWF/MTV era, little known Memphis wrestler Wayne Ferris embraced the "Honky Tonk Man" act and made breaking guitars over his foe's heads a regular part of the wrestling scene. Today, Jeff Jarrett carries on that tradition in WCW. As Double J in the WWF, Jarrett performed with country rockers Sawyer Brown and made a catchy song "Be My Baby" which, in actuality, was sung by another man with southern roots, the Road Dogg, Jesse James Armstrong.

The roots of rock and wrestling even go back to the days of Sam Phillips' Sun Studios. In the mid-'50s, wrestler Sputnik Monroe was a regular member of the studios' coffee club. There he watched Charlie Rich, Howlin' Wolf, Johnny Cash, Jerry Lee Lewis, Carl Perkins and Elvis Presley lay down some of the greatest rock music ever cut. As legend has it, Monroe took Phillips' rock rebelliousness to the wrestling arena and became a civil rights activist by refusing to perform in Memphis unless Black Americans were allowed equal access to the main floor seats. As rock and wrestling both gained regional exposure, black wrestling acts such as Sailor Art Thomas, Bobo Brazil, Ernie Ladd, Earl Maynard, Dory Dixon and later Rocky Johnson, Junkyard Dog and Tony Atlas, all became regarded as valued main event acts. Years later, Phillips looked back in glee and said, "I knew we had it all in Memphis." Man, was he ever correct.

In the mid 1960s, Phillips churned out Sun Studios' last big hit. It was "Keep on Dancing" by the Gentry's. Needless to say, the rock-and-wrestling connection was alive and well. The Gentry's lead singer was none other than manager "The Mouth of the South" Jimmy Hart. The album, and single, are popular among collectors of both wrestling and rock. It was the fifth and last disc made by the group and thanks to the novelty of Hart signing, was re-issued worldwide on compact disc.

By the mid to early '80s, rock and wrestling were joined at the hips. Wrestlers began to use entrance music to give them star appeal. Sylvester Ritter took riffs from Jim Croce's "Bad Boy Leroy Brown" and became the Junkyard Dog. Michael "P.S." Hayes borrowed the look and spirit of legendary Lynard Skynard's "Freebird" and went on to super stardom. Hayes, Terry Gordy and Buddy Roberts were main event stars in front

Records by the Rhythm Rockers, $25. Photo courtesy of Mick Karch.

A Sgt. Slaughter autographed record sleeve for "The Turnbuckles," $35. Photo courtesy of Mick Karch.

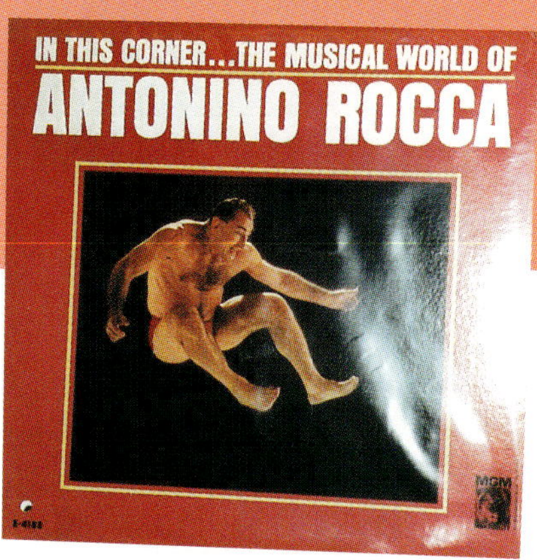

An Antonino Rocca album from 1965, $45. Photo courtesy of Dr. Bob Bryla.

A CD of "Slammin' Wrestling Hits," 1998, $10.

of standing-room-only crowds throughout the United States as the electric tag team, "The Freebirds." Eventually, as "P.S.," Hayes cut a cult song called "Bad Street USA" which still rates high among collectors. Wade Curtiss was a rocker in the '50s who briefly hit the charts and became a wrestler. Although he did quite well, he never became a major star. Curtiss' 45s are ultra-rare and collectors can expect to pay $40.

Verne Gagne's AWA was considered to be a conservative territory that took few risks. But by the late '70s, Gagne, too, caught up with the rock 'n' roll phenomenon. Buck "Rock 'n' Roll" Zumhoff entered arenas dressed in sequins looking like a Las Vegas Elvis and carried a boom box to the ring the size of a Volkswagen. To this day, Zumhoff and his fans believe his place in history should be preserved as the sport's first true rock and roller. Zumhoff was so popular, he was often out-cheered by another struggling rocker, Hulk Hogan (who played bass in the rock band Cherry), who was his regular tag-team partner. Several years later, Jim Brunzell, a dynamic tag-team wrestler, embraced rock hero Bruce Springsteen's music and recorded the picture disc called "Matlands" to the tune of Springsteen's '80s' hit, "Badlands." Today, few "Matlands" discs have survived, but if you can track down a copy, expect to pay about $20.

Last, but not least, the AWA's rock and wrestling connection boasted a tune from Jesse Ventura. His "Body Rules" tune is a much sought-after picture disc that also is quite rare. Minneapolis resident Matt Potts of Aardvark Records recently sold his copy of "Body Rules" for $75. Potts, a big fan, and once a member of the rock band the Loose Rails, dedicated the band's album "Red Turns to Green" to the late Bruiser Brody. In Minneapolis, there's even a band called "Bruiser Brody." No one can deny the roots of rock and wrestling. At the core of Minneapolis' rock and wrestling connection is Terry Katzman. He has been a local wrestling commissioner, co-promoted Rock and Wrestle for the Homeless events, was a sound man for the punk seminal rockers Husker Du (band frontman Bob Mould eventually became part of WCW's booking team), produced the Lemonheads and owns the locally renowned music shop, Garage D'or Records.

In recent years KISS, the Misfits and the Insane Clown Posse have capitalized on the rock-and-wrestling connection. The Posse even have an album titled "The Great Malenko," in honor of wrestling's late super-trainer Professor Boris Malenko. Country crooner Chad Brock completed WCW's Power Plant wrestling school and tried his luck in the ring before hitting big on the country charts in 1999. Brock's wrestling tapes are in demand by country fans who find his prior career choice amusing, if nothing else.

There have been other wrestlers who found time to record a song or two. Exotic Adrian Street issued several 45s, Freddie Blassie's "Pencil Necked Geek"($35 to $50) is a timeless classic, NRBQ did an entire album with Lou Albano, the Valiant Brothers cut a song or two and the WWF,

Fred Blassie records, $35 each.

ECW, and WCW have had hit albums based on wrestlers' entrance music. In the '70s, country comic Ray Stevens charted with "The Blue Cyclone." In the late '50s, Elvis look-alike Frank Townsend wore music notes on his trunks and had been known to sing a tune before his match. Jerry Lawler recorded the barroom classic, "T-R-O-U-B-L-E" years later, before Travis Tritt dreamed of playing before sold-out crowds. Vivian Vachone sang in French about being the queen of wrestling. The Fabulous Moolah, who was part of MTV's rock-and-wrestling venture, married fellow grappler Buddy Lee. When Lee hurt his back, he went into promoting WWF road shows and became a top country-music manager. Even Curt Hennig appeared to have a hit on his hands with last year's favorite, "I Hate Rap." Sorry, Master P.

Many bands made songs about their wrestling heroes. The Nova's hit it big with "Do The Hammerlock" sung in a voice emulating The Crusher. The record, now worth $50, became a top-requested song in the Midwest and even broke the highly respectable Billboard Top 100. If the Crusher had his way, he would have probably done a rendition of "The Beer Barrel Polka." But the Nova's song remains popular among collectors. The Cleavers did a song called "Playboy Buddy Rose" and the Turnbuckles did "Super Destroyer Mark II," $15. Certainly, other regional acts have cut wrestling-related songs as well. Insiders remark that the late Big John Studd cut a country album sometime during his career. If so, that record is very rare and would surely top the price lists at fan conventions for $20. Wrestler Sweet Daddy Siki has also made musical hits, which can be had for $20. In Japan, the combination of women's wrestling and pop music go hand in hand.

The paths of rockers and wrestlers have often crossed and will continue to do so. Wrestlers seem to be fascinated with being accepted by the mainstream and rockers continue to be fascinated by pro wrestling. For many, like the Sandman, Honky Tonk Man or Zumhoff, the rock alliance helped them become main event performers. For some, like rapper Master P, getting into wrestling was nearly career suicide. The appeal will forever be present. Nothing else encompasses America's freedom of expression and passion like pro wrestling and Rock and Roll.

Some select records

Hulk Hogan and the Wrestling Boot Band, 1995 $5.00

WWF Full Metal the Album (theme music) $20.00

Wrestlemania the Album (theme songs) $25.00

WWF The Music Volume 2, 1997, Koch Records $25.00

Stone Cold Metal Music, Mars Entertainment, (various artists), 1998 $25.00

WWF Volume 1: The Wrestling Album, 1985 $20.00

WWF Volume 3: Official Themes of the WWF, 1999 $20.00

WWF Volume 4, 1999 $20.00

WCW Slamjam, Grand Theft productions, 1992 (theme music) $20.00

Freebirds Badstreet USA, Grand Theft Productions, 1987 $15.00

Badstreet USA the Video, 1984, Grand Theft productions $20.00

ECW Extreme Music CD, CMC Records, 1998 $20.00

chapter 10

Autographs

Autographs are fun for collectors. They are special because, if you are an autograph seeker yourself, it allows you an opportunity to meet the wrestler and come away with a lifetime memory. Wrestlers are unique among professional athletes in that they are easily accessible for signings and they usually don't hold fans up for hostage like some big league ballplayers.

In the 1990s, every wrestler—from heel to babyface—is willing to sign. But that wasn't always true. Back in the '50s, '60s and '70s, when wrestling was much more close-lipped, the bad guys really didn't sign autographs. They were under a strict case of conduct that in public they would continue their "persona" like they played on TV. Nowadays, it's just as easy to get a Scott autograph as it is a Buff Bagwell signature. Top bad guys from the Golden Age are worth a lot more because of that.

Most autographs can be found for anywhere from $5 to $100. Only a few, like Andre the Giant, can fetch even more. But for the most part, collecting wrestlers' autographs is an easy, worthwhile investment. Royal Duncan is an avid signature collector and has also published various sporting event programs. But his biggest motivation is his collection of autographs. As Bill Cosby once prophetically stated, "It started out as a child," and so did Duncan's collection. Duncan began by keeping the first signature he ever got—boxer Jack Dempsey—who his father met while at a New York steakhouse. Thirty years later, Duncan has more than 3,000 individual autographs, with most of them being from wrestlers.

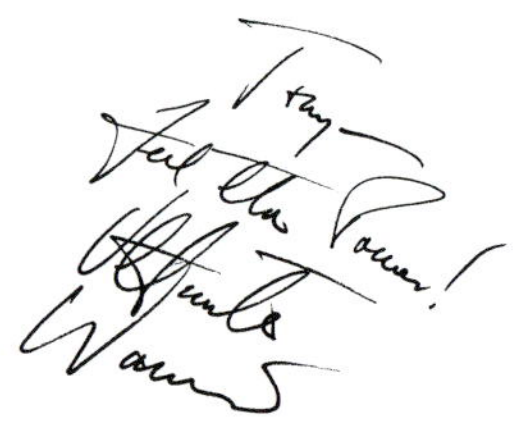

Some signatures from Tony Friedman's collection include this autograph from Ultimate Warrior.

Vince McMahon.

George "The Animal" Steele.

Bret "Hitman" Hart.

"Too Sexy" Brian Christopher.

Jimmy Hart.

"Rocket" Owen Hart.

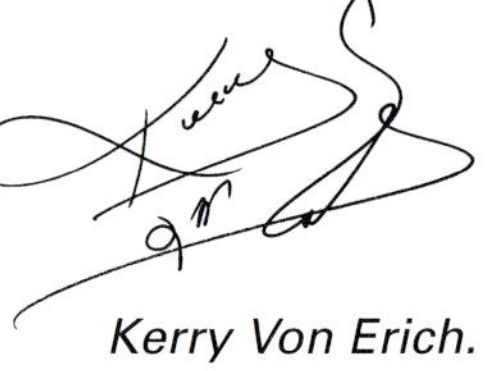

Kerry Von Erich.

Rick "Dog Face" Steiner.

Sgt. Slaughter.

Abdullah the Butcher's signature is worth $35.

Adrian Baillargeons' autograph is worth $35.

An autograph of Andre the Giant, shown here with the Musketeers, can fetch up to $120, possibly more.

Tony Friedman is a newer autograph collector. His passion has been tracking down WWF stars at the local hotels where they stay when in town for an event. "I usually stake out the lobby or bar after the matches," said Friedman. "They're always pretty good about it." Friedman's prized signatures are one each of Vince McMahon and the Ultimate Warrior. "Vince was so kind and generous, he even asked me if I wanted a picture. Warrior had his sunglasses on and didn't say much." He also has autographs from Rick Rude, Bret Hart, Hulk Hogan and more. As Friedman has found, the prices of signatures of wrestlers who have passed on increase dramatically. Owen Hart and Brian Pillman signatures are getting as much as $50. Bruiser Brody and Andre the Giant, two giants who died young, have valuable signatures—a testament to the overwhelming love that fans still have for them.

Other ways that autographs increase in value is when a wrestler appears under different names. Take Minneapolis collector Mick Karch. He has a picture signed by Bob Remus, the Super Destroyer and Sgt. Slaughter. Although he became a legend as Slaughter, Mr. Remus signed all three of his "names." Also, autographs of wrestlers like the Blade Runners (who later went on to individual success as Sting and Warrior) or Oz (who later used the names Diesel and Kevin Nash) are big on collector's lists as well.

In the list below, keen fans may realize that some wrestlers appear twice, with different names, of course.

1-2-3 Kid $25
Abdul Wizal $15
Abe Kashey $25
Abudah Dein $18
Abdulah the Butcher . . .$35
Ace Steele $8
Adam Bomb $12
Adrian Adonis $25
Adrian Street $15
Ahmed Johnson $20
Aja Kong $10
Akeem $30
Akio Sato $4
Akira Maeda $30
Akira Taue $12
Al Costello $25
Al Madril $20
Al Perez $12
Al Snow $20
Al Tomko $10
Alex Karras $20
Alex Wright $12
Alexis Smirnoff $15
Alfred Hayes $15
Ali Baba $75
Amish Roadkill $6
Angelo Mosca $15
Angelo Poffo $20
Angelo Savoldi $13
Animal $10
Anne Gunkel $15
Antonio Rocca $100
Argentine Apollo $30
Arn Anderson $15
Arnaold Skaaland $22
Art Barr $25
Art Neilson $20
Asya $10
Atsushi Onita $35
Austin Idol $10

The autograph of Superstar Billy Graham, shown here with The Wizard, is worth $25.

If you have the signature of Bill "Mr. M" Miller, it's worth $25.

Avalanche $12
Avatar $20
Ax $10
Axl Rotten $10
B.A. $25
B.B. $20
Baby Doll $10
Bad Man Jose Quintero . .$35
Bad News Allen Coage . . .$40
Bad News Brown $30
Balls Mahoney $12
Bam Bam Bigelow $15
Barbarian $8
Baron Scicula $20
Baron Von Raschke $20
Barry Horowitz $10
Barry Orton $15
Barry Windham $10
Bart Batten $10
Bart Gunn $10
Bart Sawyer $6
Bastion Booger $12
Batman $30
Bearcat Wright $22
Beef Wellington $20
Beetlejuice $35
Ben Sharpe $15
Bert Prentice $19
Bertha Faye $12

Beryln $14
Betty Grabel $25
Beulah $15
Big Bossman $10
Big Bubba Rogers $25
Big Daddy Falcone $12
Big Daddy Ritter $30
Big Daddy Siki $35
Big Dick Dudley $10
Big Juicer $5
Big K $20
Big Van Vader $25
Bill Alphonso $10
Bill Apter $10
Bill Dromo $15
Bill Dundee $8
Bill Eadie $25
Bill Irwin $12
Bill Melby $25
Bill Mulkey $12
Bill Watts $18
Billy Anderson $5
Billy Blaze $4
Billy Gunn $19
Billy Jack Haynes $12
Billy Kidman $17
Billy Longson $40
Billy Red Cloud $25
Billy Robinson $40
Billy White Wolf $30
Black Gordman $20
Black Tiger $18
Blackjack Lanza $12
Blackjack Mulligan $16
Blade Runners $35
Blue Blazer $200

Blue Demon Jr. $25
Blue Demon $75
Blue Meanie $10
Bob Armstrong $12
Bob Backlund $20
Bob Brown $15
Bob Caudle $10
Bob Geigel $15
Bob Mulkey $10
Bob Orton $12
Bobby Blaze $4
Bobby Bradley $6
Bobby Dean $10
Bobby Duncum $15
Bobby Duncum Jr. $30
Bobby Eaton $10
Bobby Fulton $10
Bobby Heenan $30
Bobby Jaggers $15
Bobby Managoff $50
Bobby Shane $35
Bolo Mongol $25
Boo Bradley $13
Booker T $19
Boris Barishnikoff $25
Boris Malenko $25
Boris Zukoff $12
Boyd Pierce $17
Brad Anderson $9

The Crusher's autograph fetches $25.

Brad Armstrong $10
Brad Batten $10
Brad Rheingans $12
Bradshaw $12
Brady Boone $35
Brandi Alexander $20
Brandon Baxter $6
Brazo De Ora $15
Brazo DePlata $18
Bret Hart $25
Brett Sawyer $8
Brian Adams $10
Brian Armstrong $10
Brian Blair $10
Brian Christopher $8
Brian Knobs $12
Brian Lee $10
Brian Pillman $55
Brickhouse Brown $10
British Bulldogs $25
Bronko Lubich $20
Bronko Nagurski $80
Brother Love $20
Bruce Hart $12
Bruce Reed $12
Bruce Swayze $12
Bruise Brothers $20
Bruiser Bedlam $8
Bruiser Brody $110
Bruiser Mastino $6
Bruno Sammartino $18
Brute Bernard $30
Brutus Beefcake $8
Buck Robley $12
Buck Zumhoff $5
Buddy Landell $8
Buddy Lee $15
Buddy Roberts $8
Buddy Rogers $45
Buddy Rose $10
Buddy Wayne $7
Buff Bagwell $24
Bugsy McGraw $11
Bull Bullinski $15
Bull Nakano $30
Bull Pain $5
Bulldog Brower $33
Bushwacker Butch $12
Bushwacker Luke $12
Bushwackers $15
Butch Miller $12
Butch Reed $10
Buzz Sawyer $8
Buzz Stern $8
C.W. Anderson $10
Cactus Jack Manson $35
Cactus Jack $25
Canadian Wolfman $65
Candi Divine $15
Candyman $25
Carlos Colon $20
Carlos Colon Jr. $15
Chad Brock $10
Charles Robinson $11
Charlie Norris $6
Chavo Guerrero $15
Chaz $10
Cheetah Kid $15
Chick Donovan $8
Chicky Starr $15
Chief Big Heart $15
Chief Don Eagle $25
Chigusa Nagayo $35
Chris Adams $12
Chris Benoit $20
Chris Candido $12
Chris Champion $10
Chris Colt $25
Chris Cruise $6
Chris Jericho $20
Chris Love $25
Chris Markoff $20
Chris Taylor $35
Chris Tolos $25
Chris Von Erich $50
Chris Youngblood $10
Christian $12
Chyna $20
Ciclone Anaya $14
Cocoa Samoa $7
Col. DeBeers $15
Col. Robert Parker $10
Colorado Kid $10
Conquistador $15
Count Billy Varga $18
Cousin Junior $10
Cousin Luke $12
Cowboy Bob Ellis $35
Cpl. Kirschner $5
Crash Holly $15
Crush $10

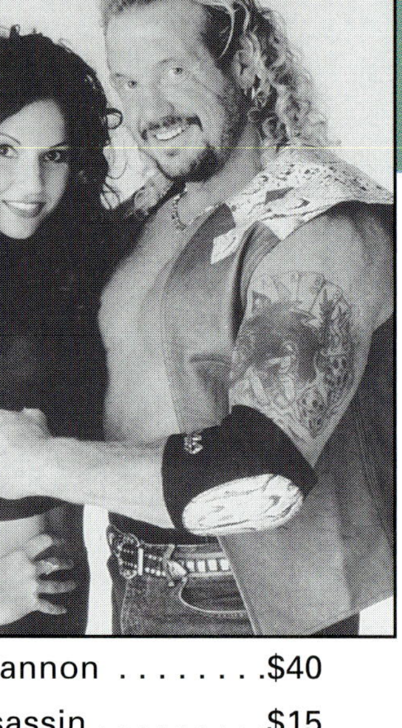

Kimberly and Diamond Dallas Page: Her autograph is worth $20; his is worth $25.

Expect to pay $20 to get the autograph of Elizabeth.

Crybaby Cannon $40
Cuban Assassin $15
Curly Cutler $100
Curt Hennig $15
Curtis Thompson $10
Cyrus $10
D.C. Drake $12
D.J. Peterson $15
Dale Lewis $10
Damien $10
Damien Demento $13
Dan Kroffat $8
Dan Severn $16
Dances with Wolves
Dudley $13
Danno O'Mahoney $50
Danny Davis (ref) $20
Danny Dominion $9
Danny Hodge $50
Danny McShane $16
Danny Spivey $12
Dave Brown $15
Dave Hebner $10
Dave Taylor $5
Davey Boy Smith $18
David Cash $5
David Crockett $9
David Flair $12
David Sammartino $12
David Schultz $45
David Sierra $6
Dean Higuchi $15
Dean Ho $12
Dean Malenko $8
Debbie Combs $15
Debra $20
Del Wilkes $15
Demolition $10
Dennis Condrey $8
Derrick Dukes $8
Derrick King $6
Destroyer $75
Devil Masami $25
Dewey Robertson $20
Diamond Lil $10
Dick Beyer $35
Dick Hutton $40
Dick Murdoch $20
Dick Shikat $75
Dick Slater $12
Dick Steinborne $25
Dick the Bruiser $25
Dick Togo $10
Diesel $30
Ding Dong #1 . . . .$35
Ding Dong #2 . . . .$25
Dingo Warrior $25
Dino Bravo $20
Dirt Bike Kid $7
Dirty Dick Raines $25
Dirty White Boy $11
Dirty White Girl $12
Disco Inferno $15
Dixie Little Cloud $40
Dizzy Ed Boulder $15
D-Lo Brown $15
DOA $10
Doink the Clown $8
Don Jardine $20
Don Kernodle $16
Don Leo Jonathan $50
Don Muraco $12
Don Stevens $22
Don Owes $20
Dory Dixon $35
Dory Funk Jr. $18
Dory Funk Sr. $60
Doug Fernas $8
Doug Gilbert Jr. $10
Doug Gilbert Sr. $35
Doug Somers $12
Downtown Bruno $15
Dr. Jerry Graham $18
Dr. Ken Ramey $15
Dr. Tom Pritchard $20
Dr. X $35
Droz $30
Dude Love $25
Duke Keomaka $30
Dump Matsumoto $25
Dustin Rhodes $18
Dusty Rhodes $25
Dutch Mantell $15
Dutch Savage $10

Goldberg's autograph is holding strong at $35.

The value of Hulk Hogan's John Hancock is $40.

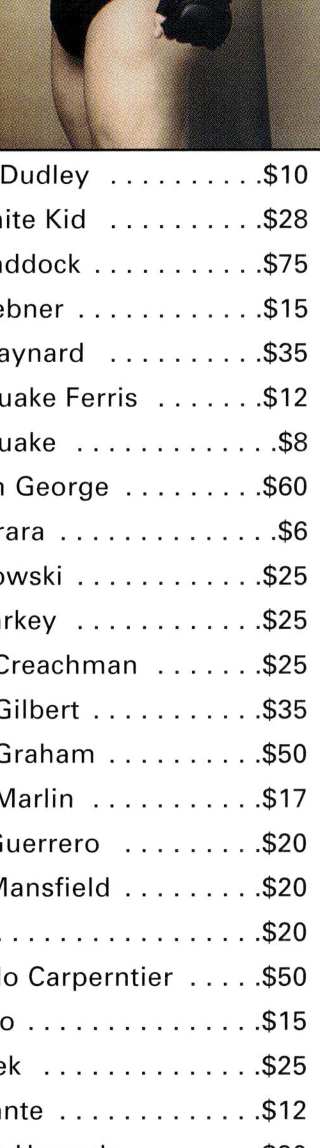

D-Von Dudley $10
Dynamite Kid $28
Earl Caddock $75
Earl Hebner $15
Earl Maynard $35
Earthquake Ferris $12
Earthquake $8
Ed Don George $60
Ed Ferrara $6
Ed Lisowski $25
Ed Sharkey $25
Eddie Creachman $25
Eddie Gilbert $35
Eddie Graham $50
Eddie Marlin $17
Eddy Guerrero $20
Eddy Mansfield $20
Edge $20
Eduardo Carperntier $50
El Brazo $15
El Canek $25
El Gigante $12
El Gran Hamada $20
El Gran Markus $16
El Santo $100
Emil Dusek $6
Equalizer $8
Eric Bischoff $20
Eric Embry $6

Eric the Red $40
Erin O'Grady $10
Ernest Miller $13
Ernie Dusek $6
Ernie Ladd $20
Evad Sullivan $20
Evan Keragous $15
Everett Marshall $50
Fabulous Moolah $15
Fantastics $25
Firefighter Chip $15
Fishman $20
Fit Finlay $12
Flying Fred Curry $15
Frank Baillargeon $35
Frank Dusek $6
Frank Gotch $75
Frank Townsend $75
Frankie Hill $15
Fred Blassie $50
Freddy Miller $15
Frenchy Martin $20
Fuerza Guerrera $15
Gama Singh $20
Gangrel $10
Gary Albright $35
Gary Capetta $10
Gary Hart $12
Gary Royal $5
Gary Young $5
Geeto Mongol $15
Gene Anderson $35
Gene Lebell $20
Gene Okerlund $10
Gene Stanley $30
General Adnan $12

Geno Hernandez $45
Gentleman Chris Adams . .$25
George Gordienko $30
George Scott $10
George Steele $15
George Takano $12
George Weingeroff $15
Getto Mongol $25
Giant Haystacks $20
Gino Hernandez $25
Glenn Osborne $10
Gobbledy gooker $50
Godfather $15
Godwinns $10
Goldberg $35
Golden Terror $20
Goldust $35
Golga $30
Gordon Solie $12
Gorgeous George (woman) .$15
Gorgeous George $150
Gorilla Monsoon $50
Gory Guerrero $30
Greg Gagne $9
Grand Wizard $25
Great Dane $20
Great Goliath $20
Great Muta $20
Great Tenyru $55

One-time world tag-team champs Jackie Fargo, left, and Don Stevens. Fargo's signature is worth $50, while Stevens is worth $22.

In an unusual demonstration of strength, staged during a live TV show in Pittsburgh, Canadian Joe LeDuc holds off eight men who try in vain to pull his arms apart. It's stuff like this that make LeDuc's autograph worth $45.

Greg Valentine $15
Grizzly Smith $15
Gus Sonnenberg $120
Guy Mitchell $15
Gypsy Joe $16
Hacksaw Reed $17
Haiti Kid $35
Haku $8
Hans Herman $15
Hans Schmidt $35
Hard Boiled Haggerty $25
Hardcore Hak $25
Hardcore Holly $8
Harley Race $22
Harold Sakata $30
Hawk $10
Headhunter #1 . . . .$20
Headhunter #2 . . . .$20
Heavy Metal $10
Hector Garza $15
Hector Guerrero $20
Hellraisers $5
Henri de Glane $50
Hercules Ayala $25
Hercules Cortez $25
Hercules $8
High Voltage $12
Hillbilly Jim $10

Hiro Hase $15
Hiro Matsda $20
Hiro Saito $10
Honky Tonk Man $10
Horace Boulder $7
Horace the Psychopath . . .$10
Horst Hoffman $17
Howard Finkel $15
Hugh Morrus $10
Hugo Savinovich $20
Hurricane Castillo $20
Hurricane Castillo Jr. $12
Ian Rotten $10
Ian Xavier $3
Iceman Parsons $20
Ilio DiPaolo $30
Inferos $25
Iron Mike Sharpe $10
Iron Sheik $20
Italian Stallion $10
Ivan Kalmikoff $25
Ivan Koloff $40
Ivan Putski $18
J.B. Trask $1
J.J. Dillon $12
J.R. Ryder $3
J.T. Smith $10
J.T. Styles $6

J.W. Storm $5
Jack Armstrong $12
Jack Brickhouse $55
Jack Brisco $20
Jack Dalton $10
Jack Dusek $6
Jack Foley $45
Jack Victory $7
Jackie $12
Jackie Fulton $10
Jacques Rougeau $20
Jake Millimen $12
Jake Roberts $10
Jamie Dundee $7

Johnny B. Badd's autograph is worth $15.

Kevin Nash's autographs are pushing the $40 mark.

A signature of wrestling legend Gene Kiniski is worth $50.

The signature of Ken Patera is worth $10.

Jason the Terrible $15
Jay Strongbow $10
Jazz $12
Jean Leveque $20
Jeep Swenson $15
Jeff Jarrett $15
Jerry Blackwell $20
Jerry Brisco $15
Jerry Flynn $11
Jerry Jarrett $15
Jerry Lawler $25
Jerry Lynn $12
Jerry Morrow $7
Jerry Oates $15
Jerry Oski $12
Jerry Saggs $15
Jerry Valiant $20
Jesse Barr $10
Jesse James $20
Jesse James Armstrong . .$17
Jesse Ventura $50
Jetty Christy $7
Jim Barnett $15
Jim Browning $50
Jim Brunzell $10
Jim Cornette $8
Jim Crockett $10

Jim Duggan $11
Jim Herd $30
Jim Londos $120
Jim Niedhart $14
Jim Powers $5
Jim Ross $8
Jim Steele $8
Jimmy Backlund $10
Jimmy Garvin $12
Jimmy Golden $11
Jimmy Hart $15
Jimmy Jack Funk $24
Jimmy Snuka $12
Jimmy Valiant $12

Collecting the autographs of the Von Erich clan will get you more than $100. Individually, Kevin's signature is worth $25, David's is worth $40 and Kerry's is $45.

Jody Hamilton $8
Joe Blanchard $30
Joe LeDuc $45
Joe Malenko $20
Joe Panzandeck $40
Joe Savoldi $12
Joe Scarpa $10
Joe Scarpello $11
Joe Snyder $8
Joe Stecher $50
Joel Gertner $14
Joey Morella $25
Joey Styles $6
John Rambo $13
John Studd $45
John Tenta $20
John Tolos $25
Johnny Ace $10
Johnny Barend $15
Johnny Eagles $7
Johnny Grunge $10
Johnny Love $3
Johnny Polo $30
Johnny Powers $35
Johnny Rich $10
Johnny Rodz $12
Johnny Rougeau $50

Lex Luger's autographs fetch $25.

The autograph of Lord Littlebrook is worth $40.

Johnny Smith $8
Johnny Valentine $55
Johnny Valiant $10
Johnny War Eagles $7
Johnny Weaver $13
Jonathan Boyd $25
Jonathan Holiday $10
Jonnie Stewart $12
Jose Gonzalez $20
Jose Luis Rivera $10
Jules Strongbow $12
Julio Magnifico $5
Jumbo Tsuruta $55
Junkyard Dog $25
Jushin Liger $25
Justin Credible $10
Juventud Guerrera $12
Kabuki $20
Kama $20
Kamala $30
Kane $26
Kanyon $15
Karate Kid $10
Karl Gotch $150
Karl Kalmikoff $20
Karl Pope $8
Karl Von Hess $13
Kato Kung Lee $35
Keiji Muto $30

Kelly Kiniski $20
Ken Johnson $10
Ken Mantell $10
Ken Shamrock $20
Ken Timbs $12
Ken Wayne $12
Kendall Windham $8
Kendo Nagasaki $13
Kenny Jay $15
Kenny Yates $15
Kensuke Sasaki $12
Kenta Kobashi $20
Kentuckians $35
Kerry Brown $9
Kevin Kelly $6
Kevin Lawler $8
Kevin Sullivan $15
Killer Khan $20
Killer Kowalski $12
Kim Duk $20
Kimala $45
Kimala II $13
Kimona $20
King Curtis $40
King Kong Bundy $35
King Mabel $15
Kinji Shibya $22
Kip Frey $20
Kokina Maximus $20
Koko B. Ware $10
Konnan $15
Kosrow Vasari $30
Kronus $10
Krusher Broomfield $35
Krusher Kowalski $15
Kurt Angle $27

Kurt Von Brauner $10
Kurt Von Hess $13
La Fierra $18
La Parka $11
Lady Blossom $50
Lance Russell $25
Lance Von Erich $20
Larry Heinimi $20
Larry Hennig $15
Larry Santo $6
Larry Shane $10
Larry Sharpe $12
Larry Simon $35
Larry Zbyszko $20
Lars Anderson $20
Lash LaRoux $9
Lazer Tron $50
Lelani Kai $15
Len Denton $10
Len Montana $25
Lenny Lane $10
Lenny Montana $40
Leo Burke $9
Leo Nomellini $25
Leon White $50
Les Thatcher $10
Les Thornton $10
Lioness Asuka $25
Little Bear $50

The signature of Rocky Johnson will get you $15.

Road Dogg's signature hits the $20 mark.

Little Coco $10
Little Guido $10
Little Kato $10
Lizmark $25
Loch Ness $20
Lodi $10
Lord James Blears $25
Lord Layton $15
Lord Oliver Humperdink . .$20
Lord Steven Regal $12
Lord Zoltan $10
Lou Albano $15
Lou Thesz $35
Louis Siclo $60
Luke Brown $15
Luke Graham $35
Luna $15
Mad Man Pondo $6
Madusa Micelli $10
Mae Young $15
Magnum T.A. $25
Mahkan Singh $12
Man Mountain Mike $30
Mando Guerrero $20
Mankind $25
Manny Fernandez $15
Mantaur $9
Marc Mero $12
Marissa Mazzola $10

Mark Ash $6
Mark Dudley $10
Mark Henry $15
Mark Lewin $22
Mark Rocco $12
Mark Starr $8
Mark Tendler $10
Mark Youngblood $10
Martin $20
Marty Janetty $10
Marty O'Neil $50
Masa Fuchi $15
Masa Funaki $13
Masked Superstar $25
Matt Borne $10
Matt Burns $5
Maurice Vachone $25
Maxx Payne $20
Mel Phillips $15
Meng $10
Merced Solis $30
Michael Cole $8
Michael Hayes $12
Michele Starr $8
Mick Foley $35
Mick Karch $8
Mideon $5
Mighty Igor $20
Mighty Inoue $20
Mighty Mo $8
Mighty Zulu $11

Miguel Perez $14
Mike Boyette $15
Mike DiBiase $25
Mike George $7
Mike Graham $15
Mike Jackson $4
Mike Jones $20
Mike Lozansky $8
Mike Mazurky $25
Mike Rotunda $8
Mike Shaw $7
Mike Tenay $5
Mike Von Erich $40
Mikey Whipwreck $12
Mil Mascaras $22
Mini Max $20
Miss Texas $12
Missing Link $25
Missy Hyatt $15
Misty Blue Simmes $20
Mitch Paradise $5
Mitch Ryder $2
Mitch Snow $12
Mitsu Irakawa $30
Mitsuhara Misawa $50
Mongolian Stomper $17
Monster Singh $30
Moondog Mayne $25
Moondog Moretti $7
Moose Cholok $15
Moose Morowski $8

An autograph of Ric Flair goes for $50.

Scott Hall's autograph is worth $27.

The signature of Scotty the Body is worth $20.

Mosh $8
Mr. Fuji $8
Mr. Hughes $10
Mr. M $50
Mr. Moto $25
Mr. Perfect $15
Mr. Pogo $15
Mr. Saito $35
Mr. Wrestling I $20
Mr. Wrestling II $20
Nacho Bererra $35
Nailz $30
Nasty Boys $12
Negro Casas $25
Nelson Royal $5
New Jack $15
Nick Bockwinkel $20
Nick Kiniski $20
Nicolai Volkoff $10
Nicole Bass $12
Nightmare Dan Davis $12
Nikita Koloff $12
Nikolai Volkoff $10
Nobuhiko Takada $12
Nord the Barbarian $15
Norman Smiley $12
Norman the Lunatic $15

Norvell Austin $18
Oklahoma $15
Ole Anderson $30
One Man Gang $10
Orion $6
Otto Wanz $35
Outback Jack $19
Owen Hart $65
Ox Baker $25
Oz $50
Pampero Ferpo $35
Pat Barrett $25
Pat Patterson $10
Pat Tanaka $20
Paul Bearer $10
Paul Boesch $25
Paul Christo $12
Paul Christy $8
Paul E. Dangerously $10
Paul Ellering $12
Paul Jones $12
Paul Neu $15
Paul Orndorf $10
Paul Roma $5
Paul Vachone $25
Pedro Martinez $25
Pedro Morales $25

Pepper Gomez $20
Pepper Martin $20
Percy Pringle $12
Perro Aguayo $25
Perry Saturn $10
Peter Polaco $15
Pez Whatley $7
Phil Hickerson $12
Phil LeFlon $8
Pierroth $15
Pit Bull #1 . . . .$10
Pit Bull #2 . . . .$10
Pitrata Morgan $22
Plowboy Frazier $15
PN News $15
Precious $12
Predator $8
Prime Time $5
Primo Carnarra $100
Prince Albert $12
Prince Iakea $10
Princes Little Dove $15
Psicosis $15
Queen Kong $7
Ralph Halpern $15
Randy Gusto $6
Randy Savage $30

While the autograph of Stone Cold Steve Austin is in demand for $40, the autograph of Stunning Steve Austin, as he was called in his WCW days, is worth $75. Stunning Steve is shown here with Jeanne.

Wrestling legend Ed "Strangler" Lewis' autograph hits the mark at $100. Lewis, once a heavyweight champion, left the ring to run a successful restaurant and cocktail bar. In this 1945 photo, he puts a toe-hold on a lamb chop.

Ranger Ross $7
Raven $20
Ravishing Ronnie $13
Ray Candy $15
Ray Gunkel $25
Ray McCartney $15
Ray Steele $40
Raymond Rougeau $20
Razor Ramon $35
Reckless Youth $10
Red Bastein $25
Red Berry $55
Red Lyons $25
Red Rooster $50
Red Sutton $30
Reggie Lisowski $50
Reggie Parks $25
Rene Goulet $15
Reno Riggins $8
Rey Mysterio Jr. $15
Rhino $10
Rhonda Singh $15
Richard Charland $15
Rick Bassman $4
Rick Link $5
Rick Martel $5
Rick Patterson $10
Rick Rude $60
Rick Steiner $10

Ricky Chosu $55
Ricky Fuji $15
Ricky Morton $15
Ricky Santana $5
Ricky Starr $40
Ricky Steamboat $15
Rikidozan $110
Rikishi Fatu $25
Rip Hawk $10
Ripper Collins $20
Ripper Savage $12
Rob Van Dam $16
Robert Gibson $15
Rocco Rock $10
Rockin' Robin Smith 30
Rocky Delassera $10
Rocky Hamilton $10
Roddy Piper $25
Rogeau Brothers $20
Roger Kirby $8
Ron Bass $10
Ron DuPree $15
Ron Fuller $15
Ron Garvin $10
Ron Ritchie $10
Ron Simmons $20
Ron Starr $10
Rufus Jones $10
Rusher Kimura $18

Russ Francis $15
Rusty Brooks $5
Ryuma Go $20
S.D. Jones $5
Saba Simba $35
Sable $40
Sabu $20
Sailor Art Thomas $50
Sal Bellomo $13
Sal Graziano $10
Salofa Fatu $25
Sam DiCero (Super Maxx) .$12
Sam Houston $6
Sam Meneker $20
Sam Muchnick $25
Sam Steamboat $40
Samoan Samu $5
Sandman $15
Sandy Barr $10
Sandy Scott $10
Sapphire $10
Satoru Sayama $50
Saturn $10
Saul Weingroff $20
Savanah Jack $10
Savio Vega $6
Scandor Szabo $50
Scary Sherri $35
Scorpio $8

Scott Armstrong $12
Scott Casey $6
Scott Hudson $5
Scott Irwin $25
Scott Norton $8
Scott Putski $6
Scott Steiner $8
Scott Taylor $8
Scotty Levy $20
Scotty Riggs $8
Scrap Iron Gadaski $13
Sean Waltman $25
Sgt. Slaughter $12
Shane Douglas $10
Shane McMahon $24
Shawn Michaels $25
Sheik Farhat $50
Sherri Martel $25
Shinya Hashimoto $10
Shiro Koshinaka $10
Sho Funaki $10
Shotgun Gage $5
Sid Vicious $15
Sign Guy Dudley $10
Siki Afa $15
Silver King $20
Siva Afi $15
Skandor Akbar $10
Skull Murphy $30
Sky Hi Lee $15
Slick $12
Soldat Ustinov $7
Sonny King $20
Sonny McMahon $35
Sonny Rogers $12
Soul Taker $15
Spike Dudley $20
Spike Huber $5
Spiros Arion $25
Sputnik Montroe $25
Stan Gagne $15
Stan Hansen $25
Stan Kowalski $15
Stan Lane $10
Stanislaus Zbyszko $100
Stephanie McMahon $35
Steve Armstrong $12
Steve Austin $40
Steve Blackman $10
Steve Casey $40
Steve Corino $5
Steve Doll $9
Steve Druk $35
Steve Gatorwolf $10
Steve Keirn $15
Steve Lombardi $10
Steve McMichael $15
Steve Olsonoski $4
Steve Regal $5
Steve Stanley $30
Steve Strong $10
Steve Williams $8
Stevie Ray $12
Sting $30
Sunny $20
Sunny War Cloud $15
Sunshine $12
Super Calo $12
Super Crazy $15
Super D $25
Super D Mark II $20
Super Parka $7
Super Zebra Kid $45
Swede Hanson $15
Swedish Angel $25
Tajiri $10
Taka Michinoku $12
Tammy Lynn $10
Tarzan Goto $13
Tarzan Tyler $25
Tatanka $12
Tatsumi Fujinami $55
Tazz $20
Ted Arcidi $10
Ted Arcidi $10
Ted Dibiase $15
Ted Oates $6
Teddy Long $12
Terminator Cro $15
Terminator Riggs $12
Terminator Wolf $12
Terri Runnels $15
Terry Bolder $55
Terry Funk $13
Terry Garvin $25
Terry Gordy $10
Terry Taylor $12
Test $15
Tex McKenzie $12
The Big Show $20
The Coach $35
The Crusher $40
The Genuis $10
The Goon $13
The Grappler $8
The Hater $8
The Juicer $20
The Maestro $11

The Patriot $20
The Rock $30
The Samoans $12
The Spolier $25
The Terminator $13
The Wall $11
Thrasher $8
Thunderbolt Patterson . . .$15
Thunderfoot $10
Tiger Ali Singh $12
Tiger Chung Lee $20
Tiger Conway Jr. $11
Tiger Conway Sr. $15
Tiger Mask $30
Tiger Singh $25
Tim Brooks $5
Tim Flowers $10
Tim Horner $15
Tim Hunt $2
Tim Woods $25
Tiny Lister/Zeus $30
Tiny Mills $25
Tito Santana $10
T-Joe Khan $15
TNT $25
Todd Champion $15
Todd Morton $7
Todd Pettingill $11
Tojo Yamamoto $16
Tokyo Joe $20
Tom Zenk $8
Tommy Dreamer $15
Tommy Gilbert $30
Tommy Rich $17
Tommy Rogers $10
Tommy Young $15
Tonga Kid $25
Tony Altamore $20
Tony Atlas $12
Tony DeNucci $2
Tony Falk $3
Tony Galento $45
Tony Garea $13
Tony Leone $12
Tony Marinara $3
Tony Marino $12
Tony Parisi $25
Tony Shiavone $8
Tony Stecher $25
Torrie Wilson $15
Toru Tanaka $25
Tracy Smothers $10
Triple H $25
Troy Graham $11
Truth Commission $15
Tug Taylor $10
Tugboat $10
Tully Blanchard $14
Typhoon $10
Uganda $12
Ultimate Warrior $35
Ultimo Dragon $20
Ultraman $12
Undertaker #2 . . . .$50
Undertaker $45
Val Venis $25
Vampiro $20
Van Hammer $10
Verne Gagne $25
Vic Grimes $6
Vic Steamboat $10
Vic Venom $6
Victor Jovica $20
Victor Rivera $25
Vince McMahon $20
Vince Russo $12
Vincent $10
Vinnie Vegas $50
Viscera $10
Vivian Vachone $30
Waldo Von Erich $40
Wally Karbo $22
Warlord $7
Warren Bockwinkel $35
Wayne Farris $15
Wayne Munn $75
Waynona Little Heart $50
Wendi Richter $12
Whipper Watson $75
Wilbur Snyder $15
Wild Bull Curry $50
Wildman Jack Armstrong .$12
Wolf Hawkfield $10
Wolfie D $7
Woman $18
Woody Strode $35
Wrath $15
X-Pac $20
Yojo Anjo $20
Yokozuna $8
Yoshi Fujiwara $25
Yukon Eric $50
Yvon Robert $50
Zebra Kid $30

chapter 11

The Internet

Like a secret fishing hole or quaint coffee shop, a true collector knows of that special, secret place that he or she can go to find that one certain gem that will make their collection complete.

First, there is the attic, where dad or big brother stashed their old mementos over the years. Then we have the local flea market or garage sales, where one can find just about anything if the stars are in line and luck is on our side. Of course, we can't forget the underground network of fellow fans that everyone knows. One can have a lot of success going to the ones he or she knows—like a friend of a friend—and find that special something. But now, with the boom of the Internet, wrestling fans are finding that going online is the best way to hunt for the right item at the right price, day or night.

There are several sites worth mentioning. The best of the best is, of course, eBay—the 'Net's premiere auction site. If you've never heard of, or used, eBay, it's pretty simple, really. First log on to its website (www.ebay.com). Users register their name and e-mail address into the database and that's all that's required to buy a product. Just enter a keyword for the item you are looking for, such as, "Rock action figure" and every item that falls into that category will appear. Look through what each seller is offering and make a bid, like a real auction. Check back each day and see if any other people have made any higher bids. You can bid as often as you like. If you have the winning bid, it's up to you to negotiate with the seller over how much the item will be sold for, who will pay for shipping, and how you will receive it. You can make an unlimited number of bids for an unlimited number of items. Most bid periods are over in a week, so don't expect to "win your bid" right away. And even if you place the winning bid, you aren't obligated to buy. So, if you have second thoughts, no problem.

During a recent look, a fan could simply enter the keyword "wrestling" and be steered toward an astounding 2,500 different pieces of pro-wrestling merchandise and collectibles. Everything from never-used tickets to a 1940s' Gorgeous George match from Los Angeles to a "Stone Cold" Steve Austin autograph to canceled checks signed by people like Lou Thesz. In fact, if it's at all possible, there may be too many items. Certainly, with the right timing, any fan can find exactly the right item he or she needs.

A fine bonus to eBay is the ability to see the items before you make a bid. Many sellers have photos posted on the site for users to view. It's great for checking if it's really the item you want. The prices are fairly reasonable, too. When we peeked on eBay recently, we found an entire set of the Remco AWA action figures and wrestling ring from 1985 and bidding was starting at around $70—certainly a fair price for such a rare commodity. Most event programs sell for around $10-$20, but expect to pay a higher price for older, rarer and more significant programs or ones that are autographed. Advertising posters from old-time wrestling shows, like the kinds that we all remember from our local VFWs or Boys Club, are readily available and sell anywhere

Some fanatic wrestling fan recently forked over $10,000 for Sunny's old breast implants.

Many cool Sable collectibles can be found on the Internet.

Official merchandise for Sting, shown here in his earlier wrestling days, can be found at the WCW's website.

from $20-$50, depending on which wrestlers were advertised on the poster. Ones with photos or graphics are higher priced but well worth it if you are looking for, say, any item with Harley Race or Bruno Sammartino on it. More contemporary items like action figures are abundant here, if that's your area of interest. Video tapes are also quite popular as well.

More sites have popped up in recent years which sell the most current, mass-produced wrestling-related collectibles like those licensed by the World Wrestling Federation and World Championship Wrestling. Highspots (www.highspots.com) and Figures Inc. (www.wrestlingsuperstore.com) are two sites which boast an incredible amount of wrestling goodies, with fan friendly accessibility and service.

Highspots is our choice for finding anything related to Japan and Mexico's Lucha Libre. Original masks made of high-quality material and craftsmanship sell for about $50. Fans can find most of the newer-styled masks including replicas of ones worn by Rey Mysterio, Ultimo Dragon, La Parka, and Thunder Liger. Mexican and Japanese dolls seem to be Highspots' specialty and new items are posted on its website regularly. This is also a good site to find the most up-to-date foreign-packaged videos of some of the more obscure promotions in the Orient like Big Japan, Frontier Martial Arts, and Ultimo Dragon's Toryumon group.

Figures Inc., meanwhile, is the place to go if you're looking for anything related to WWF and WCW post-1985. It has virtually everything you need, from out-of-stock dolls to wrestling music to T-shirts. If it doesn't have it available through its online catalogue, Figures Inc. can put in a special order for you as well.

Of course, the granddaddy of finding the most current merchandise is the WWF and WCW websites. Why wait on line (at the arena shows, that is) for just a few of the hundreds of items that are available, when you can buy everything you want from one place?

At the WWF site (www.wwf.com) fans can find great T-shirts of harder-to-find grapplers like Edge, Christian, the Hardy Boyz and D-Lo Brown. Guys like Austin (who claims to design all of his own merchandise), the Undertaker, Mankind and the Rock have hundreds of different items for sale.

At WCW's site (www.wcw.com) the big names like Sting, Dallas Page, Lex Luger, Kevin Nash and Hollywood Hogan have a staggering amount of items for sale. These probably aren't going to be true collector's items one day, but they are fun novelty gifts, to be sure. Mugs, full lines of clothing, sleeping bags, toys and virtually everything a fan can think of are available here. Most of the items can't be found anywhere else. So, if fans want it, this is the only place to find it.

With the success of wwf.com, many independent wrestlers are beginning to see the benefit of the Internet and are starting their own websites to market their own merchandise. As you can see by the list that follows, the number of wrestlers using this vehicle to sell their stuff is ever-growing. For an up-to-date list, check out Georgiann Makropoulos' column on 1Wrestling.com

Fans of Canadian Crippler Chris Benoit can check out http://www.chrisbenoit.com.

Can't get enough of Buff Bagwell? Check out his site at http://www.buffstuffinc.com.

(www.1wrestling.com). Here, the wrestlers market themselves no differently than the ones in the big promotions. Joel Gertner, Chris Candido, Taz, Sunny, Sable and the Ultimate Warrior just to name some, have lots of neat items. Recently, Sunny even sold her—gasp!—old breast implants with an asking price of $10,000. Now that's what we call a serious piece of memorabilia.

With any purchases online, it's probably smart to do a little homework on the person you are buying from. The quality that you get is not always the quality that was promised. Our experience with wrestling collectors has by and large been reliable and honest. Below, is a current listing of wrestlers with websites. Most have collectibles for sale. Some of these sites are just fan-run websites. But they are all fun and informative:

Wrestlers online

Abudadein
http://www.abudadein.com

Afa and the Samoans
http://www.wildsamoan.com

Gary Albright
http://www.typhoonmedia.com/AIRPLEX

Arn Anderson
http://www.arnanderson4ever.com

Kurt Angle
http://www.goldwrestler.com/

Ted Arcidi
http://people.ne.mediaone.net/hartnett/arcidi/index.html

Steve Austin
http://www.stonecold.com

Mean Marc Ash
http://www.angelfire.com/nc/marcash/

Bob Backlund
http:// www.backlund2000.com

Penny Banner
http://www.geocities.com/colosseum/sideline/6292/penny.html

Nicole Bass
http://www.thevalkyrie.com/bass

Brandon Baxter
http://pages.prodigy.com/starlink/baxter.htm

Steve Blackman
http://www.rdsnet.com/~blackman/

B. Brian Blair
http://www.brianblair.com

Boni Blackstone
http://hometown.aol.com/ReecyClair/bonihome.html

The Blue Meanie
http://www.thebluemeanie.com/

Killer Tim Brooks
http://members.aol.com/unipromos/wrestle

D-Lo Brown
http://www.dlobrown.com/

Michael Buffer
http://www.letsrumble.com/

King Kong Bundy
http://www.kingkongbundy.com/

The Bushwhackers
http://www.wrestlingclassics.com/bushwhackers

Tammy Lynn Bytch (Dawn Marie)
http://www.wrestlingman.com/dawnmarie/

Chae (Nitro Girl)
http://www.chae.com

Chastity
http://www.chastitywrestling.com

Chad Collyer
www.chadcollyer.com

Steve Corino
http://www.stevecorino.com

Cyrus (Don "The Jackal" Callis)
http://freeweb.digiweb.com/sports/thejackal/

Christopher Daniels
http://www.christopherdaniels.com

Ted DiBiase
http://www.milliondollarman.com/

Danny Doring
http://wrestlingnation.com/doring/

Justin Credible puts a choke hold on Sabu. More photos of Justin in action can be found at http://www.ThatsJustinCredible.com.

Shane Douglas
http://www.shanedouglas.com

Tommy Dreamer
http://members.aol.com/ECWTommy2/arena.html

Dudley Boyz
http://www.thedudleyboyz.com/

Bobby Duncum, Jr.
http://www.bobbyduncumjr.com/

Frank Dusek
http://www.wrestlingclassics.com/dusek

Francine
http://www.francineecw.com

Dory Funk, Jr.
http://www.dory-funk.com/

Fyre (Teri Byrne)
e-mail address: wcwfyre@worldnet.att.net

Verne Gagne
http://www.awawrestling.com

Gorgeous George III
http://www.geocities.com/Colosseum/Court/5702/GORGEOUSGEORGEIII.html

Joel Gertner
http://davidfj.simplenet.com/gertner

Goldberg
http://www.jackhammer.net

Superstar Billy Graham
http://www.capital.net/com/bayeco/ssbilly1.html

Eddy Guerrero
http://www.eddysucks.com/

Billy Gunn
http://www.billygunn.com/

Randy Hales
http://pages.prodigy.com/starlink/hales.htm

Hardy Boyz
http://www.mattandjeffhardy.com/

Bret Hart
http://www.brethart.net/

Headshrinkers
http://www.typhoonmedia.com/Head

Headshrinker Samu
http://www.typhoonmedia.com/Samu

Bobby The Brain Heenan
http://www.bobbythebrain.com/

Ulf Herman
http://welcome.to/UlfHerman

The Honky Tonk Man
http://www.wrestlingnation.com/honky/

Missy Hyatt
http://www.leehiatt.com/missy/missy.html

Antonio Inoki
http://www.antonio-inoki.com

Kanyon
http://www.twc-online.com/custom/Kanyon

Steve Keirn
http://www.baylink.net/Keirn

Jason
http://jasonknight.cjb.net

AC Jazz
http://www.amycrawford.com/

Chris Jericho
http://www.chrisjericho.com/

Judge Jeff Jones
http://www.JudgeJeffJones.com

Paul Jones
http://www.wrestlingclassics.com/paul_jones/

Steve Keirn
http://www.baylink.net/Keirn

Kimona
http://www.dabeffy.net/kimona/

Konnan
http://www.konnan.com/

Killer Kowalski Jr.
http://www.angelfire.com/ma2/kowalskijr/

Killer Karl Kox
http://web2.airmail.net/slots2

Buddy Landel
http://www.ddtdigest.com/landel/

Jerry Lawler
http://www.kinglawler.com/

Stan Lee
http://members.aol.com/stanthemanlee

Legion of Doom
http://www.lod2000.com/

Lash LeRoux
http://weirdopalooza.com/lash.html

Lodi
http://www.lodipage.com/

"El Sexsisto" The Latin Lover
http://members.aol.com/SEXSISTO1/index.html

Adrian Lynch
http://members.aol.com/alynch69/welcome.html

Madusa
http://www.madusa.com

Rocky Maivia
http://www.geocities.com/~rockymaivia

Dutch Mantel
http://wrestlingnation.com/tbrmag/dutch/dutch.html

Dawn Marie
http://www.wrestlingman.com/dawnmarie

Rena Mero
http://www.RenaMero.com

Kevin Nash
http://www.kevinbigsexynash.com/

Natasha
http://www.angelfire.com/nj/natashadahmer

Nitro Girls
http://nitrogirls.com

Super Nova
http://www.wrestlingnation.com/supernova

Diamond Dallas Page
http://www.thediamondmine.com/

Ken Patera
http://www.tcguide.com/kenpatera/

Scrap Iron Adam Pearce
http://scrapiron.hypermart.net

The Pitbulls
http://www.ThePitbulls.Com

Rod Price
http://web2.airmail.net/bobb/rod.html

Harley Race
http://www.harleyrace.com/

Rik Ratchet
http://hometown.aol.com/kknight4/ratchet/index.htm

Reckless Youth
http://www.reckless-youth.com/

Stevie Richards
http://www.stevierichards.com

Jake "The Snake" Roberts
http://www.jakethesnakeroberts.com

The Rock
http://www.TheRock.com

Axl Rotten
http://www.axlrotten.com/

Samu
http://www.typhoonmedia.com/Samu/

Macho Man Randy Savage
http://www.machoman.com

Dan Severn
http://www.the-beast.com/

Frank Shamrock
http://www.frankshamrockusa.com/

Larry Sharpe
http://www.monsterfactory.com

The Original Sheik
http://www.primenet.com/~ferante

Jimmy Superfly Snuka
http://www.superflysnuka.com

Ricky "The Dragon" Steamboat
http://www.ricksteamboat.com/

George "The Animal" Steele
http://www.georgesteele.com

Scott Steiner
http://www.bigpoppapump.com

Adrian Street
http://www.bizarebazzar.dotstar.net/

Suicidal Youth
http://brianjmacdonald.home.mindspring.com

Taz
http://www.tazmission.com

Lou Thesz
http://thesz.scoopscentral.com

Dick Togo
http://dicktogo.homepage.com/

Tygress (Nitro Girl)
http://www.vanessasanchez.com

The Undertaker (comic book)
http://www.theundertaker.net/

Jimmy Valiant
http://www.Jimmyvaliant.com

Rob Van Dam
http://www.robvandam.com/

Jesse Ventura
http://www.jesseventura.com/

Von Erichs
http://www.vonerich.com/

The Ultimate Warrior
http://www.ultimatewarrior.com/

Mikey Whipwreck
http://www.showdown.net/whipwreck

Steve "Dr. Death" Williams
http://members.tripod.com/DRDEATH123/

Torrie Wilson
http://www.torriewilson.com

Tom Zenk
http://www.tomzenk.com

Balls Mahoney & Axl Rotten
http://www.strictlyecw.com/ballsandaxl

Promotions and territories

AAW All American Wrestling
http://www.allamericanwrestling.com/

Atom Smashers Wrestling Federation
http://www.aswf.com

APW
http://www.allprowrestling.com

APWF Allied Powers Wrestling Federation
http://apwf.scoopscentral.com

AWA Superstars of Wrestling
http://www.awastars.com

Bad to the Bone Wrestling
http://www.angelfire.com/ky/bbw

Buffalo Wrestling Federation
http://www.bwf-wrestling.com

All things Taz can be found at http://www.tazmission.com.

California Championship Wrestling
http://www.neckbreaker.com

CPW Championship Pro Wrestling
http://cpwwrestling.com

CWF Champion Wrestling Federation
http://www.champion-promotions.com/

Combat Zone Wrestling
http://www.czwwrestling.com

Deep South Wrestling
http://www.angelfire.com/la/DeepSouth/

EWF Empire Wrestling Federation
http://www.ewf-wrestling.com

ECPW (Gino Caruso's promotion-NJ)
http://www.ecpwwrestling.com

ECCW Extreme Canadian Championship Wrestling
http://www.ECCW.com

ECW Extreme Championship Wrestling
http://www.ecwwrestling.com

ECWA
http://www.ecwaprowrestling.com/

EWA
http://www.ewawrestling.com

FIW
http://fiwwrestling.com

Florida Championship Wrestling
http://www.fcwwrestling.com/

Florida Extreme Wrestling (FEW)
http://go.to/few

Heartland Wrestling Association
www.hwaonline.com

Independent Championship Wrestling
http://www.icwchampions.com

IWA Independent Wrestling Alliance
http://www.angelfire.com/nc2/iwaprowrestling

Independent Wrestling Federation Please Re-Bookmark This Site!
www.wrestlingiwf.com

Independent Promotion of Green Bay, WI
http://acw.webjump.com/

Infinity Wrestling Federation
http://www.theiwf.8m.com

IPW
http://ipw-hardcore.com

Iron Ring Wrestling
http://members.aol.com/IRWOffice/wrestling.html

ISPW
http://www.ispwwrestling.com

Jersey All Pro Wrestling
http://www.angelfire.com/yt/japw/show.html

KYDA
http://www.KYDA.com

Lakeshore Wrestling Organization
http://www.angelfire.com/mi/lakeshorewrestling/

LIWF (Long Island Wrestling Federation)
http://liwf.cjb.net

Lunatic Wrestling Federation
http://www.lwfwrestling.com

Mason-Dixon Wrestling
http://www.whoowrestling.com/mdw

MCW
http://www.marylandwrestling.com

MEWF Mid Eastern Wrestling Federation
http://indywrestling.interspeed.net/mewf/

Mid Southern Pro Wrestling
http://www.mspwonline.com/

Millennium Wrestling Alliance
http://www.mwahq.com

NAWA
http://www.nawawrestling.com

NCW Northern Championship Wrestling
http://ncw.qc.ca

NDW New Dimension Wrestling®
http://www.ndwwrestling.com/

New England Wrestling
http://www.newenglandwrestling.com/

New Jack City Wrestling
e-mail:newjackcitywrestling@yahoo.com

NEW Northeast Wrestling
http://www.northeastwrestling.com

Northeast Wrestling
http://www.newrestling.com

NWA/CWA
http://members.aol.com/SportsEnt/dates.html

NWA/ECCW
http://www.ECCW.com

NWA New England
http://www.nwane.com

NWA/New York
http://www.geocities.com/Colosseum/Bench/2240/index.html

NWA/UK Hammerlock
http://www.hammerlock-wrestling.com

NWA Southwest Wrestling
http://www.nwa-southwest.com/demo2.html

NWA West Virginia/Ohio
http://www.piledriverpress.com/nwa/wvohio

NWL National Wrestling League
http://www.NWLwrestling.com

PCW Pennsylvania Championship Wrestling
http://www.pcwprowrestling.com

Stampede Wrestling
http://www.stampedewrestling.com/index.htm

Steel City Wrestling
http://204.171.105.152/SCW/SCW.HTML

TWA Texas Wrestling Association
http://www.twawrestling.com/

3 Rivers Wrestling
http://www.angelfire.com/biz2/3RW

United Independent Wrestling Alliance (UIWA)
http://www.uiwa.com/

United States Wrestling Federation
http://www.wrestlingnation.com/uswf/

United Wrestling Coalition
http://www.uwcwrestling.com

WWF
http://www.wwf.com

WCW
http://www.wcw.com

World Legion Wrestling
http://www.worldlegion.com

World Professional Wrestling Federation
http://www.wpwf.com

World X-treme Wrestling
http://www.XtremeWrestling.com
XPW—http://www.xpwrestling.com

Yankee Pro Wrestling
http://hometown.aol.com/YPW98/index.html

CONTACTS

Highspots
P.O. Box 35493
Charlotte, NC 28235-5493
(704) 334-5807
http://www.highspots.com

P.M. Video
P.O. Box 6890
Seffner, Florida 33583

RF Video
P.O. Box 797
Langhorne, PA 19047
(215) 891-9404
http://www.rfvideo.com

R & B Collector's World
420 Wildwood Ave.
Pitman, NJ 08071
1-800-318-2147
http://www.rnbcollectors
world.com

John McAdams (videos)
P.O. Box 1126
Sanbornville, NH 03872
JnMcAdam@aol.com

Sportsworld (autographs)
429 Broadway
Everett, MA 02149
(617) 387-7220
http://www.sportsworld-usa.com

Dr. Bob Bryla
1912 Sunset Ave.
Utica, NY 13502
(315) 733-1846

Figures Inc.
P.O. Box 19482
Johnston, RI 02919
(401) 946-5720
Fig Inc@aol.com

Norman Kietzer
527 South Front St.
Mankato, MN 56001
(507) 344-8913
kietzer@mctcnet.net
http://www.mctcnet.net/~kietzer

Tom Burke (collector and buyer)
31 Groveland St.
Springfield, MA 01108-2920

MANIAX (Japanese collectibles)
2-19-8 Nishamagome
Ota-ku
Tokyo, Japan 143

Royal Duncan (world title histories book)
7600 North Galena Road
Peoria, IL 61615
Send $55 check or money order

Dennis Coraluzzo (poster collector and promoter)
14 Margeaux Court
Woodbury, NJ

Mick Karch (announcer and collector)
P.O. Box 2247 Loop Station
Minneapolis, MN 55420

Steve Tierchel (Ventura action figures)
(612) 850-0912
(612) 342-0017

Chris Perry
201 Country Club Road
Newport News, Virginia 23606
(757) 595-8016
chris42005@aol.com

Mike Rogers
2740 SE Lewellyn
Troutedale, OR 97060
Monthly newsletter and result for $1

Cauliflower Alley Club
c/o Kurt Lauer
HCR 33
Box 107
Rolla, MS 65401-9808
Write for more information

CHAOS Comics
1-888-CHAOS13
Call for info on WWF comics

Sheldon Goldberg
Mat Marketplace
(617) 327-3945

Rhino Records
(makers of picture discs and videos)
1-800-432-0020

International Wrestling Institute & Museum
c/o Mike Chapman, curator
Newton, Iowa
(515) 526-8836
(515) 791-1517

Brian Elliot (doll collector)
http://members.tripod.com/~actionfigs/figures.html

chapter 12 To Know Your Role, You Must Know Your Past

Today, the average fan recognizes three major wrestling federations: World Wrestling Federation (WWF), World Championship Wrestling (WCW) and Extreme Championship Wrestling (ECW). Others are known as "independents." There are at least a dozen independent promotions operating out of Minnesota alone, and more than 100 "indies" in the United States, 20 in Canada, six in Puerto Rico, more than 20 in Japan, several in Europe, Australia, South America, Great Britain and probably more in countries you've never heard of.

Most of the independent stars will never get the chance to make it to the Big Three, but who can blame a dreamer. It's a big jump to go from performing in front of 12 paying customers at a remote VFW to performing at Madison Square Garden before a standing-room-only crowd.

However, to the collector, the independent promotions offer vital, priceless memorabilia. Origins of the stars we see today are defined in the independents and that's why they are of premium value to collectors.

Basically, from the 1950s to the mid-'80s, every geographical region had what is affectionately called a "territory." As the Crockett family's NWA (now WCW) and Vince McMahon's WWF began to tour nationally in the early '80s, the territories began to dwindle. Soon, most simply folded. Today, territories are on the rebound in the form of the indies. These groups maintain a lifeline to the three major federations. The next Rock, Stone Cold, Goldberg or Sandman may be out there in your hometown.

So, to honor the days of old, the following is a very brief synopsis of various territories and the stars that helped them stay alive. Hopefully, this will lead you in the right direction when looking for that special item. Happy collecting...

American Wrestling Association

The Verne Gagne-owned AWA was one of the premiere territories from 1960-1986. The AWA's training camp produced top stars like Ricky Steamboat, Ric Flair, Big Van Vader and Jim Brunzell. Rarely did the AWA stray from its tried-and-true formula for success. When it did, it went for muscle-bound crowd pleasers like Hulk Hogan or Superstar Graham.

Big-Time Wrestling

Big-Time's heyday was the '60s and '70s in the Motor City. It lived and died with the Sheik and Bobo Brazil. Much of Big-Time's fun can be seen on the classic movie, "I Like to Hurt People." Like most other promotions of the day, it used top free-agent talent like Andre the Giant, Dusty Rhodes and Terry Funk.

The Central States

Based in Kansas City, former wrestler Bob Geigel spearheaded the group. Bruiser Brody was a top main event star there. Reverend turned WWF manager, Slick, also got his start there, as did Mitch Snow, Curtis Hughes and D.J. Peterson.

Chicagoland Wrestling

This legendary group was headed by Fred Kohler and later Bob Luce. From the 1920s-'60s, Chicago's Amphitheater and Soldier Field held some of the sport's biggest matches. Superclash at Comiskey Park had several classic matchups on the card which was commercially released. On that card, Stan Hansen and Rick Martel wrestled throughout the infield and dugout in what was a hardcore match before its time.

Continental Championship Wrestling

Based in Alabama, the Continental/Southeastern promotion was headed by Ron Fuller (WCW's Col. Robert Parker), who had about a zillion cousins and sons wrestle as well. The Samoans, Ted DiBiase, Dirty White Boy, Jimmy Golden and Nightmare Danny Davis were regulars in the mid-'80s. Strongman Doug Furnas got a start there, as did the Road Dogg. It hung tough as a territory, but folded in the early 1990s.

CWA (Germany)

The CWA is Otto Wanz' Germany-based promotion. The German strongman weighed well more than 300 pounds and enjoyed hiring other large men to wrestle. Tapes of his AWA title reign and the clips where Wanz rips a phone book in half and then is attacked by the Heenan family are classics. Nowadays, mid-level stars like Cpl. Kirschner, Derrick Dukes, the late Larry Cameron and Fit Finlay have made nice paydays in CWA.

Extreme Championship Wrestling

Before it became ECW, the territory, in the Northeastern U.S., had many incarnations behind promoters Dennis Corraluzzo, Joel Goodheart, Tod Gordon and Paul Heyman. The initials ECW are responsible for some high-profile cards in recent years. Blood baths, balcony leaps, hardcore wars, barbed wire fences, busted tables, T&A, shoot interviews, scaffold matches and a myriad of mayhem is available here.

Florida Championship Wrestling

The Florida-based promotion led by Eddie Graham, prior to his suicide, was a major player in the '60s, '70s and '80s. Ric Flair, Blackjack Mulligan, Dusty Rhodes, and later, Rick Rude, Barry Windham and Kevin Sullivan, were mainstays. Scott Hall and Lex Lugar got their first title pushes in Florida.

Global Wrestling Federation

The first incarnation of Global, a Florida-based territory, was that of a publicly held company. The few TV tapings it had in 1987 offer eclectic fun and are rather hard to find. The second Global, based in Dallas, was headed by Joe Pedicino, who was savvy enough to nab an ESPN contract. It aired for a from 1990-91 and stressed good, quality wrestling. Buff Bagwell, Lightning Kid and Jerry Lynn's first national exposure came with Global.

International Championship Wrestling

The ICW is a small, but crowd pleasing, promotion in the New England region. In the '70s and early '80s, an ICW promotion ran shows in the Memphis territory using the greats of the era, including a young, agile Randy Savage.

IWA (Puerto Rico)

After years of being a WWF liaison between Puerto Rican, Japanese and Mexican promoters, Victor Quinonnes has established his own group in Puerto Rico, utilizing the best free agents on the island, Japanese and Mexican stars, independent talent and stars on loan from the WWF. In the 1970s, Eddie Einhorn booked his own IWA in the Northeast. Ernie Ladd, Mil Mascaras, Ivan Koloff and Eric the Red were found here.

Memphis Wrestling

Although the names and faces have changed at times, Jerry Lawler has truly been the "King" of Memphis wrestling. He has been involved in virtually every top-grossing main event, has pioneered many of the elements that are seen on the Big Two's shows today and has had a part in developing 30 percent of today's top stars. Today, Lawler is running Memphis Championship Wrestling and Randy Hales is promoting for Power Pro Wrestling.

National Wrestling Alliance (Music City)

Local businessman Bill Behrens and longtime fan and promoter Bert Prentice have turned the dormant Nashville area into a booming territory. As part of the NWA, Music City sees many of the top indie stars come through the area. Recently, Terry Taylor, Brian Christopher, Jerry Lawler, the Fabulous Ones and even the legendary Jackie Fargo have stopped by to say hello. The NWA has several regional affiliations, including Ohio Valley Wrestling and Texas Southwest Wrestling out of Dallas.

Mid-South Promotions (UWF)

Bill Watts' Mid-South promotion was phenomenally successful throughout Oklahoma and Louisiana in the early '80s and continues to be one of the most popular groups for collectors. His Mid-South wrestling show became syndicated and eventually aired on WTBS. In the late '80s, he duplicated that success by forming the Universal Wrestling Federation, which went head to head with Jim Crockett's NWA and the WWF. Mid-South gave Jim Ross his first spot as an announcer. Watts developed young talent.

Montreal Wrestling

Numerous promoters have done well in Montreal. The Rougeau name is synonymous with wrestling in that region. The brothers recently began promoting cards featuring long-time area draw Richard Charland and Abdullah the Butcher. Papa Raymond was a top scientific grappler of the '60s and '70s. Dino Bravo and Rick Martel were also top draws in the region. It was here that Martel first teamed with Tom Zenk and became WWF stars as the Can-Am Connection.

Mid-Atlantic

This was an NWA promotion headed by Jim Crockett and based out of the Carolinas. Main events were often blood baths. Ric Flair, Ricky Steamboat, Wahoo McDaniel, Greg Valentine, Ole and Gene Anderson, Sgt. Slaughter, Magnum T.A., Roddy Piper and the Youngbloods were stars for the group. The Valentine-Piper dog collar showdown is a must-see for any collector.

Pacific Northwest/Portland Championship Wrestling

This long-standing organization (1940s to 1990s) was one of the more successful territories ever. Portland's owner Don Owens happened to be one of the dullest announcers of all time, which makes him a cult favorite. A who's who of pro wrestling sauntered through that area: Scott Norton, John Nord, JW Storm, Scotty the Body (Raven), the late Brady Boone, Curt Hennig, Rip Oliver, Brian Adams, Don Leo Jonathan, Col. DeBeers, Tom Zenk and Al Madril. Jesse Ventura even cut his teeth for Mr. Owens.

Pro Wrestling America

Although the AWA ruled the Midwest, Minneapolis super-trainer Eddie Sharkey saw an opening and seized the opportunity in 1985, forming this renegade group. In the early years, Mad Dog Vachone, Steve Regal, the Fantastics, Bruiser Brody, Tim Flowers, Tom Zenk and Nord the Barbarian main evented.

Smoky Mountain Wrestling

Based in the blue hills of Kentucky, SMW provided an outlet for up and coming talent and veterans in the early 1990s. For modern-era wrestling, no group outside ECW spawned more superstars than SMW: Chris Candido, Tammy Sytch (Sunny), New Jack, Balls Mahoney, Brian Lee, the Heavenly Bodies (Jimmy Del Ray and Tom Pritchard), Terry Funk, Tim Horner, Tracy Smothers, Chris Jericho, Lance Storm, Cactus Jack and the Hardy Boys all stopped by.

Stampede Wrestling (Calgary)

Led by Stu Hart and his eight wrestling sons, the action spanned from the '50s to the present. Stampede's alumni reads like a wrestling Hall of Fame: Abdullah the Butcher, Larry Cameron, Bret, Bruce and Owen Hart, Dynamite Kid, Davey Boy Smith, Johnny Smith, Bad News Brown, the Mongolian Stomper, Terry Funk, Gene Kiniski, Steve Blackman, Brian Pillman, Masa Chono, Jushin Liger and Norman the Lunatic.

Texas All-Star/Southwest Wrestling

This promotion, run in the Southwest by promoter Joe Blanchard and son Tully, was an eclectic group deeply rooted in high-paced, often bloody, matches. Its heyday was from 1983-85, when it was seen on the USA Network. Ironically, the network canceled the show for its excessive violence. Vince McMahon came in and took the time slot, and the rest is history.

Texas Wrestling Federation

The TWF opened in early 1999, as a result of Shawn Michaels' retirement and subsequent move to being a trainer. He, Jose Lothario and Sho Funaki (of Kaientai fame) both train the up and comers for the new group.

World Wrestling Alliance

The WWA was headed by Dick the Bruiser throughout the '70s and had television air play throughout the Indiana area. Wilbur Snyder, Steve Regal, Spike Huber, Bobo Brazil Jr., Tex McKenzie, and the Bruiser himself were regulars.

World Class Championship Wrestling

From 1982-87, no promotion was more feverishly loved than Fritz Von Erich's WCCW, based out of Dallas-Ft. Worth. Memorabilia from this area is still in great demand. The Freebirds, Bruiser Brody, Chris Adams, Iceman Parsons, Kabuki, Killer Khan, One Man Gang, the Simpson Brothers, Precious and Jimmy Garvin and others helped make WCCW an historic and exciting promotion.